A student's guide to Writing Business Reports

The ability to prepare an effective report is a vital skill for anyone building a career in business

by Zoe Robinson and Stuart Pedley-Smith

KAPLAN

PUBLISHING

British library cataloguing-in-publication data
A catalogue record for this book is available from the British Library.
Published by:
Kaplan Publishing UK
Unit 2 The Business Centre
Molly Millars Lane
Wokingham
Berkshire
RG41 2QZ
ISBN 978-0-85732-207-4

© Zoe Robinson and Stuart Pedley-Smith

First edition published 2010

Printed and bound in Great Britain.

We are grateful to the Institute of Chartered Accountants in England
& Wales for permission to reproduce extracts from the Broadsword
case study.

Contents

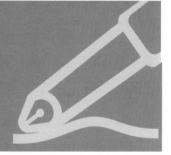

About this book

The ability to prepare an effective report is a vital skill for many professionals. Whilst the majority of reports contain a number of standard elements, the exact structure of the document and the approach taken to writing it will differ significantly depending on the specifics of the situation.

Rather than trying to be all things to all men (or women), and not doing a good job for anyone, this book will focus specifically on business reports. That is to say, reports whose aim is to analyse business issues, maybe identifying potential solutions to those issues, and to ultimately reach conclusions and provide some recommendations. For these reports, the key success criteria is the effective presentation of a commercially sound argument that is communicated in a style that is both professional and business-like. To do this, we must focus not just on the writing of the report but on the whole process of preparing a report including the planning and the development of commercial reasoning.

With this scope in mind, we feel there are three main 'groups' of people who will benefit from reading this book:

1. Those writing a dissertation for a business or finance-related undergraduate or postgraduate degree;

2. Those sitting an exam for a business or accountancy-related professional qualification where a potential requirement is to prepare a report;

3. Anyone working in the business or finance sector who is required to write reports as part of their job.

Although the core skills will be the same, regardless of who is writing the business report, we must recognise that each of the three groups above may well need to make small changes to their approach or perform additional processes as a result of the situation they are in. Key drivers of this are:

*   Time limitations that will be strict for those sitting a professional exam but less so for the other groups;

*   The availability of information and the ability to perform additional research;

*   The scope of the report, which will be predefined for those sitting an exam and maybe those in business, will be more flexible for those writing a dissertation.

So, to ensure you get guidance relevant to your situation, each chapter will end with some specific pointers for each of the three groups, ensuring that you can directly transfer what you learn from this book into practice.

How to use this book

To get the most from this book, we would recommend you start by reading the chapters in order. This will give you a good understanding of all of the stages of preparing a report and how they fit together. However, the structure of each chapter means that once completed, you will be able to dip into the book, using it as a reference guide to support your report writing attempts.

Each chapter contains a number of examples and illustrations to demonstrate the points being made and to give the book a more commercial and practical feel. However, to fully master any skill there is no substitute for practice. We have therefore included a case study, using a company based in the travel sector, to allow you to do just that.

Some initial background information on this company is presented after the introduction to this book. You do not need any detailed knowledge on the travel industry; the information presented will be sufficient. As we progress through the chapters, we will add to the information provided, building a bigger picture as we go, much as would happen throughout the report writing process. At each stage, small exercises will allow you to develop and practise your skills and to help you gain a better understanding of the most effective approach to writing reports.

You may choose to read the initial background information now, attempting each exercise as you complete each chapter. Alternatively you could read through the whole book, leaving the case study exercises to be tackled as a mini 'report-preparing' project at the end. Which approach you take, or whether you choose to attempt all of the case study exercises or not, will depend on the time you have available and what additional opportunities you will get to practise the techniques before preparing your first 'proper' report. Regardless of your approach, the answers to all of the exercises can be found in the final chapter of this book.

About the authors

This book is a result of a collaboration between Zoe Robinson and Stuart Pedley-Smith, both of whom have considerable experience of breaking down the process of preparing reports into a series of simple steps for finance professionals approaching the final stage of their exam journey.

Having qualified as a Chartered Accountant with PricewaterhouseCoopers, Zoe experienced first-hand the problems encountered when preparing business reports as a novice. All the recommended books and computer-based training packages seemed to focus on single elements of the overall process, often placing great emphasis on the words used or the structure of the report, and neglecting the need for a plan or a meaningful thought process. As she moved into the world of training, Zoe began to specialise in the final level case study style examinations, and quickly recognised that if a student was unsuccessful in this type of exam, it was often their ability to prepare a report that was the cause rather than their underlying technical knowledge. After years (she doesn't like to be reminded of how many) of helping students achieve success, Zoe now works for Kaplan Publishing as the Content Specialist for the case study exams set by the ICAEW and CIMA. In this role she assists many students through their final exams, both as a tutor and as the author of the study systems used by tutors and students worldwide.

After qualifying in the accounting profession, Stuart moved into industry and was required to produce monthly financial reports. These reports were to provide the board with an overview of the company's financial position at the end of each month. They were rich in financial detail but probably lacked the intuitive commentary that would only come with age and a lot more commercial experience. In the years that followed Stuart was given opportunities to learn those commercial skills, working in several different industries, and ultimately by running his own company. Like Zoe, he now prepares final level accountancy students to sit their case study exams and believes that the skills they learn during this stage of their academic development are probably the most valuable and are highly prized by the companies they work for. He specialises in learning and development within Kaplan and lectures on a variety of related subjects.

Acknowledgments

There are many people who have helped with a specific task or who have contributed in other ways to making this book possible.

Perhaps the most significant contributor has been Oliver Seed, whose incredible attention to detail, methodical approach and amazing diligence meant no stone was left unturned. He was assisted by David Brearley, Paul Robinson and Pete Saunders, all of whom we are grateful to for ensuring we have dotted every i, crossed every t and got our hyphens in the right place.

However, this book is the result of many years experience working with students who have needed to write a report as part of an exam process. The process outlined has developed over time and the tips given have been collected from working with both students and fellow tutors. So, perhaps most importantly, we'd like to say a big thanks to all of our past students and the people we work with who, whether knowingly or unknowingly, have inspired our thoughts, ideas and methodology.

Stuart dedicates this book to his Mum, for always having confidence in him.

Zoe dedicates this book to her husband, Paul, and wonderful sons, Jamie and Sam, because without their unquestioning support, this book would never have been written.

Broadsword case study

We are grateful to the Institute of Chartered Accountants in England and Wales (ICAEW) for permission to reproduce extracts from the Broadsword Case Study material. The copyright remains with the ICAEW.

Introduction

Introduction

It was only when we began to teach report writing as part of the training required for final level accountancy students that we fully realised how easily the facts in an argument can be lost if they're not constructed and presented in the correct way. Full of great ideas, students would often jump in, dumping their thoughts onto the page but failing to do justice to their work.

An effective business report should present commercially sound arguments in a style that is both professional and business-like

A key success criteria for any business report is the effective presentation of commercially sound arguments in a style that is both professional and business-like. The aim of many reports will be to persuade the reader, and to do this, the arguments must be convincing and well thought out. This can only be achieved when we recognise that preparing a report is about much more than picking up your pen (or more often nowadays, sitting in front of your computer) and writing.

Note our choice of words in that last sentence: 'preparing' a report, not 'writing' a report. The distinction is crucial. It is a lucky and rare individual who is able to deliver an effective report without putting in the ground work. We've all heard the saying "to fail to prepare is to prepare to fail". If a report is not planned, and its contents not fully considered, it will often fail to achieve its objective. With this in mind, it's important to regard the preparation of a report as a process, not a writing exercise.

Before we go any further in looking at the process of preparing reports, it's worth taking a step back and asking some more fundamental questions.

What is a report?

A book is really just a long report and so when we decided to write this book, we practised what we were about to preach and developed a plan. Our starting point was this question – what is a report?

It surprised both of us when we found it difficult to answer. We each had our own ideas, drawn from our own experiences of writing reports and teaching the process to others, but these ideas didn't fully match up. Does a report have to contain recommendations? Yes argued Stuart, no argued Zoe; it depends was the middle ground compromise. So, what is so hard about this question that two people, with a combined total of over 25 years experience of teaching report writing, find it so difficult to answer?

Well, according to the Oxford English Dictionary, a report is 'an account given of a matter after investigation or consideration'. Now, this is quite a generic definition. It could encompass anything from a chat on the phone with your friend about last night's TV to a 20,000-word document outlining the findings of a judicial enquiry.

If we were to focus our scope a little, concentrating on written reports in the business and finance sector, does this help? To some extent, yes. This now reveals some aims that all reports would most likely have. These would include:

- conveying information (although not necessarily new information); and

- reaching a conclusion on the meaning of that information (but not necessarily providing recommendations directing the reader to take further action).

Most importantly though, a document cannot be regarded as a report without the existence of an objective that it is trying to achieve. This objective will always be to provide answers to a number of questions posed directly or indirectly by the reader. All elements contained within a report will relate back to this objective, leading the reader towards the answers they seek. So, if a Board of Directors requests a report on the issues facing their company, indirectly they want the report to tell them what to do to address the issues. If your report is to detail the findings of an investigation (an audit perhaps), it must answer the questions "what was found" and "what are the implications of the findings"?

The objective of a report will always be to provide answers to a number of questions posed by the reader

Why write a report?

In part, this is linked back to the overall objective of the report. However, a report is not the only way in which the information could be conveyed, the conclusions expressed and the objective met. So, why a report instead of say, a presentation or a discussion?

Perhaps the main reason is the formality of a report. By committing things to paper (or more commonly now, an electronic document), in an ordered and considered fashion, it is less likely that misunderstandings will arise in the future. It can easily be referred back to in order to clarify a point or confirm understanding and gives a permanent record of the matters covered.

There is also something that changes when writing a report. The author becomes more aware of the formality and so is forced to think through their argument, conscious of the fact that there will be no second chance to get it right, as might be the case with a conversation or presentation.

When the word appears on the page, that is it. It has to convey the very essence of the argument and has to move seamlessly from one paragraph to the next, as a conversation might between good friends. And so, the process of preparing a report helps the author distil their argument so that they are not only understood by the recipient of the report, but by the author themselves.

What makes a good report?

Now this is a slightly easier question to answer. At a base level, a good report is one which achieves its primary objective and answers the questions the reader wants answering.

A good report should be ordered and considered, clear and concise

However, it's not quite as simple as that. We also need to have regard for why a report format was selected over and above other formats. This introduces the idea that it must be ordered and considered to ensure there will be no misunderstandings in the future. By this we mean it should be clear and concise, it must have a logical flow and structure and most importantly, it must be planned to ensure all of these features are present.

At the heart of every good report is the author's ability to communicate. The reader has to follow the argument and the rationale behind what is being said. They of course, do not need to agree but the message should be loud and clear.

How to write a good report?

Many (although not all) reports will need to persuade the reader that the answers provided, be it opinions expressed or the recommendations suggested, are correct. Constructing the necessary persuasive arguments to ensure your reader has faith in your solutions can only be achieved if your report is planned out before you start writing.

To ensure your report achieves its objective you must plan and think, as well as write

Writing a good report, and in particular a business report, is about more than just the words you use. In order to ensure your report achieves its objective you must complete three distinct phases of an overall process; plan, think and write.

PLAN – the starting point in the process is to establish the primary objective of your report. You will need to consider who you're writing to, what their background is and what they will be expecting from the report. Next, you must develop a plan of the content in your report. You will need to review what information you already have and whether you will need, or are able to get, any additional information. Finally you will have to manage your time effectively to ensure you meet the objectives in the time available. Key to this will be a realistic assessment of what can be achieved.

THINK – it could be argued that you can't write anything down until you've first thought about what you're going to write. It's all very good having lots of information, but what does it all mean, or perhaps more importantly, what might it mean? You will need to process the information you have, considering its commercial impact. Very often within business reports, this may mean performing some numerical analysis and considering the implications of your results. This stage also involves exercising judgement to formulate your 'answer'. What are the key messages you want to convey and, if relevant, what will your conclusions and recommendations be?

WRITE – even the writing phase is not straightforward. An obvious element will be the language you use, your writing style, grammar and spelling, but more fundamental will be the structuring of your report to give it a logical flow.

Why is report writing a good skill to have?

Regardless of purpose or style, it is a fact that reports are one of the most common forms of business communication. If you want to get on in business, the skill of report writing is something you will need to develop.

Nowadays, learning this skill begins as young as seven years old, with primary school children being taught the basics of what a report should look like, and what headings could be used. However, it probably isn't until university that most people would be called upon to independently write their first 'proper' report.

As you progress up the career ladder, the skill will be required more and more, yet often you can feel under-prepared or lacking in experience to know where to begin.

It is no coincidence that many professional bodies (including the Institute of Chartered Accountants of England and Wales, the Institute of Chartered Accountants of Scotland, the Chartered Institute of Management Accountants and the Chartered Institute of Public Finance and Accountancy amongst others) set a final 'case study style' examination where students are expected to submit a report. This gives all of these bodies the knowledge that their members have sufficiently developed this vital business skill.

And so, as you embark on advancing your career, we're sure this book will assist you in developing the right skills to create some great reports.

If you want to get on in business, the skill of report writing is something you will need to develop

The Case

In order to help explain how best to apply some of the advice given in this book, a case study has been included. This case study develops as you work your way through the chapters, such that by the end of the book, you will have the complete picture and will feel confident to tackle writing the final report.

Some initial background information on the case study is included below, further sections will be provided within subsequent chapters.

Your role

You are an executive in the Corporate Development department of Broadsword plc, a UK group listed on the London Stock Exchange with business interests throughout the worldwide travel industry. Your department is responsible for assisting the Board of Broadsword to establish and implement the Group's corporate development strategy.

Broadsword's business model

The Group makes the majority of its money in the way that you might expect – that is, by arranging holidays for guests at a cost per individual trip that is lower than the price which the guest is prepared to pay.

Costs are kept low by the fact that flights, hotel bookings and other incidental costs are always likely to be cheaper when purchased in bulk. However, profitability is also enhanced by:

- good buying practices. For example, establishing long-term, trusting relationships with hoteliers and airlines. These relationships are especially helpful should something go wrong; and

- establishing and maintaining efficient business processes throughout the organisation. These processes ensure that all key activities – buying, staff recruitment and management, flight and hotel booking procedures, guest handling and liaison and the delivery of the product in every way – run as smoothly and fluently as possible.

The Group also makes money through its good name and reputation; guests come back because of the high standards and are particularly loyal if, when something goes wrong, the problem was handled well. This means that guests are prepared to pay a little more – and sometimes a lot more – for a holiday because it is supplied by Broadsword.

However, certain parts of the Group's market have now matured and are no longer as rapidly-expanding and innovative as once they were. Examples are traditional beach holiday package tours to countries such as Spain, Portugal, Italy and Greece.

The Group continues to serve these markets for the reason that, in total, they are in most cases still large. This means that the total margin made from the sector as a whole will always be significant even if the margin per individual holiday is only small. It is also worth remembering that guests for these holidays eventually seek a change; and such loyal customers will often remain with Broadsword even though they might take trips to other parts of the world.

Divisional structure

The Group is organised into the following divisions:

- package holidays: (i) short-haul (Europe) and (ii) long-haul

- winter holidays

- group holiday and charter products

- cruises

- adventure and specialist holidays

- on-line flight and hotel booking services (NB: Broadsword does not own any hotels or aircraft).

Revenue and gross profit by destination for the year to 31 December 2009 may be analysed as follows:

Segmental analysis - Nicelife

	Revenue 2009 £m	Gross profit 2009 £m
Short-haul package (UK & Europe)	135.7	1.4
Long-haul package	88.4	2.6
Total package	224.1	4.0
Winter holidays	109.6	2.4
Group / charter	277.8	20.5
Adventure / specialist	112.0	14.7
Flight / hotel booking	2.5	0.1
TOTAL	**726.0**	**41.7**
Short-haul	471.2	27.6
Long-haul	254.8	14.1

Competitive pressures

There are now several substantial competitors who benefit greatly from economies of scale – firms such as Thomas Cook and TUI, both of which have grown significantly in recent years through mergers and acquisitions. Such competition has inevitably caused some parts of the market, primarily short-haul package holidays, to be highly sensitive to price, as similar offerings eventually become difficult to differentiate.

Further competitive pressure has been triggered by the difficult economic conditions that have led to a fall in the number of worldwide travellers (as measured by international tourist arrivals) of 4% in 2009 and a decline in receipts from tourism of around 6%. This downturn has been particularly pronounced for long-haul destinations and the premium niche products where operators have been forced to discount heavily following an over-commitment on hotel and flight bookings.

Industry trends

In recent years, it has become increasingly apparent to the directors that future growth in the industry will be greatest in sectors away from the mass market (e.g. adventure / specialist holidays and long-haul), where buyers are far less price sensitive. Profitability in these sectors tends to be better than for traditional package tours, although the differential has been less marked throughout the global economic turmoil. However, industry experts predict that these sectors will be very popular once the economic recovery begins.

A further welcome trend appears to be emerging; more holidays are being booked independently by travellers direct with Broadsword, via the internet. The disadvantage that Broadsword has suffered from not having a chain of captive travel agencies, therefore seems now to be coming gradually to an end. Broadsword's larger competitors are even considering whether they now need to retain a large estate of travel agencies if internet sales are going to achieve their expected exponential growth.

Ownership structure

Having been privately owned until 1992, Broadsword obtained admission of its shares to listing on the London Stock Exchange. The Group remained in the majority ownership of its three founders until 2002, when further new shares were issued via an institutional placing. Today, about 43% of the Group's shares are in the hands of the public, of which 9% are owned by a leading institutional investor. All of the original founders have now retired, but they still own approximately 40% of the Group's equity. The remaining 17% is owned by (over 3,000) current and former employees.

plan

Identifying what to write about

This section will contain

Chapter 1

The objective of your report

In this chapter

We want to examine the objective of your report. Unless you understand the overall aim of your report together with the factors affecting what your reader is expecting your report to do, it is difficult to ensure your report delivers in the way it should.

Key to the delivery of an effective report is to funnel down from the general to the specific and through to the identification of your user's 'bottom-line' questions; those questions they really want your report to answer. Answering these questions should be viewed as your report's objective and in this chapter we'll show you how to discover them.

The 'original brief'

Let's imagine you've been asked to write a report, the 'original brief' of which is to review the performance of a particular company. Does this tell you exactly what your report needs to do? Are you able to understand the objective of your report from this brief?

Very often, the original requirements of a report will be vague and unclear. They tell you something about the subject of the report (in this case the performance of a particular company) but do little to help you consider the precise content or the direction your report should take.

Yet figuring these things out is the crucial first step towards ensuring you deliver a report that meets the user's expectations. To do this you will need to delve a bit deeper, funnelling down from the general to the specific in order to truly understand the objective your report must achieve.

The aim of a report

The starting point is to consider the aim of your report. In the introduction we noted that all reports have two aims in common; conveying information and reaching a conclusion. Does this mean these are the only aims of a report?

All reports must convey information and reach a conclusion

Remember, these are the two aims that are common to, or consistent, between all reports. They are however quite generic in their nature, with each one encompassing a wide variety of potential requests. By drilling down further, by considering the type of information being conveyed and the way in which a conclusion will be used, we can reveal a more detailed list of aims that business reports often have.

Conveying information

By distinguishing between the type of information being conveyed, we can reveal three further aims:

Providing a summary – The report could be acting as a summary, pulling together or rounding-up many other sources of information into one document. For example, a summary of competitors' pricing strategies.

Communicating findings – Often in this situation, the information will be new to the reader, perhaps the findings of an investigation or a review, and the aim of the report is to deliver the facts and the implications of these findings. For example, communicating the results of a customer satisfaction survey.

Presenting analysis – This could either relate to new information that has come to light or existing information that has never been analysed in this way before. For example, analysis of a proposal to build a new factory.

Reaching conclusions

A conclusion is an option not a view based on reasoning. If a report has no conclusion it should be questioned whether a report format was required. Even if the information conveyed was just a collection of information already in existence, a conclusion on the reliability of each piece or on the impact of the information will be required.

A conclusion is an opinion or a view based on reasoning

Often, the user of the report will be looking for more than this and will seek to use this conclusion as a form of guidance. Considering the way in which the conclusion will be used leads to some further aims:

Persuading the reader – Many reports will outline an argument for or against a course of action or a point of view. In this situation, the aim of the report is to persuade the reader that the action being suggested or the view being taken is the right one.

Aiding decision-making – Very often a user will look to a report to help them make an informed decision, as a result of which, action will be taken. Reports with this aim will need to evaluate alternative solutions in order to equip the reader with all of the necessary facts.

Giving recommendations – Some reports go that one step further, actually providing the user with a set of recommendations on the actions that should be taken. This type of report can really be viewed as a combination of the previous two; if a user is to follow the suggestions, they will need to be persuaded that this course of action is the best and that no other solutions would be better.

We're in no way saying that these are the only aims of a report. However, within the business arena, these are the aims for which a report format is most frequently required.

Factors influencing the specific purpose of your report

An awareness of the aim of your report is a good start, but it won't be enough to ensure your report hits the mark in the eye of your reader. You must also consider a range of factors that will help to reveal exactly what the reader of your report is looking for, how they intend to use your report and what their expectations are. These factors will guide you towards the specific purpose of your report. Without this 'user focus' your report is unlikely to deliver everything it should. The factors to consider are:

Taking a 'user focus' approach will help to reveal what the reader is looking for and what their expectations are

1. **The context**

    The first factor to consider is the situation surrounding why the report has been requested. Has it been triggered by a particular event or events or is it a more run-of-the-mill request? Have any precedents been set? To what extent will action be needed as a result of what is written in the report? As well as influencing the specific purpose of your report, context will also be important when you're processing information, considering the commercial implications and forming conclusions and recommendations.

2. **The author**

    The next factor to consider is the position held by you; your background, experience and your role. In what capacity are you being requested to write this report?

Example

The Chartered Institute of Management Accountants (CIMA) recently made some changes to their final level case study exam. Previously students were asked to adopt the role of a management consultant, engaged by the client to advise on the issues facing the business. This has now been changed so that students are acting as a management accountant working for the business itself.

Although this change doesn't really impact on the look or feel of the report, it does impact on the content. As a management accountant, your report should focus more on the delivery of numerical analysis and the interpretation of that information into layman's terms. There will be less covered on the general strategic direction of the business; that would be more the jurisdiction of a management consultant.

3. The reader

The final key factor affecting the 'bottom-line' questions is the user or reader. Exactly who are you writing to? More importantly, why have they commissioned this report? Points to be considered will include:

Their background – How much do they already know about the subject of your report? Will you need to spend time setting the scene or will this information already be known to them?

Their experience – Do they have much experience of business? Will they be aware of any technical jargon that you may use or will you need to explain things in more depth?

Their perspective – What are their views likely to be on the issues being addressed by the report? For example, if you were writing a report on the valuation of a business, you would need to approach this differently depending on whether you were advising the buyer or the seller.

'Bottom-line' questions

By considering the factors noted above, you get a fairly good idea of the specific purpose of your report and what your reader is expecting. But it is possible to funnel down even further to reveal a clearer set of goals, almost a tick list that will make it easier to plan, easier to manage your time, easier to gather information, analyse, think, conclude, structure and write. In fact, it will make the whole process of preparing your report much easier.

'Bottom-line' questions are those questions that the reader wants your report to answer

In the introduction, in addition to noting the common aims of business reports we also commented that all reports must fulfil an objective; that of providing answers to the questions posed directly or indirectly by the reader. The identification of those questions that the reader is looking to have answered by your report - let's call these the 'bottom-line' questions - is the end of your funnelling process.

The 'user focus' funnel

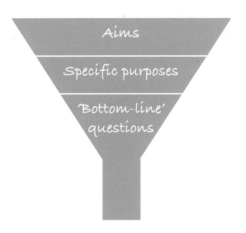

Answering the 'bottom-line' questions will always be the object of your report

Remember, the objective of any report will always be to answer these 'bottom-line' questions.

Example

Let's imagine a situation where you're an external business consultant, appointed by a business owner to advise on the potential sale of their company. The owner set up the business five years ago and is the only shareholder. He has recently received an unsolicited offer from a competitor for £3 million but knows that another competitor may also be interested in acquiring the business. He has no other job lined up and has no previous experience of this sort of situation.

Like all business reports, the broad aims of the report are to convey information and reach some conclusions but, by funnelling down, we can see more detailed aims of:

- Providing a summary of the process involved in selling a business.

- Presenting analysis on the likely value of the business.

- Aiding decision-making so the owner feels able to make an informed decision over the potential sale.

- Giving recommendations on whether the owner should sell or not.

Factors that will affect the specific purpose and content of the report include the following:

- The offer was unsolicited and so in this context the business owner is not in a position of having to sell.

- You've been appointed as a business consultant (i.e. an expert), and so you will need draw on your experiences but make sure you communicate your findings and opinions in a way that a layman will understand.

- You're advising the owner of the business and so you won't need to provide much background information on the business. However, he does not have any previous experience of this sort of transaction and so your report will need to contain information on the sale / acquisition process. Also, since you are advising the seller, you should argue towards the highest justifiable valuation.

But, we can go one better than this. By concentrating on what we're referring to as 'bottom-line questions' you can really ensure that your report delivers everything the user will be wanting and, more importantly, expecting.

So, what might the 'bottom-line' questions be in this situation? The obvious one would be:

'Should I accept the offer of £3 million?'

However, further consideration will also reveal:

- 'How do I make sure I get the most when selling?'

- 'Is £3 million the most I'll get or might I get more by selling to someone else?'

- 'What will I do for work if I sell?'

Identifying the 'bottom-line' questions

Some 'bottom-line' questions may be easy to identify but others may need more work to reveal.

For those writing a report in business, possibly for a client or their boss, the easiest option is to simply ask. When the report is commissioned, take some time to chat to the user about their expectations, the reasons why they've requested the report and ultimately, what questions they want the report to address.

For those writing a dissertation, you should discuss the 'bottom-line' questions with your project supervisor. The beauty of this situation is that more often than not, you get to control the setting of the title and scope for your report. Focusing on the 'bottom-line' questions will be even more valuable in your situation as it's easy to lose direction and focus when provided with such a free rein.

The easiest way to identify the 'bottom-line' questions is to ask, "if I were the reader, what would I want to know?"

It is the student sitting an exam that will likely find it hardest to reveal the 'bottom-line' questions. The only information you have is that given to you in the exam paper, and it is up to you to interpret its meaning. The easiest way to do this is to imagine yourself in the position of the reader. If you were the businessman in receipt of an offer for his business, what would you want to know? What would be of concern to you?

Example

You have been asked to prepare a report on the proposed closure of local branches by a well-known high-street bank. By closing nearly a third of their UK branches, located in small towns and villages throughout the country, the bank expects to increase operating profit by over 25%. Following closure of their branch, customers will be advised to contact the bank's new call centre, located in India, or to travel to the nearest branch which could sometimes be located more than 20 miles away.

Now consider how the 'bottom-line' questions might alter depending on who you were reporting to?

Shareholders will be concerned about their wealth which is directly linked to the profitability of the company. Their 'bottom-line' questions will be 'what impact will the strategy have on operating profit this year?' and 'will this effect be expected to continue in the longer term?'

Employees will be concerned about job security. Their 'bottom-line' questions will more likely be 'will there be redundancies?' or 'will I have to transfer to another branch?'

Customers will have a different set of concerns. Issues such as how they will withdraw or deposit money or even whether they should consider moving their custom to another bank.

Interestingly, a report addressed to the Directors would perhaps need to consider all of the above. They have a duty to manage overall stakeholder conflict and the ultimate success or failure of a strategy will come down to how it is perceived amongst all stakeholders.

This is a very useful technique that we will re-visit in more detail in chapter 4 when we start to consider the 'think' stage of our overall process.

Without this it is unlikely that your report will achieve its objective. After all, if you don't know what the questions are how can you expect to provide the answers?

Once you've identified these 'bottom-line' questions they, along with the underlying aim and the factors affecting the specific purpose of your report, will determine many of your report's fundamentals such as the structure, the look and feel, and most importantly the content. They will also give you a way of measuring the effectiveness of your report; if your report answers the questions, it has met its objective.

A detailed understanding of the questions being asked by the reader is the best place to start when preparing any report

The value in your report

Often the real value in your report is in the conclusions and recommendations you provide and good conclusions and recommendations cannot be provided without a sound commercial thought process underpinning them. This is the 'think' stage of the overall process (more details of which are in chapters 4, 5 and 6). Neither can good conclusions and recommendations be given if you don't know exactly what you should be concluding on or what you should be recommending about. By identifying a series of 'bottom-line' questions, it is much easier to ensure that your report is delivering what it needs to and that it has value to the recipient.

You can't add real value without knowing what you should be concluding on or what you should be recommending about

Remember, these 'bottom-line' questions are those questions that the user really wants answering by the report. By phrasing them as questions you provide a clear mandate for your report.

The Case – a chance to practise

Following on from the information contained at the start of this book, you now have an opportunity to apply what you've learnt in this chapter to the case study.

The Directors of Broadsword feel that, given the current environment, the best way to expand the business may be to acquire a competitor. Many companies are going through difficult times and they believe this could present an excellent opportunity for Broadsword to increase shareholder wealth.

At a recent Board meeting, your boss, the Corporate Development Director, reported on one such competitor; Nicelife.

Nicelife has experienced a near 15% decline in revenue over the past year and has reported net operating losses in both of the past two years. This was despite some quite radical steps to keep costs under control, which included a major redundancy programme when the company shed around 20% of its non-seasonal staff. This came as a surprise to the employees although many of those dismissed have since found new positions in the industry, including a number who have moved to Broadsword. Nicelife has continued to operate well in this difficult period, even though the head count is much reduced.

Nicelife is currently owned by its senior management team and Judo, a group of venture capitalists. Their respective holdings were 50:50 until 1 December 2008, when Judo invested a further £10m and the ratio changed to 30:70.

You have been asked to prepare a report on the potential acquisition of Nicelife by Broadsword. Consider how the 'bottom-line' questions addressed by your report would differ if you were reporting to:

- the shareholders of Broadsword
- the shareholders of Nicelife
- the Competition Commission
- the employees of both companies

Specific applications

 Exam based

When writing a report as part of an exam requirement you need to consider the objective of your report on two levels. On the one hand, it is important to go along with the 'role play' scenario that often you'll be presented with. You'll need to think carefully about the position you're being expected to adopt, who you are writing to and the context of the report in order to discover the 'bottom-line' questions and deliver them.

On the other hand though, you need to bear in mind that you're trying to pass an exam. The examiner will have laid down some criteria that the markers will look for within your script and to ensure a pass, you must deliver them. This may require you to suspend your thoughts on how you would prepare this report in reality and, to some extent, 'play the game' with what you produce.

Example

The Chartered Institute of Management Accountants (CIMA) case study paper specifies nine criteria against which students will be assessed. One of these is 'technical' where students need to use approximately five technical models throughout their script, relating these models to the issues being covered. In reality, it is unlikely that any report from a management accountant to the Board of Directors would make reference to models such as Mendelow's matrix or Maslow's hierarchy of needs, but in this instance, students must move away from reality and deliver what the examiner is wanting.

When trying to pass an exam, the starting point is to ensure you understand the criteria against which you'll be assessed

When trying to pass an exam, the starting point of your planning process, even before you consider your user and their 'bottom-line' questions, is to ensure you understand the criteria against which you'll be assessed and the competencies the examiner is wanting you to display.

Having found out what you need to do, you must constantly refer to these throughout your planning process to check you are delivering.

 Dissertation

The precise process for preparing a dissertation will vary depending on whether it is an undergraduate, graduate or MBA assignment. So the first thing to stress is that you must carefully review any guidance issued by the university or institution where you are studying. This will provide detailed rules and helpful suggestions on how to select your topic and how to present your final document. That said, there are some helpful points we can make here that will be relevant to all.

When it comes to establishing the 'bottom-line' questions of a dissertation, the process is quite different to a report prepared in an exam or for someone in business. This is because the questions can be directly controlled by you. You, and you alone, will have to select a topic, assert an argument or find a statement to defend.

One may think this should make it straight-forward. Surely, if you get to set your own 'bottom-line' questions, it should be much easier to ensure you address them? Not necessarily.

As a student, you are used to having the scope of an assignment laid out for you; so when you are given complete freedom to select whatever you want, it can be difficult to decide. The key is to choose your topic wisely. So here are some top tips to follow when selecting the topic of your dissertation.

When selecting the topic of your dissertation you must be clear on the aims of your research

- Try to structure your title around an underlying question or hypothesis (a statement you are defending or central argument you are asserting). This will make your objective much clearer and you will find it easier to keep this thesis at the forefront of your mind as you plan and write.

- Be clear about the aims of your research. Try to limit these aims to three at most. Any more and your dissertation will start to lose focus. Draw up a statement of the overall nature of any original work along with a list of objectives for your work. This will help you assess progress as you work on the project.

- Don't take on too much, or be too ambitious in what you will be able to achieve in the time available. As a general rule, the narrower and more specific the better. See chapter 3 for more guidance on time management.

- Choose a topic that interests you as this will make the whole process more pleasurable. More importantly though, don't lose sight of what is being examined. The majority of assessors will be looking for evidence of your skills as a researcher as well as the application of the knowledge learned on your course. It is important that your topic gives you sufficient opportunity to do this.

- Take your time to decide. When you have an idea, carry out plenty of research to determine the availability of information and the extent to which the topic has been covered by previous research.

Often within post-graduate and, in particular, MBA dissertations, students will focus on a topic related to the company for which they now work. It's important to note that a report produced for your company is unlikely to represent an acceptable dissertation without significant alteration. A dissertation will require much more background information since it will be read (and more importantly assessed) by people who aren't familiar with the specifics of the company. It will also need to go into far more detail on the academic arguments and technical theories, perhaps taking a more reflective or critical line than would be expected in a business report. This should be evident by comparing and contrasting the purpose and 'bottom-line' questions, which will be very different for these two pieces of work.

 ## Business report

A report prepared in business will typically be for your boss or for a client. Either way, it's important to remember that they are paying for this. Whilst this means they may be more demanding or have higher expectations, it also means they will be more willing to invest the time ensuring you know exactly what they want you to do. It's a corny expression but time is money in business, and a report that does not achieve its objective will be a waste of both their time and yours.

When writing a report in business, take the opportunity to clarify your user's expectations

Take the time and seize the opportunity to clarify their expectations. Ideally, this should be over more than one meeting as this gives you the opportunity to consider their requests in more depth, perhaps perform some initial investigative work, and go back with further questions.

Try to end your discussions with an unequivocal list of questions they want your report to address. By stating the scope of the report in this way, both you and the recipient of your report will be clear on the 'bottom-line' questions from the outset.

In a nutshell...............

The starting point of the report writing process is to pin-point the objective of your report. This will involve funnelling down through the generic aims of the report, on to assessing the factors affecting the specific purpose of your report and ending with the identification of the 'bottom-line' questions that the reader wants answering.

The most common aims of business reports are to:

- Convey information in order to:
    - provide a summary
    - present analysis
    - communicate findings.
- Reach conclusions that:
    - persuade the reader
    - aid decision-making
    - give recommendations.

The specific factors that will need to be considered include:

- the context of the report
- the author (i.e. who you are and what your role is)
- the reader (their background and experience in the area the report is covering).

To identify the 'bottom-line' questions you should put yourself in the position of the reader and ask yourself; what would you want to know? This 'user-focused' approach will provide a clear mandate for your report.

Answering the 'bottom-line' questions should be viewed as the objective of your report and so, once identified, you can begin your planning process, placing these questions at the very heart of your plan.

Chapter 2

Your content plan

In this chapter

We will consider the importance of planning the content of your report, and how this will help ensure it achieves its objectives. We'll also cover how to prepare your plan, looking at things such as how to efficiently gather and record information, what to do with the information you have and how to decide whether you need any more.

Gathering, processing and reviewing information are necessary elements of the report preparation process. All require a logical approach, an organised recording system and self-control to not go over the top.

This chapter will show you how to achieve all of these by working through a simple three step cycle. At the heart of and under pinning this cycle is the need to document your findings and your thoughts. So after considering the importance of documentation, we'll provide some practical tips on how to structure and use a planning sheet to drive the content of your final report. Each stage of the cycle will be examined to ensure you have a clear understanding of what needs to be achieved along the way.

The importance of having a plan

Having identified the objective and established the mandate for your report, we next need to consider how best to deliver it. This is where your plan comes in.

In the introduction we defined a report as 'an account given of a matter after investigation or consideration'. It would therefore be naive to think that, having identified the objective of your report, you can just start writing and deliver in full. As a minimum, you will have to gather some information and process it before you commit pen to paper (or finger to keyboard as is more often the case). Without this processing you have not 'investigated' or 'considered' anything.

Furthermore, you will need to consider how best to present the information, whether there is a logical order, whether some points should be prioritised above others, and how best to construct your argument. All of these points and more will be covered by a plan.

The starting point, and indeed central point, for any plan will be the report's objective - answering those 'bottom-line' questions. This ensures you place this at the heart of everything you do from here forward.

You should not add anything to your plan if it is not directly linked to answering the 'bottom-line' questions. This will focus your mind and ensure you stay on track and don't deviate away from meeting your user's expectations. This is particularly important when writing a report under time constraints since you won't have time to waste on unnecessary diversions.

In chapter 1, we noted that a potential aim of a report is to persuade the reader that a certain conclusion or recommendation is the right one. To do this you will need to build a sound case or construct an argument to support your assertions; you cannot simply real off lots of facts in a random order and expect the reader to piece it together. This is another area where a plan is essential. During the process of preparing a report you will uncover facts and think through implications in what may be a haphazard fashion. By noting them all within your plan, you can more clearly see the linkages or the path that must be taken to build the argument. Once identified, you can spell out this path within your report in a much more ordered fashion.

Finally, a plan will ensure your report covers everything it has to. It's very easy to finish writing a report and realise that a great point you'd thought of earlier has been accidently missed out. This is particularly frustrating if a report is hand-written as inserting it in the appropriate place can be difficult. Even when typing your report, inserting a new point may require the surrounding text to be re-written in order for the section to make sense. A plan, if used properly, will help to ensure this never happens to you again.

So, as you can see, preparing a plan before you write has many advantages. The key question is - are there any disadvantages?

Often students will approach us with statements like "I never plan – it just feels like a waste of time". Such declarations do reveal one potential problem. A plan will only deliver everything we've noted if constructed properly. It's therefore important to take some time to develop this skill if you're going to unlock the benefits we've noted above. This book will show you how.

You should not add anything to your plan if it is not directly linked to answering the 'bottom-line' questions

A plan is vital as it will ensure your report covers everything

Planning is never a waste of time if a plan is constructed properly

The planning cycle

Handling the information required to write your report is not a one-off event. Instead it should be regarded as a cycle that is repeated over and over until you have sufficient information to be able to fully address the 'bottom-line' questions the user wants answering. The repetition of the cycle will be a key way in which your plan will develop.

The planning cycle

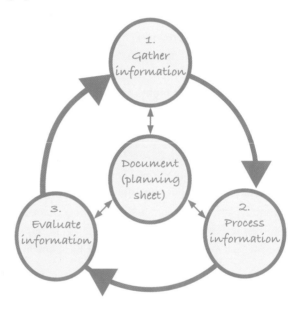

At the heart of the planning cycle is your planning sheet where you will record all of the information you collate

At the heart of the cycle is a document called a planning sheet where you will record all of the information you collate. There is nothing more likely to waste time than failing to document your findings as and when you come across them. As you gather each new piece of information it should be documented. You will then need to process that information, to reveal both the fact and its implications (see chapters 4 and 5 for more details on this), which should also be recorded or noted in some way. Finally, you must review the information you've identified to see if you have enough to answer those all important 'bottom-line' questions; documenting your reasoning as you do so (more is covered on this in chapter 6). If the answer is no, then the process starts over again, with further information gathering, processing and reviewing. This cycle will be repeated until such a time as enough information is available to allow your report to meet its objective.

The planning sheet

Earlier in this chapter, we discussed the importance of having a plan when writing a report. The documentation of the information you gather will form the spine of that plan, pulling everything together in one place, providing the framework to enable you to think commercially, draw your conclusions and formulate your recommendations before you structure your report and eventually write it. Your planning sheet is something that will be enhanced, refined and constantly referred to as your report takes shape.

Your planning sheet will be enhanced, refined and constantly referred to as your report takes shape

How should I structure my planning sheet?

There is no single correct answer to this but as a general rule, you will want to divide your report, and therefore your planning sheet, into sections, or more likely, a number of sheets. These might relate to the specific requirements of an exam or the 'bottom-line' questions your user wants answering.

However, the best structure will often depend on the situation.

Example

Let's contrast some different situations, beginning with a look at two professional accountancy case study exams. Firstly, the CIMA T4 Case Study Examination that requires students to prepare a report that prioritises and analyses the issues facing the company, evaluates alternative solutions and provides recommendations. New information is provided on a number of issues that can vary in length between a few lines to just under a page. In this situation, a planning sheet that helps to prioritise the issues can be of benefit but any specific work planning each individual issue is perhaps best attempted by making notes in the margin of the exam paper. This reduces the need to copy or transfer information from one place to another.

Now contrast this with the ICAEW Case Study, which asks students to prepare a report covering three specific requirements. Information relevant to these requirements will be provided over a number of further exhibits. Planning on the exam paper in this situation would mean information was dotted around over several pages. Students are therefore advised to have a planning sheet for each individual requirement.

When writing a dissertation, where the objectives are often more open-ended, you may find it appropriate to have a planning sheet for each chapter, with perhaps an overview sheet showing how the chapters fit together. This is the approach we have taken in writing this book, which to many intents and purposes could be regarded as simply a long dissertation.

What should my planning sheet contain?

The primary purpose will be to document the information you gather. However, as noted in both the introduction and chapter 1, often your report will have to outline an argument, persuade the reader and develop recommendations. You will therefore need space on your planning sheets for not only the facts but also the implications of those facts. These will be needed to add weight to your arguments and advice. You may also want to see clearly how facts inter-relate with each other.

Depending on your situation, you may be required to provide a reference to the source of your information. By capturing this information as you go, you can save precious time later on.

What should my planning sheet look like?

Your planning sheet will enable you to see all relevant information in one place

Again, there is no universally correct answer to this. Much of it will depend on your personal preferences, as well as your situation. The key is to remember the purpose of your planning sheet; to form the basis of your plan and to enable you to see all relevant information in one place.

Spider diagrams (or mind-maps)

Spider diagrams or mind-maps involve creating a picture showing all the information you have and how different pieces link together. They are ideal for those people who are better stimulated by pictures and diagrams and are beneficial as they allow you to see at a glance, how your argument is taking shape.

The distinction between spider diagrams and mind-maps is in their purpose. Mind-maps are usually constructed in a well thought out manner, their primary purpose being to aid recall on a subject. Often you will see plenty of illustrations and drawings together with the use of different colours to trigger your memory into action. Spider diagrams are a little less complex. They usually consist of a series of 'bubbles' and 'lines' used to show information and relationships as part of a plan to achieve something.

For the purposes of writing a report, spider diagrams are therefore usually more appropriate, particularly if you are under any form of time pressure.

At the heart of the spider diagram you should place the central theme (usually in a 'bubble'). This will most likely be one of the 'bottom-line' questions your report must address. As you gather each new piece of information, you should add a new 'bubble' and record the information. You don't need to add lots of detail – just enough to capture the facts. When you process the information you will also need to add its implication to your diagram.

Each new piece of information should be linked, either to the central theme, or to some other facts or implications which you have previously noted. If you don't feel able to make a link to something on your sheet, the likelihood is that the information is irrelevant to what you are doing (see next section).

Example

A couple of friends of yours have recently approached you looking for advice on 'going it alone' as solicitors. They are unsure how to start a business and would like your advice on the best structure for them. A spider diagram of initial thoughts could be drawn as follows:

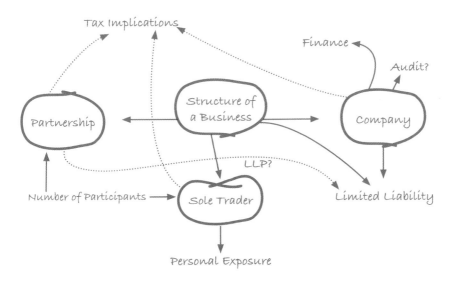

Ordered list

In contrast to the diagram approach, this method suits those people who prefer structure and lists. You will begin each planning sheet by setting up some column headings relating to the aspects you need to cover. This could be as generic as 'fact' and 'implication' or it could be something more specific to your scenario.

As you gather each new piece of information, you will make a note under the relevant column, adding further comments as you process the information and consider its implications.

Example

Using the same scenario as we looked at for spider diagrams, an ordered list could appear as follows.

COMPANY	PARTNERSHIP	SOLE TRADER
Easier to raise finance	Tax implications	Personal exposure
Limited liability so less personal exposure	Easy to add new partners	Won't fit if want to do it together
Tax implications	Legal requirement	
Legal requirements (audit)	Limited Liability Partnership (LLP) – best of both worlds?	

If your report requires you to prioritise information, you can do this as you go along, writing new pieces of information either above or below existing facts depending on their relative importance.

Lists are such a part of our everyday lives that this method is the one naturally adopted by many people. However, it is not as good as the diagram approach for showing relationships and recognising these linkages is a key element in preparing a well thought out report.

Gathering information

Prepare a 'shopping list'

Before you gather any information, start by writing out a 'shopping list' of information you would like to have. What information would you regard as essential to enable you to answer the 'bottom-line' questions, and perhaps more importantly, where can you get that information from? This 'shopping list' should be the first thing you write on your planning sheets. As you gather each piece of information, you can 'tick' it off your list, perhaps adding further items to your list as a result of what you discover.

Outside of the exam hall, you can save large amounts of time by using this technique. It will help you to focus on the relevant and dismiss the irrelevant.

In an exam situation this isn't such a crucial step since you are limited to the amount of information available. However, it can still help to focus your mind when reading through the information provided.

Start with what you already know

In any situation, be it an exam or not, you will have a certain amount of knowledge and information already within your head. The next step therefore is to 'brainstorm' what you already know, getting this information onto your planning sheets before you go any further. This will help to free up space in your brain before any new information requires processing. This brainstorming could involve recording specific facts or information already known or it could be noting down ideas on areas where further information will be required.

Before you gather any information, start by writing out a 'shopping list' of information you would like to have

Processing information

Whenever you add some information to your planning sheet, you should note down why you've added it. Try to consider the implication of that fact; the 'so what' as well as just the 'what'. Chapter 4 goes into more detail about how to think commercially and how to work through the implications of information and chapter 5 considers how this process might alter if you're dealing with numerical information. At this stage, however, we just want to stress the importance of you processing each piece of information as it is added.

It is important to capture your thoughts as you have them or else you risk losing them

When planning a report, you will often feel like a firework display is going off in your mind. Each new piece of information you identify triggers a series of 'explosions' or thought processes on what that information means or how it can be used. It is important to capture these thoughts as they happen or else you risk losing them or, worse still, spending much time feeling frustrated as you are unable to recall them.

Another key part of the processing stage is to check information for consistency or for potential conflicts. Any conflicts will need to be acknowledged in your report and ideally, should be addressed and resolved by obtaining further information.

Evaluating information

After each new piece of information has been processed, you should stand back and evaluate whether you now have enough information to be able to draw some conclusions and, if required, make some recommendations. Are you able to answer the 'bottom-line' questions? Reaching this decision will require the exercising of judgement and perhaps some further commercial thinking in order to identify and evaluate potential recommendations. How to do this will be covered in detail within chapter 6; all we wish to do now is highlight the importance of this stage within the overall cycle.

It is unlikely that you will feel able to reach conclusions after just populating your planning sheets with the information you already know and so you should consider what further information you may need and where you can obtain it. At this point, you commence the cycle again.

Example

Back to the scenario with our solicitor friends. Clearly from our initial brainstorm, we don't have enough information to be able to advise our friends one way or the other. Additional information we will need to gather and evaluate will include (but is not limited to):

- What are the legal implications of forming a company or a partnership?

- What are the tax implications of forming a company or a partnership?

- How do LLPs work and what are the benefits?

- How many firms of solicitors are set up as LLPs – is this the norm and if it is, why?

- How much finance will be required? Will more need to be raised?

Gathering new information

In the majority of situations, there will be specific new information that is fundamental to your report and that must be processed. Often this will relate to the trigger factor for your report (for example, a take-over bid, an audit or, in an exam situation, the additional information you've been provided with in the exam hall.) Perhaps the one exception to this is a dissertation although the points we're about to outline are still just as relevant.

Reading and comprehending new information can take a long time, yet often we are up against time constraints that mean we're tempted to rush this process.

Mastering the skill of speed reading

Speed reading is a collection of reading methods which attempt to increase rates of reading without greatly reducing comprehension or retention.

It is a skill that you should look to master as it can be really helpful in processing large amounts of information. This is often the case when writing reports as you commonly find yourself having to read many other written documents to ensure that what you are writing is both informed and comprehensive.

Aoccdrnig to rseearch at Cmabrigde Uinervtisy, wehn yuo're wirting in the Enlgish lagnauge, it deosn't mttaer in waht oredr the ltteers in a wrod are, the olny iprmotant tihng is taht the frist and lsat ltteer be at the rghit pclae. The rset can be a tatol mses and you can sitill raed it wouthit a porbelm. Tihs is bcuseae the huamn mnid deos not raed ervey lteter by istlef, but the wrod as a wlohe.

Tihs is one of the rseanos seped radaindg wokrs and is so evfecftie

The truth is you probably already use speed reading techniques to some extent. Think of a time when you looked at a document or article and the volume you were faced with seemed daunting and you were perhaps unsure if it was even worth reading at all. What did you do? Glance at the headings, pick out the key words, turn the pages quickly whilst scanning for something that would catch your eye. These are speed reading techniques, all you need to do is make the approach a little more structured and focus your attention more precisely.

The most important trick about speed reading is to know what information you want from a document before you start reading it

The most important trick about speed reading is to know what information you want from a document before you start reading it. If you only want an outline of the issue, then you can skim the document quickly and extract only the essential facts. If you need to understand the real detail of the document, then you may need to read it slowly enough to gain the full understanding you need.

Key words

40-60% of the words on a page are neither critical nor important. So, it stands to reason that if you could figure out which are the key words you could scan past the other words and let your mind fill in the blanks. Train your mind to find these key words and you'll add even more speed to your reading. The average reader ploughs through somewhere between 250 and 350 words per minute for easy material. The ideal reading speed, however, is probably between 500 - 700 words per minute, and can be achieved by using some of the techniques below. Some people can read even faster. The world speed reading competition has individuals reading 1,000 - 2,000 words per minute although there is some lack of comprehension at this rate, and this is a key point.

Technique

- Prepare - what do you want from the book or document, what are you looking for and how important is each part? It is never a bad idea to write this down.

- Preview - familiarise yourself with the structure, look briefly at the cover of your document and see what it tells you about the subject. Look at the table of contents to understand the flow and run through the document briefly, one or two seconds per page is all you need. Make a note of how it is put together, what parts interest you and highlight what you want to explore in more detail.

- Use a technique to read faster - most of these techniques involve moving an object, a pencil or even your finger, from left to right and back again. Below is some specific guidance.

Sit at a table or desk with the text held between 15 and 18 inches in front of the eyes. Eliminate distractions, noises, and anything that will compete for your attention while you do this exercise.

Trace your fingertip underneath the printed text lines starting at ¾ of an inch from the left hand margin to ¾ of an inch from the right hand margin at a steady even speed. The finger, scanning beneath the text of each and every line acts as a pacer which eyes will naturally follow. Humming a tune out loud can be effective in that it occupies the speech centres of the brain. This part of the brain can only really do one thing at a time, so this makes it impossible to mouth words or imagine mouthing words. Mouthing words (or what is referred to as sub-vocalisation) is one of the main reasons some people read more slowly.

Practice the exercise for about 15 minutes a day. After a few days the reading experience will become more natural and your speed will cease to be limited by the speed limits of spoken speech.

The big debate around speed reading is comprehension verses speed. So in that planning section try to identify what is crucial, something that if you misread could result in a significant problem or mean that you miss a key point. For these more important areas you should perhaps slow down and focus your attention on the key words by underlining them. This not only makes them more visible but the very process of underlining will help promote those words in your mind so making it more likely that their significance will not be missed when your brain gets going on putting the whole case together.

So in summary, speed reading is very useful if not essential in allowing you to process large amounts of information, but when you are dealing with something technical that needs your full attention, you would be wise to slow down. And don't forget, as you speed read your way through new relevant information, document it along with any thoughts you have about the significance of that information. Continue the cycle by evaluating whether you have sufficient information and if you need more, where it will come from.

When dealing with something technical, you would be wise to slow your reading down

Further reading

'Speed reading in a week' by Tina Konstant. Hodder Arnold; 2nd Revised edition (27 Sep 2002).

The Case – a chance to practise

Building on the information you've already been given in the introduction and chapter 1 regarding Broadsword's interest in Nicelife, you can now practise the techniques we've covered in this chapter. You will be writing a report to your boss in the Corporate Development Department. Although you may have identified a range of potential 'bottom-line' questions in your answer to the chapter 1 exercise, your boss has now specifically asked you to prepare an initial report investigating two of the key areas the Board of Broadsword would need to consider before it can reach a decision on whether to acquire Nicelife.

At a meeting with your boss to discuss the content of the report, you have agreed that the 'bottom-line' questions your report will answer are.

- How does Nicelife's performance compare with Broadsword's over the last two years? Specifically, your boss wants to understand why Nicelife has incurred losses over that period.

- What will be the likely reaction of the Competition Commission to an acquisition?

Your boss has given you the following information, which he obtained from the internet as a starting point for your investigations.

Start by preparing a shopping list of information you feel you will need to be able to answer the 'bottom-line' questions. Then move on to populating your planning sheets with the information you've already been given in the introduction to this book.

Next, review the new information provided on the next three pages, using speed reading techniques, and make a note of relevant facts. At this stage, don't worry about interpretting those facts (we'll cover that in chapter 4). You should also identify any further information that you will require to complete your report.

Document your answer on a planning sheet.

The UK Competition Authorities: How they work

This paper provides a summary of the broad principles that apply for the protection of both consumer and supplier.

General concepts of competition

Market competition is a simple and efficient way of guaranteeing products and services of excellent quality at competitive prices. Suppliers (producers and traders) offer goods or services on the market to meet customers' demands. Customers seek the best deal available in terms of quality and price for the products they require; this best deal emerges as a result of a contest between suppliers.

Competition policy aims to ensure wider consumer choice, technological innovation and effective price competition by ensuring that companies compete rather than collude, that dominant companies do not abuse their market power and that efficiencies are passed on to final consumers.

The UK competition framework: What is the Competition Commission?

The Competition Commission (CC) is one of the independent public bodies which help ensure healthy competition between companies in the UK for the benefit of companies, customers and the economy.

They investigate and address issues of concern in mergers and acquisitions (hereafter referred to as mergers) - when larger companies will gain more than 25% market share and where a merger appears likely to lead to a substantial lessening of competition in one or more markets in the UK.

Competition Commission Guidelines

The CC will be asked to investigate a merger if there is or may be a 'relevant merger situation' that has resulted, or may be expected to result, in a 'substantial lessening of competition'.

A 'relevant merger situation' is created if one of the following thresholds is met:

- the value of the UK turnover of the enterprise acquired (or to be acquired) exceeds £70m (the turnover test); or

- the share of supply of goods or services in the UK or in a substantial part of the UK held (or to be held) by the merged enterprise is at least 25% (the share of supply test).

After gathering information the CC must consider five questions. The first two questions seek to establish whether an investigation is required, the last three assess whether a remedy is required.

The two 'initial merger questions' are:

- whether a relevant merger situation has been (or will likely be) created; and if so

- whether the creation of that situation has resulted, or may be expected to result, in a substantial lessening of competition within any market or markets in the UK for goods or services.

An important element in deciding whether a merger results in a substantial lessening of competition is to define the relevant market or markets. There are normally two dimensions to the definition of a market: a product dimension and a geographic dimension. There is inevitably an element of judgement involved in defining the market and the CC will adopt the methodology most appropriate in the context of the relevant merger situation.

If they answer both questions in the affirmative, there is an anti-competitive outcome from the merger and the Commission must go on to consider remedies.

The three 'remedies questions' (for both completed and anticipated mergers) are:

- whether action should be taken by the Commission;

- whether the Commission should recommend the taking of action by others; and, in either case,

- what action (if any) should be taken and what is to be remedied, mitigated or prevented.

Typical remedies include:

- divestment of assets, business units, sectors, or entire businesses

- 'behavioural undertakings' by one or more parties

- 'monitoring' – i.e. the requirement to provide specified information about (say) prices or the terms and conditions of sale, as and when requested by the Director General of Fair Trading.

In arriving at its decision on remedies, the CC may request that the merger parties themselves, and/or other third parties (including relevant regulators), submit their proposed remedies to prevent the substantial lessening of competition.

If the CC decides that remedies are required, they will consult with relevant parties on the choice and form of these measures and then set out their decision on remedies in their final report. Following publication of the final report they will work with relevant parties to prepare undertakings or orders that give effect to their requirement.

Following its decision on remedies, the Commission can clear the merger, subject to the remedies being undertaken. However, it may decide that no remedies are sufficient to prevent a substantial lessening of competition: in such a case, it will prohibit the merger.

Specific applications

 ## Exam based

Once you have processed all of the information in your head and all of the information presented to you in the exam, your final review must conclude that you have enough information to answer the 'bottom-line' question. After all, you have no other potential sources of information available to you!

Always re-read the exam paper to check you haven't missed any information

Sometimes, students feel that they could still do with more information, and perhaps feel frustrated or angry as a result. The first thing to do in that situation is check that you haven't missed anything. Re-read the exam paper again just to check. If this doesn't reveal anything then you'll just have to get on with it regardless.

The important thing is to reach conclusions, and give recommendations (if required), based on the information you do have. As a general rule, examiners do not give significant marks to those who sit on the fence. See chapter 6 on conclusions and recommendations for more detail on this area.

 ## Dissertation and business reports

Outside the exam hall, the review of the information collected is a far more important step in the overall cycle.

If you still don't feel like you have enough information to fully address the 'bottom-line' questions you must identify what further information you require and just as importantly, where and how you can get it. You will need to carry out some further research and it's important to carefully consider the best way to do this. Broadly, you have two options:

Desk research

Desk research is the gathering and processing of existing or 'secondary' data. This may use information such as existing company reports or other information in the public domain, as well as internal company information depending on the circumstances.

To carry out successful desk research, you should assume that the work has already been done; it just needs to be located. You must think laterally and keep an open mind. Make sure you document what you look at throughout the process and follow up leads, however vague they may seem.

A word of warning though. Whilst desk research is a lot easier in the 21st century than it ever has been in the past, it is also a lot harder to sift the relevant from the irrelevant. Be careful not to waste time reading lots of information that adds little value to your overall report.

Finally, don't forget that you must refer to any of the published material you use and/or directly quote from (see chapter 7 for more details). You can save a lot of time by ensuring you note all of the relevant details at this stage.

Field research

Field research involves the collection of new (primary) information direct from respondents. It is usually more expensive than desk research and so is often only performed if desk research fails to deliver all of the necessary information.

There are three main types of field research:

• opinion research: to determine people's opinions on issues

• motivation research: to determine why people do what they do

• measurement research: to quantify research so that sample results can be extrapolated to a target population.

Specific techniques for performing such research include interviews, trial testing, observation and questionnaires. Of these, questionnaires are probably the most common. Care must be taken when setting the questions and in particular, you should think about how you plan to analyse the data obtained. Often, some form of sample will need to be selected and this can either be done randomly or can be based on a quota, where certain characteristics of the sample are pre-determined.

In a nutshell..............

Preparing a content plan is an effective way of ensuring your report answers the 'bottom-line' questions, contains an argument that flows logically from one point to the next and covers everything it needs to.

Regardless of your situation, writing a report that meets its objective will not be possible unless you process all of the necessary information. You will need to repeat the planning cycle several times until you are happy you have all of the information you require to answer the 'bottom-line' questions. The cycle contains three key stages.

- Gather the next piece of information.

- Process that information so you are clear about the facts and their implications.

- Review the information you have and exercise judgement to determine whether it is sufficient to answer your 'bottom-line' questions. If the answer is no, you must repeat the cycle again.

At the heart of this cycle is a document called a planning sheet where you will record all of the information you collate.

The purpose of your planning sheet is to enable you to see all relevant information in one place. It is something that will be enhanced, refined and constantly referred to as your report takes shape. It will also help you to avoid unnecessary repetition of work later on.

Before you populate your sheet with any information, start by writing out a 'shopping list' of the information you would like, and think about where each piece of information can be obtained.

You should then begin by considering what information you already know before adding to this by gathering new information. Each piece of information must be processed and it is important to capture your thoughts as you have them or else you risk losing them. As you populate your planning sheets you will need to think about the most appropriate way of structuring your sheets; common methods include spider diagrams and ordered lists.

Techniques such as speed reading can be used to help review large volumes of information quickly and efficiently.

Chapter 3

Your time plan

In this chapter

We're going to explore one of the most fundamental elements of writing an effective report – time management.

Time management and prioritisation are essential skills for dealing with many situations in life but in report writing they are crucial. Whether you're sitting an exam, writing your dissertation or are up against a deadline for a meeting, you never have the time you need to write the report you want to write.

With this in mind, this chapter will look at some key aspects of good time management. We'll show you how to prepare a realistic time plan or schedule that plays to your personal strengths and weaknesses; we'll consider techniques to help you stick to it; how prioritisation can be the answer to many time problems, before looking at how to prioritise effectively.

And finally, in recognition of the fact that things don't always go to plan, we'll provide guidance on how to recover if your timings start to slip.

The importance of having a plan - and sticking to it!

In chapter 2 we talked about the importance of planning and how much easier the writing process can be if you prepare a detailed plan. However, the focus on this was in planning the content of your report. What we haven't done so far is consider the time you spend preparing your report: how much time should be spent planning, and how this should compare with the time spent actually writing your report.

We've not addressed this yet because it's like asking "how long is a piece of string?" There is no definitive answer of how long it should take to prepare a report. Very often the answer is "as long as you've got". But one thing is guaranteed - whatever time you've got won't be enough.

There is no definitive answer of how long it should take to prepare a report. Whatever time you've got won't be enough!

The problem with never having enough time is that it forces you to compromise. Something has to give. Something you would have liked to have done has to be left incomplete in order to get the report published within the deadline set. So, what do you drop?

Too frequently students find themselves in this situation and what tends to get dropped is the final stages of the planning cycle. They start off with the best of intentions, gather the information, maybe crunch some numbers, but then realise they're running out of time. "I'd better start writing or I'll never get finished" is the typical thought that comes into their head, just before they grab their pen and launch into composing the first section of their report.

Now we're sure that once you've read the contents of this book (and in particular chapters 4 and 6), you'll see the danger in this strategy. The final stages of the planning cycle are the stages where you have the commercial thought processes, where you consider the implications of your findings and where you reach your conclusions and recommendations. These are the key stages in adding value to your report. Without this the benefits of your initial planning steps are significantly reduced.

So, the student gets to the end of writing their report, just about manages to finish in time and is left with the conclusion that planning was a complete waste of time. They feel they didn't see any benefit from the time they invested at the start of the process. Is it any wonder they reach this conclusion when they skipped the most important part?

To ensure the whole process works as it should, it's important that alongside your plan for the content of your report, you also have a time plan, let's call it a schedule, that clearly shows the activities or tasks to be completed, the amount of time available for each, as well as a deadline for each stage.

You need to operate two plans, one for the content of your report and one showing the activities to be completed and the time needed for each

Example

If you decide in your content plan that you need to perform some calculations to support your argument, your time plan (or schedule) would detail how long you expect to spend performing those calculations.

Having such a schedule, and more importantly sticking to it, will ensure you complete all the necessary stages in preparing an effective report.

Devising a schedule – the 4 steps to success

Now you appreciate why a schedule is so important, the next key question is how do you devise one that works? Allow us to introduce the four steps to scheduling success.

Step 1 Identify the time available

This has to be the best place to start. Look at the amount of time available between now and the deadline for the submission of your report. Then, try to be realistic about how much time you'll be able to devote to preparing the report. Consider what other commitments you may have, and the amount of time they are likely to take. Consider also how much time you're willing to invest in preparing the report.

Try to be realistic about how much time you're willing to devote to preparing the report

If you're sitting an exam, this step in generally quite easy. If it's a four hour exam then that's the length of time you've got. Perhaps those who will find this the hardest are the ones preparing their dissertation. Background information on your objectives will often be given many months before the submission date. With such a large amount of time is can be difficult to assess with any accuracy the amount of time you'll be able to invest. More guidance is given on this later in this chapter.

One of the most important factors affecting your ability to stick to your schedule is being realistic in your assessments of the time required for each activity

One of the most important factors affecting your ability to ultimately stick to this schedule is how realistic you are in these initial assessments. Try to avoid setting yourself up for a fall later down the track by over-committing at this stage in the process.

Step 2 Consider what has to be completed

Everyone has come across the expression 'time management'. But when you think about it, this really is quite a curious idea – can time really be managed? Regardless of what you do, there will always be 24 hours in a day, 7 days in a week. Not a lot can be 'managed' in this context. So the term 'time management' isn't really about managing time, it's about choosing what you do in that time.

'Time management' isn't really about managing time, it's about choosing what you do in that time

Having decided how much time you have available to prepare the report, you now have to decide what needs to be achieved in that time. Your overall goal will be to produce a report that answers the user's 'bottom-line' questions, but what will you need to do in order to meet their expectations?

We know from chapter 2 that you'll need to spend some time planning your report and some time writing it. As a general rule of thumb (and this is very broad brush) an equal amount of time should be spent on each. But this still doesn't seem very helpful. If the total time you have available is 80 hours, to have a schedule saying 40 hours planning, 40 hours writing will not help you stay on track. You need more detail.

Ask yourself this; what do I need to achieve in order to answer these 'bottom-line' questions? Try to be as detailed as you can by breaking things down into stages. The rest of this book will help you with this, as it outlines the different stages in the overall process of preparing a report, so for example, what information will I need to gather (see chapter 2) and what calculations will I need to perform (see chapter 5). Set yourself smaller objectives or goals that can be obtained along the way – this will make the whole task seem far more manageable.

As you progress in the project you will be able to re-visit this, adding further detail as you become aware of it. The more detail you can give, the more accurate your assessment of timings will be. For that is what you're aiming for here. For each stage or element you should estimate how long it will take you to complete. Again, it is important that you're realistic in these assessments and that you take account of your personal strengths and weaknesses, ensuring you allow sufficient time for tasks which you know might not be your strong point.

Step 3 Relieve the time pressure

Now it may be that when you add it all together, the total time needed comes to more than you have available. It's important to address this as early as possible rather than burying your head in the sand and hoping the problem will go away.

In this situation there are a number of options available to you. These include:

- Re-assess your timings to see if you might be able to reduce the time needed in some areas. Consider how critical each task is and whether you might be able to cut back. But remember, you must still be realistic in your assessments.

- See if there are any areas where you might be able to speed up or become more efficient with practice. Remember, your estimates of the time needed should take account of your personal strengths and weaknesses but it may be possible to address these weaknesses, thereby speeding up the task. This is particularly relevant for those sitting an exam where practising mock exams can improve your skills before the real thing. More on this later in the chapter.

  Your estimates of the time needed should take account of your personal strengths and weaknesses

- Prioritise the tasks based on what is essential to answering the user's 'bottom-line' questions, and those that would simply be nice to have. By completing the essential tasks first you can be sure you'll be able to finish the report. Any 'nice-to-have' elements can then be performed if there is any time left. We'll look at the importance of prioritisation and how to do it later in this chapter.

  By completing the essential tasks first you can be sure you'll be able to finish the report

Step 4 Monitor progress and adjust

A plan that isn't referred to might as well not exist. Be this not referring to your content plan when writing up your report or, in this instance, not referring to your time schedule when completing your project, the consequences can be huge.

As time moves on it's important that you monitor your progress against where you wanted to be. It doesn't matter whether this is a weekly update in a project expected to last several months or a half hourly update in a four hour exam – updates are the crucial first step in the battle to stay on top.

Having completed an update, you then need to react to your findings. It's no good discovering that you're two weeks behind and not flexing your schedule to reflect how you plan to catch up. A schedule will not be perfect when it's first written. You will need to make adjustments and the quicker you identify problems, the less damaging they will be to your ultimate objective.

To adjust your schedule you may need to go back to step 3, re-consider the time you expect tasks to take you, see if you can speed anything up or prioritise the remaining tasks to ensure you complete the most important ones first.

How to stick to your schedule

How many times, when studying for exams, have you thought "I know, I'll prepare a revision timetable"? So, you get a piece of paper, draw out the number of days until your exams, schedule the subjects you're going to revise, get out your different coloured highlighters and colour code it all, make it look pretty, and then realise by the time you've finished that you're already behind schedule! Sound familiar to anyone?

Or how about sitting at your desk, knowing you need to revise but then that gorgeous summer's day comes along and your mates are out having fun in the park and all of a sudden your commitment to your timetable doesn't seem quite so strong.

We've all been there. Preparing timetables and schedules is all very good but they'll only be of any use if we have the discipline to stick to them. So how do we ensure we stick to the plans we make?

A plan that isn't referred to might as well not exist

Regular updates are the crucial first step in the battle to stay on top. Having completed an update, you then need to react to your findings

In his book '**The 7 habits of highly effective people**', Stephen Covey lists one of the habits as 'Begin with the end in mind'. On a micro level this is exactly what you should do when preparing a report. Visualise the delivery of your report that addresses all of the user's needs, that meets all of the criteria against which it will be assessed, and imagine how good it will feel to have produced that. Keep that thought with you throughout the process as this will help to keep your motivation high.

'Begin with the end in mind'. What will your report look like when it's complete?

Next, set yourself small, realistic goals. By breaking down the project into smaller stages, as suggested above, you've already made a start on this. Be clear on the consequences if a goal isn't completed on time and link that back to the potential of failure in the delivery of your report.

Ensure that your goal in each stage is SMART. By this we mean Specific, Measurable, Achievable, Relevant and Time-bound. This will be important when it comes to the 'monitor and adjust' step detailed above as it'll help you assess which stages you've completed and which ones you're part way through. Also make sure that you have a strategy for how you're going to achieve each goal and complete each stage.

The final suggestion on how to stick to your schedule is, if we're honest, a bit of a cheat! It doesn't relate to the delivery of your schedule but more to how you set your schedule up in the first place. Wherever possible, build in a buffer; some contingency time that can help to absorb the consequences if things don't quite go to plan. Every successful project manager knows that including some contingencies within the plan, both in terms of time and cost, is the secret to exceeding expectations. Why should it be any different when the project is to prepare a report?

Wherever possible you should build in a buffer; some contingency time that can help to absorb the consequences if things don't quite go to plan

Prioritisation – a key skill

In step 3 of our '4 steps to scheduling success' plan above, we mentioned how prioritisation can be a key way to relieve the time pressures within a project. However, before we look at how prioritisation can be used when scheduling tasks, it's worthwhile standing back and considering why prioritisation is such a key skill to have when preparing a report.

Prioritisation is a key way to relieve the time pressures within a project

Prioritisation is the process of reviewing a list and scheduling or arranging the order in which you're going to deal with the things on that list. As noted above, it is used when you PLAN your initial time schedule but you'll also benefit from prioritising at the THINK stage of the report writing process; in particular when you exercise judgement over your thoughts and findings to draw conclusions and recommendations. And that's not it! You also use the skill again when you come to structure and WRITE your report, making sure you include the most important matters early within your report.

We'll therefore re-visit the skill of prioritisation many times within this book. At each point we'll consider the specifics of how to prioritise at that particular stage although it's worth noting now that the broad technique does not tend to alter very much.

Let's take some time now to look at prioritisation in the context of your task list.

The why

By prioritising the work you do, you ensure that you tackle the most important stuff first. This means that if, or maybe this should be when, you find you don't have enough time left to do everything, you've at least covered the essentials and are able to complete the overall project.

The tasks that are dropped are those that would be viewed as 'nice-to-have'. You may know that they're missing but since the user was never aware of your original plan, they will continue in blissful ignorance.

As you move through the planning cycle, you can re-assess what you believe to be the highest priority. This could result from the discovery of new information, and your review of the impact of this information to your user, or from the need to amend your time schedule following the completion of the 'monitor and adjust' step detailed above.

The how

If you don't have a set of criteria against which to prioritise, the whole process will fall down

Arguably this is the most important aspect of prioritisation. It's all very well understanding why you should prioritise but if you don't know how, if you don't have a set of criteria against which to prioritise, the whole process will fall down. The precise criteria you use will vary depending on your situation and the stage in the process you're at. However, in a business context, the following will provide a good starting point:

Criterion 1   Link to 'bottom-line' questions

Making the link back to the 'bottom-line' questions your report must answer is vital. Any task that will not help to answer those questions can immediately be relegated to the 'non-essential' pile.

Criterion 2   Impact

By this we mean how significant something will be or by how much it will influence your analysis or your conclusions. You might not be able to fully answer this question until you've done some work, perhaps you need to gather some information first or crunch some numbers. This is another excellent example of why your schedule may need to be adjusted as you progress through the project.

Criterion 3   Urgency

The more urgent a task or an issue, the higher the prioritisation should be given to it. Often when preparing your project schedule you'll find that some activities can't be started until another has been completed. This therefore leads to a natural prioritisation that isn't difficult to work out. When this interdependency doesn't exist, you'll need to carry out a more detailed assessment of how urgent an issue is.

Example

You've been requested to write a report on value-retailing in the fashion industry and the following 'bottom-line' questions have been agreed:

- What are the key issues affecting fashion retailers?

- What strategies are value-retailers adopting and how successful are they?

- How does the supply-chain operate for a value-retailer in the fashion sector?

- Is this a profitable sector in which to operate?

You have a week to prepare the report. In order to answer the questions, you've decided that the following tasks will need completing:

- Reading background articles and looking at some case histories on some real life players. Much of this can be accessed on the internet and this will allow you to answer the first two questions.

- Meet with an expert in the industry to understand the complexities of the supply chain.

- Reviewing the financial statements of companies operating in the sector to determine if they are profitable.

Arranging a meeting with an expert should be viewed as the top priority. It could take some time to set up and so you need to treat this as an urgent task.

Performing research on the internet should be prioritised second. It will help you answer more of the agreed questions and will also help you to prepare for your meeting with the expert. This task will have a greater impact on your ability to deliver the report.

The lowest priority task is to review the financial statements of real life companies. These are readily available so won't be difficult to access and you're only looking for one piece of information within each.

....

Help – I'm running out of time!

Even the best laid plans can go wrong. How the problem occurred isn't anywhere near as important as how you react to the problem

Even the best laid plans can go wrong. How the problem occurred isn't anywhere near as important as how you react to the problem. What has happened has happened and you can't change that so forget about the whys, put them out of your mind and focus on how to pull things around.

Now hopefully, if you've followed the guidance given throughout this chapter, any problems will have been identified as soon as they arose and will have been dealt with swiftly. Remember, the earlier you flex your schedule the less damaging it will be. But what about those last-minute crisis situations? What if your motivation has been lacking as you've gone through the project and now you're left with a small amount of time to get back on track?

The most important thing is to keep calm. Anyone who has ever had time management issues in an exam will know exactly what we mean when we talk about 'that sinking feeling'. It feels like you're being sucked down a plug-hole. The spinning begins first, and then the force of being sucked down that gets stronger and stronger until you can't resist any longer. This is quite a common feeling as panic takes grip of your body. By trying to stay calm you can help to prevent this spiralling feeling.

If you find yourself stuck on a particular task - move on to another task to release the block

The first thing to do is re-group. Try to quickly take stock of what you've completed and what still needs to be done. After this, you'll need to make a realistic assessment of what can be done in the remaining time. Link back to the 'bottom-line' questions, together with any assessment criteria if relevant, to prioritise the remaining tasks.

If you find yourself stuck on a particular task (this may have been the cause of your over-runs in the first place) try to move on to another task in order to release your block. As the saying goes, a change is often as good as a rest, and simply switching your focus for a short period may be enough to get you going again.

You may be faced with having to choose between breadth and depth. Would you prefer to cover a number of tasks or issues quite briefly or just stick to one or two but ensure you perform a thorough analysis? Unfortunately this book can't make this decision for you. It will depend on the situation you're in, who you're preparing the report for and what their perception would be.

If you're running out of time when writing up your report, there are some techniques to consider such as the use of bullet points. We'll cover this in more detail in chapters 7 and 8.

Finally, if possible, you may be able to seek some help. This could involve drafting in some additional people (only really a possibility for those writing a business report) or asking for an extension to your deadline.

Further reading

'The 7 Habits of Highly Effective People' by Stephen R Covey, Simon & Schuster Ltd; 15th Anniversary Edition (4 Jan 2004).

The Case – a chance to practise

You'll remember that in the last chapter you were told that your boss in the Corporate Development Department has asked you to prepare an initial report investigating some of the key areas the Board of Broadsword would need to consider if it were to acquire Nicelife.

The 'bottom-line' questions your report must answer are:

* why has Nicelife incurred losses in the last two years and how does their performance compare with Broadsword's in that period?

* what will be the likely reaction of the Competition Commission to an acquisition?

Prepare a list of further tasks or activities you will need to complete in order to answer these questions and consider how those tasks should be prioritised.

Specific applications

 Exam based

When writing a report as part of an exam requirement you should effectively produce two schedules.

Before the exam

Firstly, you will need a schedule of how you're going to prepare for the exam. This should include some time reviewing all relevant material and importantly, time when you can attempt practice exams to help improve your technique.

Preparing an effective report under exam conditions, and the extreme time pressure this brings, requires a significant amount of exam technique as well as the underlying knowledge and understanding that the examiner is looking for.

Imagine that you were learning to drive a car. You've studied the highway code religiously for several weeks, you've watched a DVD about how to drive and you've accompanied other drivers, watching their approach and techniques. Does this mean you should be able to get in a car and successfully drive from A to B without any problems? Of course it doesn't. The only way you can really learn how to drive is to strap on your seatbelt and get out there and practise. You need to master your driving technique in your own particular way and there is just no substitute for spending hour after hour driving around, not caring where you're going, just practising your skills. Only after investing these hours will you be sufficiently competent to be able to attempt your driving test.

Well, let us tell you that passing a case study style exam, or indeed any exam where you're expected to prepare a report, is very similar. You must invest the hours completing practice exams in order to improve your skills and hone your technique.

The day of the exam

The other schedule you'll need to prepare is a schedule of how to spend your time during the exam itself. This should give priority to those elements you know the examiner views as most important to ensure you spend the most amount of time in these areas.

Often tuition providers will provide guidance on this. However, it's important that you find a time plan that works for you. This will be an adaptation of a generic plan suggested by any tutor and specifically, should take account of your personal strengths and weaknesses.

So, for example, you might know you're quite a slow reader and so will need to allow more time than average to read through the information you're provided with in the exam hall. Alternatively, you might know that you take quite a long time to generate original, commercial ideas so maybe this stage of the planning process should be given more time in your schedule.

So what happens when, even with your schedule, you still have far too much of your report left to write at the end of the exam? The good news is that where your schedule might seem quite unachievable at the start of your exam preparation, by the end you'll be able to fit everything in. How? Well, believe it or not, the more you practise your technique and develop your skills, the quicker you will become. Something that might take you 30 minutes when you sit your first mock exam, may be completed in just 15 once you've practised four or five times.

In terms of our 4 steps to success, step 4 where we monitor and adjust is therefore very important. As you get better at different tasks, you can reduce the time needed for these and transfer that time into other, more important, more highly prioritised tasks.

The final thing to mention is the need to be flexible. More often than not a well prepared student will walk into an exam, go through their usual routine and be reasonably pleased with the result (even though they probably won't admit this to anyone – certainly not outside the exam hall!) Occasionally though, the examiner can throw in a bit of a curve ball; a slight twist that can maybe throw you off-balance. The key to dealing with this is to be able to flex your schedule to accommodate it. Know where you perhaps have a bit of slack or buffer and be prepared to use it if needed. For example, it may be that there are a few more calculations required than normal or an additional issue to analyse, either way, by being aware of aspects in your schedule that can flex, you'll be able to handle it.

When trying to pass an exam you should have two schedules, one covering how you'll prepare for the exam and one for how you'll manage your time in the exam

☞ Dissertation

Time management when preparing a dissertation will, for some, be incredibly hard. Those who are already great at planning and find it easy to be disciplined will be fine. It's the rest of us who might struggle.

The problem is actually one of too much time rather than too little. Often you'll be told about the deadline and assessment criteria for your dissertation as much as 9 months in advance. With such a long period it can be difficult to motivate yourself in the early stages. It's also a lot harder to pin down what you need to do and when.

It is important to appreciate that they give you such a long period of time because you need it. You can't afford to ignore it for a couple of months because if you do, you're bound to find yourself with too much to do in too little time.

In chapter 1 we looked at the importance of selecting the right topic and that this stage of the process should not be rushed. However, once you have settled on a chosen topic, the time management techniques outlined in this chapter must swing into action; and quickly!

One particular tool that is useful for longer term projects such as a dissertation (something to be completed over a course of weeks rather than days or even hours) is a Gantt chart.

A Gantt chart provides a graphical representation of the activities within a project and can be used in both project planning and control (so it's great for the monitor and adjust step as well as the original plan).

It's a horizontal bar chart where the length of the bar represents the duration of the activity. The x-axis of the chart contains the number of weeks or months until the deadline and each bar is entered on the chart according to when it needs to be completed.

An example of a Gantt chart

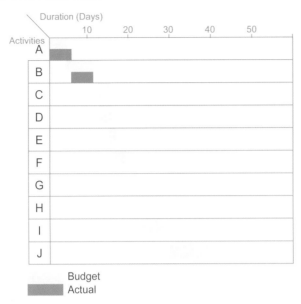

Budget
Actual

When a Gantt chart is used to help control a project it is usual to use two bars, one showing the planned duration of an activity and the second showing the actual duration.

Having some kind of 'snapshot' such as this can really help to keep track of progress over a longer period and the use of such a tool would be strongly recommended.

The use of a tool such as a Gantt chart can help to keep track of progress over a longer period

Business reports

Preparing a business report often lies somewhere in-between an exam situation and a dissertation. Typically you'll have a number of days to complete the project (rather than hours or months as is the case with the other authors). This can be a nice period of time. It's urgent enough to keep you motivated throughout but not so urgent that you feel like you're in a race against time.

When writing a business report there will sometimes be a number of people involved, not just you. You may be fortunate enough to have access to a team of researchers or there may be someone else who is going to type out your report. Equally your report may need to be reviewed by a line manager before being sent to a client. In all of these instances it will be important to liaise closely with your colleagues to make sure they're aware of your time schedule and that it works for them as well as you.

When colleagues are also involved in preparing the report you should liaise closely with them to make sure they're aware of your time schedule and that it works for them as well as you

55

If you're lucky enough to have a team of people (or even just one person) helping you on the project, you may find it easier and more motivating for them, to delegate responsibility for discrete areas of the report, rather than just specific tasks. Try to think how you would have benefitted from being given such responsibility and, if they don't have any experience of preparing reports, give them a copy of this book to help them out!

In a nutshell.............

Spending time planning can feel like a waste of time if your plan is not constructed and used properly. One of the most common reasons for failing to complete a plan is poor time management.

However much time you have to prepare your report, it's unlikely to be enough. Successful time management is not about changing the amount of time available, it's about choosing what you do in that time. It is therefore important to operate two plans, one for the content of your report and one showing the activities to be completed and the time available for each.

To help manage your time effectively you should follow the four steps to scheduling success:

1. Identify the time available. Be realistic about how much time you'll be able to devote to writing your report.
2. Consider what has to be completed and how much time each activity will take. Again, make sure you are realistic by taking account of your personal strengths and weaknesses.
3. Relieve the time pressure and prioritise tasks to ensure you cover the most important things first.
4. Monitor progress and adjust. A plan that isn't referred to might as well not exist so perform regular updates on how you're doing and make changes based on your findings.

Sticking to your schedule requires you to be focused on your goal of delivering a report that meets all of the user's expectations. Having said this, it never does any harm to build in a buffer when preparing your schedule; some contingency time that can help to absorb the consequences if things don't go to plan.

Prioritising the activities you need to complete in terms of their impact on your analysis and conclusions and the urgency of each task, will ensure that if you start to run out of time, it is the smaller, more trivial activities that are dropped rather than the ones considered fundamental to the delivery of your report. This can only be done if you have a clear set of criteria against which to prioritise. The precise criteria will vary depending on the situation but a good starting point is:

- linkage to your 'bottom-line' questions
- impact
- urgency.

think

Building commercial arguments and exercising judgement

This section will contain

Chapter 4

Commercial thinking

A student's guide to
Preparing Business Reports

In this chapter

We're going to explore how to add value to a report by thinking more commercially. One of the main purposes of any report is to present information in a logical and well thought through manner, yet logic on its own is not enough. To come up with new and innovative ideas you need more; you need to be creative. For a business report there is an additional implication that it will have a commercial bias and that the report is written with this in mind. If not there is a danger that the conclusions will not be taken seriously and the recommendations ignored.

This chapter takes on the challenge of explaining how to think more commercially and starts at the very beginning with the question, how do we think? By exploring this topic you will understand how important thinking is to the process of preparing a report. Next, we'll define exactly what it means to be commercial. This should be a little easier, yet interestingly it is more than just understanding a set of financial statements. There are many accountants who can do this, yet are not at all commercial.

And lastly we will show how thinking commercially fits into the process of preparing a report. We'll show how analysing information and then interpreting its meaning will provide the building blocks for you to ensure that your report is not only commercial but well thought through, valuable and able to stand up to the challenge of others.

Is thinking really a stage?

Although we've structured this book around three phases of an overall process; plan, think and write, the act of thinking is not limited to this middle stage. When you plan your report you will need to think in order to identify the 'bottom-line' questions, to consider the content of your report and to reveal an initial list of tasks you'll need to perform in order to prepare the report. Equally, when you write, you will need to think about the most appropriate structure for your report and how to best present your argument. But it is at this middle stage when you can expect to do most of your thinking, or at least most of your commercial thinking. It's at this stage when you've gathered some information and you've got to figure out what it means, put it all together and think about the conclusions you're going to draw. So whilst the principles we're going to cover in this chapter can actually be applied throughout the whole process, it is when considering the possible meaning of pieces of information that you'll find the specific techniques most useful.

You will need to think at every stage of preparing a report

In chapter 2 we introduced the idea of a planning cycle; that you start by gathering some information, then you move on to process that information before evaluating it to see if you are now able to answer the 'bottom-line' questions.

The planning cycle

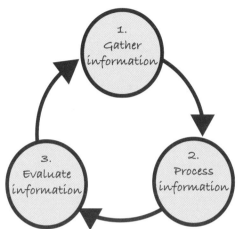

This chapter is going to focus on the 'process' stage in this cycle. The stage at which you look at the information you've collected and ask yourself, 'what does it mean?' Answering this question will require you to think commercially to identify what each piece of information might mean. It is only when you think commercially about all of the information that you begin to see the bigger picture, which then helps you evaluate, exercise judgement and start drawing some conclusions that will be of value to your reader.

Before we consider how to go about thinking commercially, it is worthwhile spending some time considering some more fundamental questions; how do we think, what are the keys to thinking more effectively and what do we mean by being commercial?

How do we think?

This is certainly a big subject for a book about report writing. Perhaps firstly we should answer the question, why do we need to understand about thinking in a book that is ultimately about the written word?

Understanding the way we think is a crucial first step in ensuring we do it properly. Your mind is a wonderful and curious thing – it works in ways that many of us never consider and if you were asked the question "how did you think up that idea?" you'd probably find it difficult to answer.

Understanding the way we think is a crucial first step in ensuring we do it properly

In writing this book, we've certainly found this the hardest chapter to tackle. Trying to convey what it is to think, and what is more, what it is to think commercially, required us to draw upon every ounce of our experiences to date. It is however, the aspect that we felt was fundamental to the difference between an acceptable report and a great report; key to this is the distinction between logical thinking and creative thinking and whether the two can be used in tandem.

Logical thinking

Logical thinking is a process of reasoning, involving some analysis and deduction

For our purposes we will define logical thinking as a process of reasoning, involving some analysis and deduction. It is logical to form your opinions based on the facts as you believe them to be at the time. You can then present the facts in an order that is sensible and sequential, such that one argument will follow the other. Used effectively this can be incredibly persuasive. It is almost as if the author is inside the head of the person reading the report, guiding them through the complex information, answering every question, leaving the reader to conclude that the answer put forward is obviously correct and perhaps the only one possible in those circumstances.

Edward de Bono, he of lateral thinking fame, has been critical of some elements of what might be thought of as logical thinking. De Bono argues that we spend too much of our time looking back at events, trying to find facts that will help us understand more about what will happen in the future. Accountants are probably guilty of this more than others. He concludes that we can arrive at what appears to be a perfectly logical answer having not explored all that we should, thinking too much of what the answer is, rather than what the answer(s) could or might be.

If we purely follow a logical thought process then we could be left with a less than comprehensive report

But does this matter when we're preparing a business report? Absolutely – yes! If we purely follow a logical thought process then we could be left with a less than comprehensive report, and be guilty of making too many assumptions based on historical information.

In looking for what the answer is we could perhaps have failed to consider what the answers could or might be? In short - there could be something missing.

Creative thinking

Creativity is the ability to generate something new, perhaps by combining, changing or re-applying existing ideas or thoughts. Some creative ideas are astonishing and brilliant, while others are just simple, good, practical ideas that no one seems to have thought of yet. Creative thinking focuses on exploring ideas, generating possibilities, looking for many right answers rather than just one, designing a way forward rather than seeking out what is true. Is this perhaps what we need to add into our logical process, a bit of creativity?

Now being creative is important, but in the commercial world we don't have the luxury of coming up with thoughts and ideas that have no real purpose. Yes, we want to be creative, but it has to be directed and applied to the task in hand.   So, how can we get the direction we need without stifling the ideas? Consider this quote from Albert Einstein.

"Innovation is not the product of logical thought, although the result is tied to logical structure."

Perhaps this holds the key; innovation and creativity are not the product of logical thought, but we need a logical structure in which to apply it. This would suggest that preparing a great report requires both logical and creative thinking.

Creativity is the ability to generate something new, perhaps by combining, changing or reapplying existing ideas or thoughts

Preparing a great report requires both logical and creative thinking

Techniques and attitude – the keys to thinking more effectively

To think effectively you need two things: a set of techniques and the right attitude to use them

To think effectively, combining both logical and creative thought, you need two things: a set of techniques and the right attitude to use them. The attitude can be thought of as your frame of mind or mood, the techniques are tools, or logical frameworks, that when applied will help structure and drive your creative thinking. There are many creative techniques, some of them you will have certainly come across before and we'll see some specific examples later in this chapter, but a theme that is common to most is that they all get you to look at the information from different perspectives.

The importance of perspective

Many creative breakthroughs occur when attention is shifted from one angle or perspective to another, and it is this shifting of attention that is key. Edward de Bono argues in favour of something he calls 'parallel thinking', that there can be many views dependant from where you look.

It's a box with a white wall

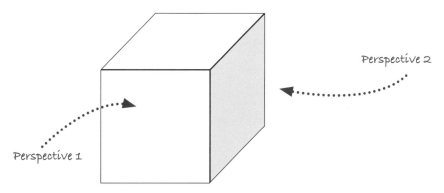

Perspective 2

Perspective 1

"It is a fact that this box has a white wall; no it doesn't, it definitely has a pink wall." Both are in fact correct; there is not one correct answer, it simply depends on the perspective you are looking from. Change the perspective and you will change what you see.

Example

Let us assume that in your role as a manager you have just reviewed the trading information for the last month and have seen that sales have fallen from £250,000 to £200,000. You want to find out what this means?

A logical thought process might lead to the conclusion that we are selling less this year than we did last year, the implication being that we are not performing as well. Now there is much merit in a simple yet logical observation but in order to gain a better understanding, to add more value to the commentary, we should look at it from different perspectives. We need to think more widely.

Look at the information through the eyes of other people or other things/objects etc. When changing your perspective don't limit your thinking to people that you know, or in fact even exist; think equally about objects and simply let your imagination run wild.

Now get yourself into the right frame of mind, relax, and re-read the information above, with one subtle but important difference, ask what MIGHT it mean, rather than what does it mean.

Look at it from the different perspectives, thinking perhaps about what it might mean for them or the objects you have chosen:

- the employees: will there be redundancies?

- the sales force: will they get their bonus?

- last year: perhaps last year was an exception

- being positive: it could be a whole lot worse

- being negative: the business is failing

- advantages: we can now offer a better service to fewer customers

- disadvantages: this could affect our credit rating

- other companies: every other company has done badly

- the budget: it's okay because we budgeted a fall

- the CEO: how to fill the gap created by this fall in sales?

- something off the wall: perhaps it's a mistake, a computer error. Maybe this is not the sales figure but the product code!

Without going through the attention directing process, your attention will follow the patterns laid down by experience

This of course is far from everything, but can you see how this process of directional thinking and changing the question to what it might mean, rather than what it does mean, opens your mind to other possibilities to give a much more in depth view as to what is happening. Edward de Bono summed it up nicely when he said "without going through the attention directing process, your attention will follow the patterns laid down by experience." What this means is that a failure to consider alternative perspectives will mean you only focus on the obvious patterns and ignore the less obvious, but potentially just as valuable ones.

The importance of attitude

Although changing perspective will help you become more creative, if you are not in the right frame of mind, without having the right attitude you may find that the above techniques won't work. You may fail to see the significance and possibly importance of what you are looking at or thinking about, you may be constrained by traditional logical thought.

You need to approach the creative process with a positive attitude; it really helps if you believe the techniques will work.

One of the reasons that some people find it more difficult to get into a creative frame of mind or develop a more positive attitude towards creativity is because they don't think or believe they are creative. If every time you need to be creative, your inner voice says, "who am I fooling; I have never been creative, I can never come up with clever ideas, I am more logical, more black and white", it is perhaps not surprising that you don't come up with anything new or different. You are in effect creating a self fulfilling prophecy.

Your inner voice plays an important part in determining how you feel, the mood you are in, and ultimately how creative you are at that moment. Try changing that inner voice to say "yes it's true, initially I find it harder to be creative, but I have my moments. I just have to put my mind to it and get into the right mood and when I do, I can generate as many ideas as anyone, I am creative."

Everyone has the ability to visualise and see things by using what is sometimes called your 'mind's eye.' The ability to visualise will not only help in getting you into the right frame of mind, but is a creative technique in its own right. When faced with a situation, look at it, walk around it, make it colourful, and if it involves people, place them in that situation. Don't be afraid to put in lots of detail, the more detailed your images the easier it will become for you to 'see' a way forward or 'find' a solution.

You need to approach the creative process with a positive attitude; it really helps if you believe the techniques will work

Your inner voice plays an important part in determining how you feel, the mood you are in, and ultimately how creative you are at that moment

What is being commercial?

It could be argued that in business being commercial is the most important skill you can possess. But what do you have to do to be commercial? A search through the appointments section of a couple of major newspapers uncovered the following adverts for Commercial Directors.

COMMERCIAL DIRECTOR WANTED

The core responsibility of the appointed candidate will be to **manage the finances profitably** across the four business units. The successful applicant will be able to demonstrate significant experience when it comes to **delivering financial milestones**, and be capable of making decisions that are both practical and commercial. Ideally they should have managed the commercial interests of similar projects and so be **familiar with the industry**.

COMMERCIAL DIRECTOR WANTED

The job entails **compiling budgets and forecasts**, reporting to the CEO on business performance, and shaping and implementing strategic activities, such as growth into international markets, or new product development. Commercial Directors require full **understanding of a company's market position, consumer trends**, and **competitors' positioning**, so analysing market data is a major part of the job. He or she may have to **establish KPI systems** (Key Performance Indicators) for measuring different aspects of an organisations performance.

So, if we were to summarise these requirements, it would seem that to be commercial you have to have:

To be commercial must have a focus on profit and an awareness of context

Aspect 1. A focus on profit

Aspect 2. An awareness of context

manage the finances profitably	familiar with the industry
delivering financial milestones	understanding of a company's market position, consumer trends, and competitors' positioning,
compiling budgets and forecasts	
establish KPI systems	

Perhaps the true measure of being commercial is your ability to combine these aspects. When issues arise that threaten the achievement of financial targets, it is often the appreciation of the context of the scenario that will help deliver practical solutions.

Let's look at each of these aspects in turn.

Aspect 1 – a focus on profit

Making profits is in effect another way of thinking; it is an objective or outcome that focuses your mind and therefore your actions. People who only do things to generate profit are often called commercial, so it would seem that making profits or having a profit motive is important. On the flip side of course, some people may think of you as mercenary, which sounds far less complimentary. Making a profit acts as a motivator, mobilising the individual or organisation to take action.

Making a profit acts as a motivator, mobilising an individual or organisation to take action

Following on from the comments above about Commercial Directors, we can drill a little deeper into what it is to be focused on profit

1. Having a good grasp of finance, understanding financial statements and what they mean.

2. Recognising that the organisation exists to make profits and hit targets, any advice we offer should reflect this.

3. Appreciating that we cannot put forward recommendations or offer advice that will result in a deviation from the planned or budgeted profits, without recognising the significance of what we are saying or coming up with a possible solution.

4. Coming up with innovative, creative yet practical ways in which the organisation can make more profit, both now and in the future.

These all have the importance of making profit and understanding how profit is calculated and generated in common. It is beyond the scope of this book to provide a detailed explanation as to how to prepare or interpret a full set of financial statements, although there is some further guidance provided in chapter 5. However, given the importance that profit plays in being commercial, we should at least look at some of the basics; what is profit, how is it created, what should you look out for in a set of financial statements etc? With this in mind the next section covers two of the most important financial statements: the Income Statement and the Statement of Financial Position. For each we will provide a 'bluffers guide' giving a simple narrative as to what some of the numbers mean and what you should look out for. Of course, some of you reading this may already have an excellent grasp of finance and so may choose to ignore this next section.

Income Statement

The Income Statement shows how a company has performed, specifically how much profit it has made in the last 12 months. So, if being commercial means making a profit, this is where we should look first. In simple terms, profit is generated when you sell something for more than it cost.

Given below is some additional information on the financial performance of Broadsword plc for the year to the 31 December 2009 and a forecast of its performance to December 2010 and 2011. Please note – this information is being provided for illustrative purposes only. You will not need to draw on this information to complete your work on the case study.

Income Statement	Year to 31 Dec 08 Actual £m	Year to 31 Dec 09 Actual £m	Year to 31 Dec 10 Forecast £m
Revenue	905.4	877.3	950.0
Cost of sales	(786.2)	(789.9)	(850.0)
Gross profit	**119.2**	**87.4**	**100.0**
Administrative expenses	(98.9)	(68.6)	(66.5)
Operating profit	**20.3**	**18.8**	**33.5**

Bluffers guide

Above are the actual figures for Broadsword plc and what they believe their future performance will be. Budgets and forecasts are produced not only to give a route map as to what the organisation aspires to achieve, but to offer constraint on spending and a quantifiable target against which future performance can be measured. There is an implication that if you are commercial, achieving the budget will be your primary focus.

Don't overcomplicate what you see; does it make a profit, the figure to look at here is operating profit; is this better than last years, (in this example, it isn't) and is it expected to make even more profit in the future (in this instance, yes)? If the answer to any of these is no, it could signal a commercial problem for the organisation.

Also look to see if the business has expanded (or will expand), are sales (revenue) growing or declining? Ideally we should calculate some ratios for Broadsword and perhaps one of its competitors, so that we have some comparison with others within the industry. Types of ratio could include: annual revenue growth, gross and operating margins etc. To find out more about ratios and how numbers should be presented in a report, see chapter 5. When reviewing forecasts we should also ask a few questions; do we think this growth is achievable, how exactly will we achieve this growth etc.

In summary look at profitability, growth in revenue and don't forget that industry norms will help improve your understanding, acting as a benchmark for your findings.

Always keep at the forefront of your mind, how any decision or conclusion you are about to make will impact on the current income statement and any forecasts e.g. more customers or price increases will improve profitability, increases in spending or price rises from suppliers will reduce profitability.

To assess financial performance you should look at profitability, growth in revenue and don't forget that industry norms will help improve your understanding, acting as a benchmark for your findings

Statement of Financial Position (Balance Sheet)

The Statement of Financial Position (or Balance Sheet) shows the assets and liabilities of the company at a point in time. In some ways this is a less useful document than the Income Statement as it is perhaps not so clear how much profit has been made. But a company cannot sustain its profitability without having sound foundations and this can be seen from a Balance Sheet. Think of the Balance Sheet as the engine that generates the profits. If you neglect the Balance Sheet an organisation can soon begin to experience problems with its future profitability.

Below is the Statement of Financial Position for Broadsword plc as at 31 December 2009.

ASSETS	£m	£m
Non-current assets		
Property, plant and equipment	19.9	
Intangibles	33.4	
		53.3
Current assets		
Trade receivables	15.9	
Cash	239.9	
		255.8
Total assets		309.1
EQUITY AND LIABILITIES		
Equity		
Share capital	50.0	
Reserves	54.7	
Current liabilities		104.7
Trade payables	204.4	
		204.4
Total equity and liabilities		309.1

Bluffers guide

As with the income statement there are some key figures that we should look at. Equity, or as it is sometimes known, shareholders' funds, shows the amount the shareholders would get if the company sold off all its assets and paid all its liabilities. This is not really the value of the company, as businesses are valued on the cash the assets generate not on the historic value of the assets themselves, but it will give you some idea. In this instance equity is £104.7m.

Gearing (the relationship between debt and equity) will give you some idea as to how risky the business is. At the moment in the UK and most parts of Europe this is of major concern for companies. The more debt you have, the more interest you have to pay, the more exposed you are, the more risk you carry. Broadsword does not appear to have any long term debt, in fact they have significant cash reserves.

Finally we should look at short term liquidity; can we pay everyone who needs paying in the next 12 months? This can best be seen by finding out if your current assets, £255.8m, are large enough to pay off your current liabilities, £204.4m, which in this example they currently are.

In summary look at shareholders funds, gearing and short term liquidity.

Of course this is a far from comprehensive analysis sufficient to prepare a commercially valuable report. But if being commercial involves having an understanding of the financial statements, and an appreciation that making a profit is key to everything a company does, then it was necessary for us to at least look at the basics.

Aspect 2 – an awareness of context

There is more to being commercial than understanding what profit is and how it is calculated. As mentioned in the introduction to this chapter; there are lots of accountants who have a good understanding of financial statements and yet are not at all commercial. So, what is missing, what don't these accountants have?

For starters they are probably lacking an understanding of the industry and the people within that industry. In situations where accountants are not integrated within the business, perhaps operating from head office, they will be unaware of the environment or context from which the figures they produce come. And if they don't understand the context, they will not be able to grasp the commercial implications of the financial information they are preparing. The result will be conclusions and recommendations that are not practical, are of little use to the reader and only add further to the belief that accountants are little more than 'bean counters'.

Context is a set of circumstances that surround the information, and includes far more than just an awareness of the industry and the people. We should take into account anything that could change the way the information looks or alters the apparent importance of one event over another.   This might include the economic climate, social trends, or the financial strength of the business to give but a few examples.

Context is a set of circumstance that surround information

It might help to think of context as an actual frame that can be moved over the information you are looking at. Around the frame are the factors that create the context and at its centre is the information itself. As you change the context, the information will begin to look very different.

The context frame

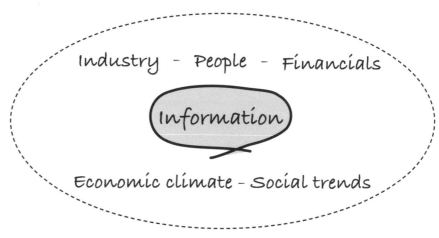

Industry – People – Financials

Information

Economic climate – Social trends

The descriptions above are perhaps a little too general; we need to drill down into the specifics. For example, what exactly is it about the industry? Are there many competitors, a strong trade union presence, is the industry in decline, is it capital intensive, highly risky? What is it about the people? Are they highly skilled, overpaid, likely to leave, demotivated? The context frame adds colour, it adds scale and texture to the information, such that it comes to life. The more detail you add the clearer the picture becomes. This in turn will help you write in a more commercial manner as your grasp of the industry and implications of what you are saying is reflected in the comments you make. Sometimes the circumstances can change so much that it might be better visualising a whole new context frame shifting over the event, changing fundamentally what it looks like and ultimately the conclusions you will form or recommendations you will make.

The context frame adds colour, it adds scale and texture to the information, such that it comes to life

One key thing to appreciate is the way in which context interacts with the creative thought process of considering perspective. By clarifying the information and viewing it in the correct context you are able to have a better appreciation of the implications of perspective. Your creative thoughts become less 'off the wall' and more refined into something that genuinely adds value and will be of use in your report.

Example

Let's look at our original example again, and consider what meaning this information might have given different contexts.

Remember – in your role as manager you have just reviewed the trading information for the last month and have seen that sales have fallen from £250,000 to £200,000. You're trying to figure out what this means?

Context 1 – The internal audit department have recently completed their review of the invoicing process and concluded that invoices were being raised and revenue was being recognised in the accounts before the products had been despatched from the factory. New procedures were implemented last month to delay the raising of an invoice until after despatch.

So, how does this change our view of things? We're no longer concerned about the value of sales in this last month. The fall is most likely a timing issue and we'd expect sales levels in the following month to return to their usual level. What now becomes of greater concern is why this issue wasn't detected earlier and whether there will be any impact on the financial results for the full year (remember, the company will have a profit target that it must hit – is it still expected to do that?)

Context 2 – Back to our original information but this time we've discovered that the sales in the previous month were exceptionally high due to a promotional discount offered to all customers. Now we view the situation in a more positive light as, again, we're not concerned that sales have dipped. We'd probably look back on sales in previous months to check that the level of sales is consistent with that seen before the promotion.

Context 3 - What about if we know that a new competitor has started trading and that £200,000 of sales in one month was the lowest level of monthly sales seen in the last three years?

Now we're worried. It would appear as if this new competitor has stolen market share from us and a thorough review will need to be conducted, looking at why customers have made the switch and what we can do to entice them back.

Obviously, this example doesn't give you sufficient information to form opinions. Your evaluation of the sufficiency of information would certainly conclude that more information is needed in all three situations.

The main reason for using this example is to demonstrate how your thoughts begin to change when you focus more closely on the context. The result of looking at the information through the context frame is that you begin to see the company and how it works more clearly.

Processing information

Let's now go back to where we started at the beginning of this chapter. Having gathered the information, we now have to process that information, by thinking commercially in order to identify what it might mean.

We now know that to think effectively we need the right attitude and some techniques that combine logical and creative thought processes and that to be commercial we need to focus on profit and ensure we appreciate the context of the information.

But whilst all this helps, it still isn't crystal clear how you convert the information you've gathered into reasoned, justified conclusions and recommendations. What would help is a nice logical system that we can follow.

> *Processing information involves analysing it to find out more by breaking the facts up into smaller parts. Then you must take those smaller parts and interpret them, identifying what they mean*

An example of such a logical system, which we'll refer to as 'the information journey', is outlined below. Firstly you need to analyse the information you have; find out more by breaking the facts up into smaller parts. Then take those smaller parts and interpret them, identify what they might mean. Taken together these two steps can be viewed as the 'process' stage of our planning cycle. From there, we can move on to exercising judgement by evaluating the information to form conclusions and give recommendations.

The information journey

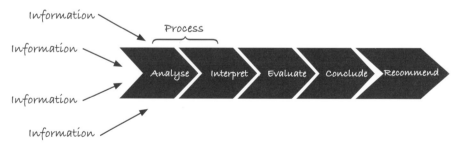

The final stages of the journey will be covered in chapter 6. For now we'll focus on the elements relating to information processing; analysis and interpretation.

Analysis

Analysis involves taking the information you have before you, breaking it up into parts and examining it.

The information you gather may take on various forms; be it a set of financial statements, a research report or the results of a survey to give but a few examples. Some information will be small – perhaps just a single fact. Others will be originally presented in a much larger document and part of your role will be to filter the relevant from the irrelevant, and pick out the key facts before you go on to consider what they might mean. Some of the information you gather will be background information that will help you to form an idea of the context, other information will be more fundamental to the questions you're trying to answer.

Due to the wide variety of information, there is not a 'one size fits all' way to approach analysis. However, there are two specific types of analysis that might be particularly useful in a business environment:

The first, is to use a business model to help present the information in a different light. We'll refer to this as strategic analysis.

The second is to prepare some calculations; let's call this financial analysis.

Not all information will need to undergo both types of analysis. Some information won't fit into either category. But these two broad types are useful in giving us some techniques, some logical frameworks to help structure our commercial and creative thought processes.

> Analysis involves taking the information you have before you, breaking it up into parts and examining it

Strategic analysis

There are of course many different types of business models that can help with your strategic analysis. However, it would be impractical to discuss them all in a book on report writing so we are going to look at just three, simply to illustrate the value they can bring. These three models are interlinked and should be used in the order presented.

PEST analysis – provides an environmental context

A PEST analysis is a technique that uses four key words, Political, Economic, Social and Technological to explore the environment in which an industry exists. It is a very simple technique that uses each key word to act as a prompt to help you think about the different factors influencing the company. By looking at the environment we are of course gaining an understanding of the context in which the company is operating.

Porter's Five Forces – provides an industry context

Porter's Five Forces seeks to analyse the industry in which a company operates. Michael Porter argued that the long-term profitability of companies within an industry is reduced by the presence of one or more strong forces or threats that affect their ability to compete.

The forces are:

- threat from new entrants
- threat from substitutes
- threat from the power of suppliers
- threat from the power of customers
- threat from competitive rivalry.

The profitability and survival of any company in the industry will depend on countering these five forces.

SWOT analysis – a specific focus on the company, and its position

A SWOT analysis is a position analysis tool that helps you analyse a business from four different perspectives:

- What is the organisation good at internally- strength?

- What is the organisation bad at internally - weakness?

- What external factors could help the organisation meet its objectives - opportunity?

- What external factors could prevent the organisation meeting its objectives - threat?

Notice that this forces you to identify what is good or bad and refines the perspective by firstly looking inside the organisation, then secondly looking outside the organisation. It avoids the trap of seeing only negatives by asking you to come up with positives, and vice versa. The result will be a much deeper and broader understanding of the business. A SWOT is a good way of producing a summary of the whole business, helping you pull together many different thoughts into one document, ideally fitting onto a single page of A4. You can then scan this page, interpret your findings and begin to think which are the most important; what threats are going to cause you problems, what opportunities should you take? To do this you will have to start making decisions which will involve using your judgement.

Financial analysis

Some form of financial analysis or calculation is often essential when it comes to preparing business reports. This will be explored in some detail in the next chapter and so at this stage only think of it as an example of analysis. Numbers are logical and although the true value lies in how you interpret them, they can be incredibly persuasive when it comes to winning an argument; they can often appear as irrefutable facts.

Interpretation

Having analysed the information we now need to explain what it might mean; we need to interpret it. You will need to draw on the creative thinking techniques, considering information from different perspectives to ensure you identify what each piece of information might mean rather than what it does mean.

Interpretation involves thinking creatively about what each piece of information might mean

As noted above, some of your analysis will have added to your understanding of the context of the situation. You should now use this context to view the other, more fundamental pieces of information and consider what the meanings might be in terms of your 'bottom-line' questions.

Your focus should be on the commercial meanings and don't forget that a key part of being commercial is about considering the impact on profitability and the company's ability to achieve budgets.

Having identified the range of possible meanings, your evaluation process will then allow you to narrow down the possibilities into probabilities. More on this in chapter 6.

Example

Before we end this chapter let us take the example we have used earlier and illustrate how what we have learned might be used.

Remember – in your role as manager you have just reviewed the trading information for the last month and have seen that sales have fallen from £250,000 to £200,000. Using the final context, you also now know that a new competitor has started trading and that this is the lowest level of monthly sales that you've seen in three years. What does this mean?

A logical thought process would suggest that sales have fallen as a result of the new competitor entering the market. However, as a conclusion this adds little value, it is fairly shallow and of minimal use. What we need is some creative thinking, coupled with some commerciality in order to consider how this has happened and what the company can do about it. As suggested earlier, this certainly gives great cause for concern and so it will be important to dig deeper, to analyse the facts in order to reveal the exact cause of the fall.

A new competitor entering the market will not, per se, lead to a fall in sales. This will only happen if the competitor is offering something we're not, if they're offering a 'better deal'. So, how might their offering be better than ours?

We need to think creatively in order to think of potential explanations. But we also know that we might benefit from a logical structure to help us think creatively. One such structure would be to think about what's known as the 'marketing mix'. The marketing mix looks at four key attributes of an item being sold; the product, price, promotion and place. It is a business model traditionally used to identify how to sell more of a product (how to market it better), but in this situation it could easily be used to identify why our competitor has been so successful.

Price   – they could have charged a lower price meaning people decided to switch. Alternatively, they could have charged a higher price, generating additional sales by creating a perceived value, or an upmarket image.

Product   – there could be something unique about their product, some attribute that ours doesn't have. It might have nicer packaging than our product, which gives the impression that something is different which appeals more to our customers. The product could have a strong brand or perhaps the competitor is an established company, with a well known brand that is entering a new market.

Promotion – they could have offered some incentive to buy the product (e.g. buy one get one free). Or they could have advertised the launch of their product heavily.

Place   – the competitor's distribution channels could be more efficient than ours. Perhaps we suffered problems meaning our goods weren't reaching the shelves in time.

Of course, we shouldn't be confined by the logical thought that the new competitor caused the fall in sales. We should consider different perspectives and open our minds to some more creative ideas that may leave us concluding that these two facts happened by coincidence. Perhaps there is another explanation for the fall such as a fall in quality or indeed any of the other pieces of contextual information suggested earlier.

Having analysed the information, having used our creative yet commercial thought processes to examine all of the different parts, we now need to interpret this information and consider what it might mean. We're going to illustrate this by looking at the price component.

Analysis	Interpretation / Meaning
Competitor charged a lower price	• If we want to match the lower price we will need to either re-engineer processes to reduce costs or accept a lower margin. • Their product could be of inferior quality.
Competitor charged a higher price	• For a higher price to attract more customers there must be a strong brand or something within the product that means people are willing to pay more. • Further investment may be needed in the brand image. • Our product may need changing / refreshing in order to compete.

Obviously, this shows the interpretation of just one of the aspects we identified from our marketing mix analysis. See if you can have a go at the others.

This provides a good illustration of how our information journey fits in with our planning cycle. Our analysis and interpretation have exploded this one piece of information into a range of potential interpretations. When we evaluate this interpretation we would decide that we just don't have enough information to be able to form our conclusions and recommendations and so the cycle begins again, and more information is gathered based on our initial analysis and interpretation.

Further Reading

'de Bono's thinking course' by Edward de Bono. Facts on File; Revised edition (Sep 1994).

The Case – a chance to practise

Why has Nicelife incurred losses in the last two years?

Using the information provided in the introduction to this book, together with the information given below (some of which was also supplied in chapter 1 but has been repeated here for ease), carry out a strategic analysis by preparing the following:

1. a PEST analysis
2. a Porter's Five Forces analysis
3. a SWOT analysis.

Don't forget to interpret your analysis by thinking commercially about what each point might mean.

Nicelife – overview

Formed in 1968, Nicelife specialised in providing package holidays to the sunny destinations of southern Europe. By 1974, these had become so popular that Nicelife joined forces with a major airline operator to form an aircraft joint venture, Fineflight. Nicelife later sold its stake in the joint venture to its partner but has retained a close relationship with Fineflight.

In the late 1990's the company undertook further expansion: holidays are now sold to an increasing range of destinations, including Australia, New Zealand, parts of Asia, North Africa, Antarctica, the US and Canada, such that by 2008 just over half of its revenue related to holidays to long-haul destinations. The company has also moved into the bespoke holiday market – both short-haul and long-haul, and by 2008 nearly 53% of revenue came from supplying Group / charter or Adventure / specialist holidays.

The company maintains relationships with many hoteliers around the world, although, given the custom nature of their offering, the commitments made with each hotel manager from one season to the next can vary considerably. Nicelife has found itself at a slight disadvantage with some hotels when it comes to making changes at short notice. This has led them to conclude that their relationship with these key suppliers may need to be improved.

In late 2008, two aircraft carrying Nicelife passengers were involved in 'near miss' incidents within the space of three weeks. It soon moved to reassure the public that these were events outside its control, but inevitably they have been partly responsible for the fall in bookings.

Nicelife has experienced a near 15% decline in revenue over the past year and has reported net operating losses in both of the past two years. This was despite some quite radical steps to keep costs under control, which included a major redundancy programme when the company shed around 20% of its non-seasonal staff. This came as a surprise to the employees although many of those dismissed have since found new positions in the industry, including a number who have moved to Broadsword. Nicelife has continued to operate well in this difficult period, even tough the head count is much reduced.

The Case – a chance to practise

Likely reaction of the Competition Commission

In chapter 2 you read about the UK Competition Authorities and how they work, and noted a number of facts on your planning sheet that you thought might be relevant to your report.

Use the techniques outlined in this chapter to analyse and interpret these facts in order to identify what each might mean.

Specific applications

The nature of this chapter means that much of what has been discussed is relevant to anyone who has to write business reports. However some elements of the commercial thinking process are of greater importance dependant on the type of report you are writing.

 Exam based

Although it could be argued that anyone who has to write a business report is under some time pressure it is the individual who has to prepare a report under exam conditions that suffers most. The problem is, thinking takes time. How much time in a three hour exam should you devote to gazing at the ceiling without actually writing or typing anything?

And yet you must organise your thoughts before writing, if not what comes out can often be confused, lacking a logical structure and so be difficult to follow. The amount of time you should allocate to thinking will differ considerably dependant on the complexity of the information and on the nature of the report you have been asked to produce. This time of course won't all be spent at the beginning of the exam, although coming up with a plan as to what you are going to write will have to be done early on. Thinking is equally not something that you can build in to do later in the exam; thinking is a spontaneous process that occurs somewhat randomly dependent upon your mood or focus.

Thinking takes time yet yo must organise your thoughts before writing, if not what comes out can often be confused, lacking a logical structure and so be difficult to follow

If you have been asked to prepare a business report, then even in an exam it will need to have a commercial bias. You will be required to think through the issues outlined in the question both logically and creatively. You will need to demonstrate the impact of any information on profits, taking into account the specific circumstances (context) in which the company is operating.

Dissertation

Time to think may not be such an issue when writing your dissertation. You will be able to reflect on what you have found, making additional notes the following day or even the following week. However given this extra time, the thought process will have to be more robust and the path of your ideas clearly referenced. You will also have more time to be creative and so should be able to come up with some truly original ideas and thoughts. With this additional time comes greater expectations.

Since a dissertation is a far more academic document, you may think that it doesn't have to be commercial, but if it is a dissertation set in a business context then it will have no value if the analysis does not reflect the practicalities and commercial realities that the reader operates in. Yes you should challenge the status quo and even raise ethical concerns as to the very nature of the profit motive and whether companies should be commercial in the first place. But if you do not at least acknowledge how the commercial world operates, your arguments will probably be dismissed and many of your recommendations ignored.

 ## Business report

Business reports clearly have to be commercial and as with dissertations although deadlines will always exist, you will certainly have more time to think about your report and its contents than a student in an exam hall. What might be most difficult to grasp here is the idea that logical thought is not the only way to think. Coming up with great ideas that will make money and solving business problems, whilst recognising that there is more than one way to do it, requires some creative thought.

Coming up with great ideas that make money or solve business problems requires creative thought

In a nutshell..............

This chapter looked at the processes involved in thinking commercially. To do this it was broken down into three sections: thinking, being commercial and then a section that brings them both together with some specific guidance on analysis and interpretation.

Thinking is essential to preparing a report; without thoughts there are no words. But it is very difficult to describe the thinking process as in practice, thoughts are random and spasmodic. To prepare good reports you need to think both logically and creatively. Logical thought leads to logical argument which is key if your report is to be persuasive. And creative thought is essential if you need to find solutions to problems and see events from many angles so that your report is well balanced and thoughtful.

But there was another requirement of this chapter; we needed to explain what it was to be commercial. Despite the term being used every day in business and in business reports, it is difficult to define. What we can say is that to be commercial you need to recognise the profit motive, and you need to be aware of the context of the information.

So, using these principles we can attempt the next steps in our planning cycle. After gathering information we need to process it to reveal what it might mean. Given the context of what it means to think commercially, we can break the processing of information down into two logical steps:

1. Analyse. Think creatively within a logical framework to break the information down and examine it. Although the type of analysis and way you approach it will vary depending on the information, two very common forms of analysis within a business report will be financial analysis and strategic analysis. Business models such as PEST, Porter's Five Forces and SWOT can be useful tools to structure your analysis.

2. Interpret. Think creatively and commercially about what the information might mean. Some information will help you understand the context in which other, more fundamental information, should be interpreted.

   After processing each piece of information, it will be necessary to evaluate both the information and your findings in order to decide whether further information is required and to ultimately reach your conclusions. This will be covered in more detail in chapter 6.

Think

Chapter 5

Dealing with numbers

A student's guide to
Preparing Business Reports

In this chapter

We're going to focus specifically on financial (or numerical) analysis. We'll consider how it can be used to assist with the review of business issues and add weight to your commercial arguments.

It is a fact - any reader of a business report will expect to see some numerical analysis. Indeed, it is impossible to form opinions on business issues without looking at the impact on things such as market share or cash resources. Of greater significance is the impact on profitability, an appreciation of which we've already said is an essential element of thinking commercially.

However, too many numbers can result in confusion, diluting the value of your report. Likewise, poorly presented numerical analysis will leave your reader struggling to understand your message, rendering your report ineffective.

With this in mind, this chapter will show you how to identify the calculations required to answer your 'bottom-line' questions. After this we'll explore two common types of numerical analysis, being financial statement analysis and financial data analysis. We'll consider aspects such as presentation and layout; factors that are crucial to ensuring your reader understands the results and your interpretation of them.

The importance of numbers in your report

Remember, the process of preparing a report involves gathering facts and information, analysing and interpreting that information by thinking commercially about what it might mean, and then using your judgement to evaluate the information in order to draw conclusions and make recommendations. In the context of preparing a business report, many of the facts requiring analysis will be numerical, and a full analysis will often involve carrying out further calculations. Be it an assessment of a company's performance based on their financial statements, comparison of market data to evaluate a potential strategy or placing a valuation on a business, to give but a few examples, all will require an element of 'number crunching' followed by a process of interpretation.

The calculation, analysis and interpretation of numbers will often be a key differentiator in assessing the value of a report

It is clear therefore, that the calculation, analysis and interpretation of numbers will often be a key differentiator in assessing the value of a report.

To ensure you perform your numerical analysis effectively and efficiently, you must have a plan.

The 4 step approach to calculations

'Jumping straight in' is a mistake often made when performing numerical analysis. The result is a smattering of data, much of which has little relevance to the purpose of the report. A lot of time can be wasted in writing out endless lists of calculations, repeating facts that the reader already knows or performing intricate adjustments that have little impact on your end result.

All of the above are easily avoided by using the 4 step approach outlined below.

1. Identify the relevant numbers.
2. Consider presentation and layout.
3. Do the calculations.
4. Analyse and interpret the results.

Step 1 – Identify the relevant numbers

In chapter 1 we discussed the importance of identifying the main user of the report and considering their 'bottom-line' questions; those questions they specifically want your report to answer. Knowledge of these 'bottom-line' questions is vital in determining which numbers you are going to analyse, and which calculations, if any, you will need to perform.

A common mistake is to carry out all possible calculations based on the information available. Although this technique can work when there are no time restrictions, it will not be a successful strategy in an exam situation.

This step therefore involves asking two key questions.

- What analysis or calculations do you need to do in order to answer the 'bottom-line' questions?

- Do you have all of the information you need to do this analysis?

The decision over which calculations to do then becomes easy – it is any calculation that you **can** do that is **needed** in order for your report to fulfil its objective.

The level of complexity of your calculations can also be linked back to the purpose of your report and the 'bottom-line' questions. The key question you need to ask is whether any additional calculation will add any value to the reader.

'Jumping straight in' is a mistake often made when performing numerical analysis

Focus only on those calculations needed to answer the 'bottom-line' questions

Example

You are presented with the management accounts (current and prior year) for a clothes manufacturer that shows the revenue, cost of sales and gross profit for each of its three operating divisions: menswear, ladies wear and childrenswear. Information on overhead costs is provided for the company as a whole, broken down into key headings such as wages and salaries, rent and rates, repairs and maintenance etc.

In terms of the "what calculations could you do" question, you could:

- analyse revenue growth and gross profit margins by division or just for the company as a whole

- analyse year-on-year movement for each item of overhead expenditure or just for the total

- allocate overhead costs to each of the operating divisions in order to evaluate operating profit by segment.

To make a decision we need to couple what we can do with what will add value, and that involves considering the original brief of the report and those 'bottom-line' questions.

- If the original brief of the report is to value the business as a whole – an analysis of performance at the company level will be sufficient.

- If the original brief of the report is to evaluate the potential closure of the childrenswear division – an analysis at divisional level, including an estimate of the incremental overheads relating to that division will be required.

- If the original brief of the report is to identify areas for potential cost-cutting, a detailed analysis of movements in overhead costs would be needed, although an allocation of overheads to divisions wouldn't necessarily add any extra value.

Step 2 – Consider presentation and layout

The two main issues covered here are how to layout your calculations and the extent to which simplifying assumptions can be made that will either save time or will allow you to perform some calculations that without these assumptions, you wouldn't be able to do. Now you may think that we're jumping the gun a little here, and that this is more to do with the writing stage of preparing reports. In part, it is, although in many report writing situations, especially for those people who are sitting an exam, you won't have time to perform the calculations and then write them up neatly. You can save significant amounts of time by giving some thought to this sort of thing before you start performing your calculations.

Layout

A good layout is one which the reader finds easy to follow but also minimises the amount of repetition of information. This is particularly important in an exam based situation where you don't have time to copy out endless amounts of facts and figures that have been provided for you by the examiner.

As a general rule, it is easier, and more professional, to present all of your calculations within the appendices of your report, and to interpret your calculations within the main body of your report (see chapter 7 for more details).

A columnar approach is often an efficient layout, especially in situations where you are comparing two sets of figures (say for example, a comparison of one year with another) or where you are making adjustments to an original set of data.

Where calculations are linked together, try to think about what numbers you will need for the latter calculations and try to structure the earlier ones to generate the required figures. Also think about the space you will need. This will ensure you leave enough space and don't need to re-write anything again. For example, consider how many rows or columns will be required before you start writing.

A good layout is one which the reader finds easy to follow As a general rule, you should present all of your calculations within the appendices of your report

Simplifying assumptions

Some simplifying assumptions in your report may speed up your calculations

It is sometimes possible to make some assumptions in your report that will speed up your calculations. Probably the most common of these are rounding assumptions (for example, only working to one decimal place or working in £'000). More intricate assumptions might relate to say the effect of tax, or the relationship between two figures.

e

Example

You've been asked to prepare a report identifying potential ways to save costs for the clothes manufacturer mentioned above. Your starting point is to be a review of how costs have changed over the past year using information from the management accounts.

Just looking at year-on-year movements will not be particularly helpful as it takes no account of the volume of activity within the business. To get a better understanding of where costs have increased or decreased, we need to identify which of the costs are variable and which are fixed. Because a line by line assessment would be very time consuming, we could make a simplifying assumption that material costs and wages and salaries are directly variable and that all other costs are fixed. We know this isn't 100% accurate (for example, some element of wages and salaries will be fixed), but it is accurate enough to enable us to perform some initial analysis to reveal areas for further investigation.

Assumptions will also be required when attempting to look into the future (perhaps to prepare or assess a forecast or when considering the impact of a suggested strategy). In such situations it is possible to add further value by considering the sensitivity of your findings to the assumptions you've taken. We'll look at this in more detail later in the chapter.

Step 3 – Do the calculations

Get your calculator out and switch your brain on. The actual number crunching should be the easy part of the process, if you've done steps 1 & 2 correctly.

Step 4 – Analyse and interpret the results

Calculations result in new information and, just like any other form of information, to utilise it effectively you must analyse and interpret its meaning as well as simply report the results. Once you've carried out your calculations, you've now got to add the value.

Remember, analysis involves taking the information, breaking it up into parts and examining it. The output of any calculation is dependent on the numbers (or variables) entered into that calculation. You must therefore examine the impact that each of the variables has had on your answer; or to put it another way, how each variable has caused your answer to change.

To analyse calculations you should examine how each variable has caused your answer to change

The key to discovering the cause is to ensure you do more than just explain the maths. Identifying the cause of a result involves asking "what has made this figure be what it is and why?" Part of considering the cause is also recognising the impact that any of your assumptions have had on the calculation. In some situations there may of course be a number of possible causes and it would be essential to gather additional information before a solid conclusion could be drawn.

Having identified the cause, you are able to better interpret what this might mean. Interpreting calculations works in the same way as any other information; you will need to think commercially and creatively to identify the range of possible meanings.

One useful tip is to explain the basis of your analysis rather than just presenting your conclusions. Why have you chosen to review these numbers and what is their significance? This will help the reader understand the process you've carried out, and ultimately, will give them greater confidence in your recommendations.

You should also ensure you note down any assumptions you've made and comment on the impact they have on your analysis.

Example

You've performed some analysis on the management accounts of our clothes manufacturer and have identified that the gross profit margin has fallen from 25% to 22%.

A poor interpretation would say "costs have increased by more than revenue".

A good interpretation would consider the possible causes and together with their potential meanings.

Analysis	What might this mean?
• Decrease in selling price per unit	• Additional competition has entered the market, forcing a reduction in selling price. • The company has recently undertaken a sales promotion. • A bulk purchase discount has been offered to a new customer.
• Increase in variable cost per unit.	• Increase in utility costs. • Increase in wastage due to new production process. • Supplier increasing prices.

Like with any other information, after you've processed your numerical information by analysing and interpreting, you will need to evaluate your findings in order to reach a conclusion. More guidance is given on this in chapter 6.

Financial statement analysis v financial data analysis

Numerical analysis can be categorised as either financial statement analysis or financial data analysis.

Financial statement analysis – the review of a company's financial statements in order to reach conclusions on profitability, liquidity, cash position or the ability of the company to satisfy investors. Given what we've said earlier about what it is to be commercial, this type of analysis will often form a key part of many business reports. The most common approach to financial statement analysis is using ratios to examine expected relationships and see how these relationships change over time.

Financial data analysis – this encompasses any other type of calculation or analysis that is not financial statement analysis. Common examples would include investment appraisal, business valuations, and forecasting cash requirements. Equally, extrapolation of questionnaire findings would fall into this category.

The distinction can be useful in determining your approach, in particular during step 2 of the 4 step process, considering the presentation and layout.

To help illustrate, we're going to look at each of these processes using our case information.

Financial statement analysis

The aim of this book is not to show you how to analyse the performance or success of a company from its financial statements (for further guidance on this topic see A Student's Guide to Analysing Corporate Reports, also from Kaplan Publishing). Instead we are focusing on how to direct and present your analysis in a way that adds value to your report.

The key to adding value is to target the specific ratios that will be of interest to your reader

A common mistake made by students is getting carried away, calculating endless lists of ratios, many of which are of little assistance in helping you answer those 'bottom-line' questions. So the key to adding value is to target the specific ratios that will be of interest to your reader. In order to do that you need to understand the 'ratio families'.

The ratio families

Ratios can be divided into a number of groups, or families, that indicate what the ratios are telling you about. The main families are:

- performance
- liquidity and working capital management
- debt and gearing
- investor.

Which family you need to draw upon will depend on the 'bottom-line' questions. So, if you want to understand why the company has made a loss (like in our case study) you will focus on the performance ratios. If you want to know if a company will run out of cash, you will draw on the liquidity ratios. Any questions surrounding the ability of a company to raise further finance will require debt and gearing ratios and finally, if you want to know whether to invest in a company, the investor ratios will be the ones you'll need. Sometimes you will need ratios from more than one family in order to see the complete picture.

Each family contains a number of ratios and again, not all will be relevant to your report. However, within each group there are some 'core' ratios that will form the building blocks of your analysis.

Performance:

Core Ratio	Calculation
Revenue growth %	Annual growth = $\dfrac{\text{Revenue in Y1} - \text{Revenue in Y0}}{\text{Revenue in Y0}} \times 100$
	Average annual growth = $\sqrt[n]{\dfrac{\text{Most recent revenue}}{\text{Historic revenue}}} - 1$
	where n = the number of growth periods
Gross profit margin %	$\dfrac{\text{Gross profit}}{\text{Revenue}} \times 100$
Operating profit margin %	$\dfrac{\text{Operating profit}}{\text{Revenue}} \times 100$

It would be rare that an assessment of performance would not require at least these three areas to be covered. The operating profit margin tells you how many pence profit is made from every £1 of revenue. The gross profit margin will reflect the costs that are directly related to the product or service whereas the operating profit margin reflects more general overheads of the business.

Liquidity and working capital:

Core Ratio	Calculation
Current ratio	$\dfrac{\text{Current assets}}{\text{Current liabilities}}$
Inventory holding period (days)	$\dfrac{\text{Inventory}}{\text{Cost of sales}} \times 365$
Receivable collection period (days)	$\dfrac{\text{Receivables}}{\text{Revenue}} \times 365$
Payables payment period (days)	$\dfrac{\text{Trade payables}}{\text{Purchases}} \times 365$

The current ratio tells you whether a company could settle all of its current liabilities (short term debts) by realising its current assets. Generally, a current ratio of less than 1 may be viewed as risky although this assessment can be very crude without an awareness of context (e.g. the industry in which the company operates or competitor benchmarks). More detailed ratios looking at each area of working capital (the number of days inventory is held in stock, the number of days it takes to collect debts from customers and the number of days it takes to pay suppliers) can help to reveal ways in which cash management can be improved.

Debt and gearing:

Core Ratio	Calculation
Financial gearing	$\dfrac{\text{Debt}}{\text{Equity}}$
Interest cover	$\dfrac{\text{Profit before interest and tax}}{\text{Interest}}$

A gearing ratio allows you to assess how much financial risk faces a business. The greater the amount of debt finance, the more committed the company is to making interest payments and this brings about risk. Interest cover gives an alternative view of gearing, and helps reveal whether the company is able to service its debt and may give an indication of its ability to raise any further debt finance.

Investor:

Core Ratio	Calculation
Return on capital employed (ROCE)	$\dfrac{\text{Operating profit}}{\text{Capital employed}} \times 100$
Earnings per share (EPS)	$\dfrac{\text{Profit after tax}}{\text{Number of ordinary shares}}$

ROCE gives a crude measure of the amount of profit earned by every £1 invested in the business (capital employed can be found by adding long-term debt and equity finance together), and EPS shows how much profit is earned for every share. Investors will be attracted by companies with high levels of ROCE and EPS.

Some golden rules

It is impossible to cover all eventualities within this book, but here are a few examples to help illustrate some golden rules when it comes to assessing what is relevant and what isn't:

• Line by line segmental analysis of revenue or profit will only be of interest if there has been a shift in the sales mix or if one of the 'bottom-line' questions involves a specific segment of the business.

• If you're trying to assess performance over a period greater than three years, calculating the average annual growth over the period may be better than presenting year-on-year increases for each variable. This reduces the number of calculations down to just one per variable and makes it easier for the reader to digest. You can always highlight any unusual years as part of your written analysis.

• Never calculate a ratio if you don't know what a figure relates to. For example, current liabilities can often be a combination of trade payables, taxation and social security and perhaps some deferred income. Unless you have a specific breakdown, a calculation such as payable days will be meaningless.

• Avoid sweeping statements that cannot be substantiated. For example, year-on-year revenue growth of 20% cannot be declared as good or bad if you don't have something to compare it with. A benchmark such as historical trends can be used although a more meaningful comparison would be based on a competitor's performance or the market movements as a whole.

Presenting ratios

The key to effective presentation of ratio analysis is context. Your reader will quickly switch off if given a list of percentage movements with no way of assessing their meaning.

Context can be provided in two main ways:

- Presentation of absolute figures alongside the ratio. So for example, rather than writing 'revenue has increased by 20%', we would write 'revenue has increased by 20% from £10m to £12m'. This helps the reader to appreciate the significance of the change and will allow them to better judge the impact and implications.

- By giving a comparison or benchmark. Using the above example, we could expand 'revenue has increased by 20% from £10m to £12m' to 'revenue has increased by 20% from £10m to £12m, which compares favourably to the average market growth of 12%'.

The next step would be to interpret your results by offering some explanations for the better than expected growth.

The final consideration is whether to show how you have calculated the ratios. Outside of an exam situation, you should always show your workings within your appendix making reference to that appendix when discussing the ratio within the main body of your report. Even in an exam, it is safer to show your workings although, if you know you'll be facing great time pressure, you could skip over the ones where you know your reader will be familiar with the ratios you're using (e.g. if they will know how a gross profit margin is calculated).

Your reader will quickly switch off if given a list of percentage movements with no way of assessing their meaning.

The Case – a chance to practise financial statement analysis

You have agreed with your boss in the Corporate Development Department that one of the 'bottom-line' questions to be addressed by your report is to understand why Nicelife incurred losses in the last two years and to review how their performance compares with Broadsword's in that period.

Given below is some financial information on both Broadsword and Nicelife. Use this, along with the other case information provided in previous chapters to compare and contrast the financial performance and position of Broadsword with Nicelife.

You will need to think commercially in order to analyse and interpret your findings.

Income Statement (extract)

	Broadsword		Nicelife	
	Year to 31 Dec 08 £m	Year to 31 Dec 09 £m	Year to 31 Dec 08 £m	Year to 31 Dec 09 £m
Revenue	905.4	877.3	848.1	726.0
Cost of sales	(786.2)	(789.9)	(793.5)	(684.3)
Gross profit	119.2	87.4	54.6	41.7
Administrative expenses	(98.9)	(68.6)	(64.2)	(51.7)
Operating profit	20.3	18.8	(9.6)	(10.0)

Statement of Financial Position (extract)

	Broadsword		Nicelife	
	At 31 Dec 08 £m	At 31 Dec 09 £m	At 31 Dec 08 £m	At 31 Dec 09 £m
Tangible assets	19.8	19.9	16.0	18.6
Intangible assets	37.6	33.4	-	-
Current assets				
Trade receivables	14.2	15.9	47.2	37.6
Cash	191.6	239.9	310.2	279.3
	205.8	255.8	357.4	316.9
Total assets	263.2	309.1	373.4	335.5
Equity	89.4	104.7	(6.9)	(5.0)
Current liabilities				
Trade payables	173.8	204.4	380.3	340.5
Total equity and liabilities	263.2	309.1	373.4	335.5

Cash flow statement (extract)

	Year to 31 Dec 08	Year to 31 Dec 09 £m	Year to 31 Dec 08 £m	Year to 31 Dec 09
Net cash inflow (outflow)	15.4	48.3	(43.4)	(30.9)

Segmental analysis - Nicelife

	Revenue 2008 £m	Revenue 2009 £m	Gross profit 2009 £m
Short-haul package (UK & Europe)	120.7	135.7	1.4
Long-haul package	155.0	88.4	2.6
Total package	275.7	224.1	4.0
Winter holidays	123.7	109.6	2.4
Group / charter	312.1	277.8	20.5
Adventure / specialist	135.3	112.0	14.7
Flight / hotel booking	1.3	2.5	0.1
TOTAL	**848.1**	**726.0**	**41.7**
Short-haul	419.8	471.2	27.6
Long-haul	428.3	254.8	14.1

Segmental analysis – Broadsword

	Revenue 2008 £m	Revenue 2009 £m	Gross profit 2009 £m
Short-haul package (UK & Europe)	428.7	518.5	32.7
Long-haul package	108.5	67.7	7.6
Total package	537.2	586.2	40.3
Winter holidays	76.6	60.7	3.1
Group / charter	91.3	75.0	12.5
Cruises	91.9	66.8	10.6
Adventure / specialist	96.2	78.5	19.8
Flight / hotel booking	12.2	10.1	1.1
TOTAL	**905.4**	**877.3**	**87.4**
Short-haul	572.8	633.4	47.5
Long-haul	332.6	243.9	39.9

Financial data analysis

Since we've just described financial data analysis as 'any other type of calculation or analysis that is not financial statement analysis', it will come as no surprise to learn that the scope of calculations and analysis covered by the process is virtually endless. It would certainly be impossible to cover all eventualities within this book.

Therefore we shall focus on some general rules to be observed. This should mean that regardless of what analysis you are called upon to perform, you should be able to get the basics right.

Reflect the detail of the situation – Don't get bogged down in the figures and neglect the situation surrounding them. This is similar to the idea of user focus that we've covered extensively so far. Keep in mind what the purpose of your analysis is. Often there will not be one single correct way to perform the analysis. How best to do it will depend on what your objective is. Your starting point must be to consider the different calculations you could do and to assess which ones are the most relevant to the situation.

Don't get bogged down in the figures and neglect the situation surrounding them

Acknowledge the subjective areas – More than with financial statement analysis, you may need to make some simplifying assumptions in order to complete your analysis. To ensure your report is taken seriously, you must provide details of what assumptions you've made and consider their validity. One very effective way of doing this is to re-perform your calculations substituting an alternative assumption. This 'what-if' approach is the most basic form of sensitivity analysis yet it allows you to quickly evaluate the impact of your assumptions and note the implications if they turned out to be wrong.

General v specific - Not all situations will require a single answer to the exclusion of all others. For example, if you were trying to value a business it would be appropriate to outline a range of answers with your conclusion, providing advice on both a maximum and a minimum valuation.

Don't stop when you've done the calculations. The real value is in telling the reader what they mean, and using them to support your argument within your report

Interpretation is the key – As with financial statement analysis, don't stop when you've done the calculations. The real value is in telling the reader what they mean, and using them to support your argument within your report. The interpretation of your analysis is far more important that the analysis itself.

Layout and explanations – Because of the vast array of analysis possible, it is more likely that your reader may not be familiar with the calculations you're performing and why. Make sure you layout your calculations so they can be easily followed, labelling each piece of information and showing the steps you're going through.

The case – a chance to practise financial data analysis

Further research into previous mergers and acquisitions within the travel sector has not revealed any precedents on the definition of the market. You have therefore decided to perform some analysis using the standard market definitions used by both Broadsword and Nicelife.

The following information has been provided on Broadsword's current market share in the different sectors in which it operates. You should use this information, along with information provided earlier to estimate the size of each market and to make an assessment of the total market share held if the proposed acquisition of Nicelife by Broadsword went ahead.

	Estimated market share in 2009
Package holidays - Short-haul (UK & Europe)	Below 2%
Package holidays - Long-haul	3%
Winter holidays	10%
Group / charter	9%
Cruises	7%
Adventure / specialist *	9%
Flight / hotel booking **	3% - 12%

* Overall market share although for certain destinations it exceeds 60%.

** Market share varies depending on the sector. The overall average is about 5%.

Specific applications

 ## Exam based

When using numbers in an exam based scenario, the emphasis must be on speed and efficiency. Your focus must therefore be on the first of the four steps, identifying only those calculations that will enable you to answer the key questions your report must address.

You must keep repetition of information to a minimum, so make sure you layout your answers to facilitate this. However, this must be balanced against ensuring your marker is able to understand and follow your calculations and thought process. Workings are therefore very important.

Be careful not to get bogged down in detail that will make little difference to your end result.

Keep repetition of information to a minimum but make sure you give enough background to enable your reader to understand and follow your thought process

 ## Dissertation

Given the more open ended nature of a dissertation, any numerical analysis will often need to begin with presenting information. Be this the result of some primary research or summarising elements of secondary research, the information must be displayed in a clear and logical manner. As is often said, a picture says a thousand words meaning graphs and pie charts can often be a clear and efficient way of conveying data. Make sure you clearly label your information, cross referencing to sources where applicable. Chapter 8 will look at the presentation of your findings in more detail.

Just because you have more time to perform your analysis, resist the temptation to do every calculation you can. Restrict yourself to those needed to address the topic of your report. Effective use can be made of summary tables when integrating your findings into your report.

 Business report

When writing a report for your boss or a client, you will be able to invest more time explaining your thought process than you would within an exam environment. The reader will often spend more time studying the report and so it is acceptable to include a bit more detail. However, this detail should be restricted to the appendices to avoid over cluttering the main body of your report.

Again, a summary of the important data can be of use and will avoid the reader having to flick around the document to find information.

A summary of the important data will avoid the reader having to flick around the document to find information

In a nutshell..............

The calculation, analysis and interpretation of numbers will often be a key differentiator in assessing the value of a business report. However, to be effective, any analysis must add value and be relevant to the purpose of the report. To ensure this, it will be necessary to plan your approach using the 4 step approach to calculations:

1. Identify the relevant numbers rather than carrying out calculations simply because you can. Focus on those needed to answer your 'bottom-line' questions;

2. Consider presentation and layout, making simplifying assumptions where appropriate and ensuring your calculations are easy to follow;

3. Do the calculation;

4. Analyse and interpret the results to reveal what your findings might mean.

The key to adding value to your analysis is to target the specific calculations or ratios that will be of interest to your reader, ensuring you provide some context to keep the review interesting.

Make sure you spell out what your analysis tells you and use your calculations to support your argument within your report. Don't get bogged down in the figures, neglecting to relate them to the situation surrounding them.

Think

Chapter 6

Exercising judgement

A student's guide to
Preparing Business Reports

In this chapter

We come to what is considered by many to be the most important part of the process, forming your conclusions and recommendations. The report has been commissioned for a reason, to provide answers to the 'bottom-line' questions. As such, your reader will be expecting something of real value.

However, to ensure your conclusions and recommendations are convincing and comprehensive there is much to do. You need to evaluate your findings, take your ideas of what information might mean and form an opinion on what it does mean. To do this you will have to exercise judgement.

This chapter has been split into four main sections; firstly a section as you might expect on judgement, what it is and where it fits into our report preparation process. Secondly we take a closer look at evaluation, and find out the distinction between evaluating information and evaluating options. For each we will examine the potential criteria against which you can evaluate to ensure you understand not only why you evaluate but more importantly, how.

Thirdly we'll look at how you form conclusions and what should be included on your planning sheet that will make writing the conclusions easier and in our fourth and final section entitled recommendations, we'll find out that recommendations are much more than simply saying "I recommend that we go ahead with this."

What is Judgement?

Judgement is the cognitive process of reaching a decision or drawing conclusions

Judgement can be thought of as the cognitive process of reaching a decision or drawing conclusions, and summarises very nicely the final part of the THINK stage of preparing a report.

In chapter 4 we introduced the information journey and established that information needs to be analysed and then interpreted. Yet you are only analysing and interpreting in order to move your thoughts and opinions towards a conclusion and potentially some recommendations. This movement and intention must always be at the back of your mind.

The information journey

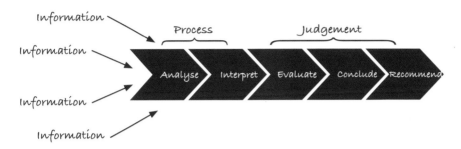

Although at the 'interpret' stage you think creatively about what each piece of information might mean, at some point you need to evaluate your findings to conclude what it does mean. Evaluation is therefore a key part of judgement and allows you to filter possibilities into probabilities, potential meanings into actual meanings.

The planning cycle revisited

In chapter 2 we introduced the planning cycle, and showed how your content plan will develop as you gather, process and evaluate pieces of information.

The planning cycle

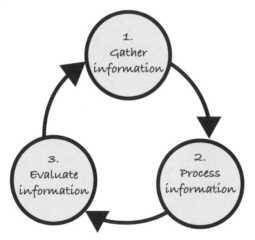

Now let's consider how the planning cycle and the information journey fit together. After gathering a piece of information, you'll process that information by analysing and interpreting, at the end of which you will have a range of potential meanings of that information. In order to assess the significance of that information and its impact on your ability to answer the 'bottom-line' questions, you will need to evaluate your findings.

After completing the cycle just once, the outcome of your evaluation will most likely be that you need to gather some more information, and so the cycle begins again. Evaluation at this stage is focusing on assessing the worth of your findings, and deciding on the sufficiency of the information you have.

As the cycle repeats you will analyse and interpret the next piece of information. But this time, when you evaluate you are doing so with the understanding gained from the first piece of information in mind. Like completing a jigsaw puzzle, you are building the picture, adding in one piece at a time. This may allow you to dismiss some of the original meanings you identified but could add further ones to your list.

At some point you must stop and break out of the cycle

In an ideal world the cycle would continue until you have gathered all of the relevant information, or completed the jigsaw. The reality, however, may be different. Due to time restrictions there will come a point when you have to stop and break out of the cycle. You may not be completely satisfied with the level of analysis or may not feel that you have gathered all the information you could, yet you cannot continue indefinitely and so will have to make do with what you've got.

When you break out of the cycle, the focus of your evaluation changes. You're no longer assessing whether you have enough information but now must pin down exactly what all your information tells you.

Breaking out of the cycle

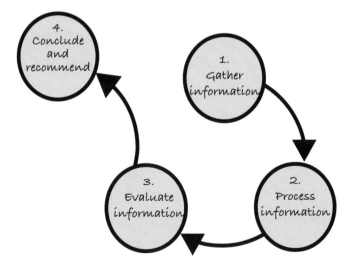

4. Conclude and recommend

1. Gather information

3. Evaluate information

2. Process information

Evaluation

As outlined above, evaluation is part of the process in helping you form a judgement. It involves assessing the worth of something by comparing it with set criteria. It is itself a process that helps the author form an opinion by filtering and prioritising the relative value of information.

As noted above you have to decide if the information you have is valuable in the context of what you are trying to do; you need to evaluate its worth. As information is combined, and the bigger picture is revealed, the meaning of the information gathered will begin to change and evolve. Identifying linkages between what at first might have appeared unrelated pieces of information and prioritising these is part of the process involved in the evaluation of information.

You also need to consider more deeply the implications of what the information is telling you. A useful way of doing this is to ask, "is this a problem for the company or an opportunity?" And although in some instances the answer is neither, when you identify problems and opportunities it helps you see more clearly the more important implications and what it is you should do next. If something is a problem; you should come up with different solutions to solve that problem; these solutions will then in turn need to be evaluated. If it is an opportunity, the opportunity will need to be evaluated. This is a different type of evaluation; here you are not evaluating the worth of the information, you are evaluating the options available.

Evaluation involves assessing the worth of something by comparing it with set criteria

Evaluating information

If evaluation involves assessing the worth of something by comparing it with set criteria, then the million dollar question is, what are the set criteria? What set of standards are we going to use to help us decide if the information we have is of use? Some criteria may be specific to the organisation and the context in which it operates, some may be related to the 'bottom-line' question; there are, however, some general points that apply in most circumstances.

Point 1: Go back to the 'bottom-line' questions

Does the information you have help in answering these questions? For example, say you had been asked to advise on a possible merger between two companies and one of your 'bottom-line' questions was, how does the culture of the two organisations differ? Information revealing that one of the companies has a bonus scheme based on divisional profits and the other has no such scheme, would be very useful. This information might indicate that one company will be highly motivated by targets, but that the other might not. This information, and its range of meanings is therefore of worth.

Point 2: Look for linkages

Can you see any linkages between pieces of information? Is there a link perhaps between the high costs of raw materials, the expansion of emerging markets and the fall in gross margin? Often to spot these linkages you need to look at the bigger picture and think creatively, let your mind wander, reading and re-reading, looking from different perspectives.

How often have you heard someone say "that stacks up"? This means they've made a link between different pieces of information and are now happier with the information they have. Linkages are important because they help to reinforce the worth of information and also allow you to start narrowing the range of potential meanings into something more solid. Anything that doesn't 'stack-up' can perhaps be put to one side.

Point 3: Be sceptical

It pays to be sceptical. Don't believe everything that is before you

It pays to be sceptical. Don't believe everything that is before you and incidentally, this includes your own thoughts. Just because you were told that the reason the new costing system is over budget is because the Procurement Director was new and did not understand the industry, does not and should not mean you put this in your report. Who was it that told you, did they have a vested interest in deflecting blame from themselves? Exactly how much difference would knowing about the industry have made anyway?

Once you've exercised some scepticism, you might feel that some information is of less value than you originally thought.

Point 4: Prioritise

You will probably be faced with far too much information, but as not all of it will be relevant, you need to begin to prioritise what is important and what is not. It will be easy to dismiss some information but without guidance as to how to prioritise there is a danger of trying to cover too much and getting bogged down. We introduced the idea of prioritising in chapter 3 and you might find some of what was said there helpful once again.

- How much does this information help answer those 'bottom-line' questions? This is more about the degree to which it is useful, not whether it is useful as was mentioned earlier.

- How big an impact does this information have? Impact in this context is about scale, how significant is the information. Does it fundamentally change your view or only slightly? You may also want to consider likelihood, especially when evaluating the potential meanings of each piece of information.

Point 5: Be objective

And finally try to be objective, logical and keep a sense of balance when evaluating. You may well already have formed an opinion but don't dismiss information at this stage simply because it does not fit your view; you might be wrong.

The implications

After evaluating the information and attempting to assess its worth, you should start thinking about the implications of your findings. One way of spotting these implications is to ask, "does this cause the company a problem or does it offer up opportunities that the company might take?"

Spotting implications is easier if you look for problems and opportunities

For example, if as part of your analysis and interpretation you have just prepared a cash flow forecast and it is showing a deficit early in 2011, the implication thrown up by this information is that the company will not have sufficient funds and will need to take some action. This represents a potential problem; can the company borrow to finance this deficit, what if they are unable to do so etc? These questions might not have appeared in your original list of 'bottom-line' questions, but given your findings, your reader will certainly be interested in the answers.

What if the information reveals that a competitor you would like to acquire has just suffered a large fall in share price and it is known that the shareholders have little confidence in the current board. This represents a potential opportunity that once again you may not have been specifically asked to comment on, but given the implication of your findings, perhaps you should now cover.

Not all information, when evaluated, will result in one of these implications. What if, as a result of your analysis of the financial position you identified that both sales and profits have hit budget this month. This is neither a problem nor an opportunity; it is simply a fact that requires no further action other than to be included in your conclusions.

The purpose of thinking like this is to help you recognise that when evaluating information there are often important implications that require more attention and further analysis, that may not have been obvious when you first started the report.

What next?

Once you have identified a problem or opportunity you cannot leave it there, you have to go onto the next stage and evaluate the options

Once you have identified a problem or opportunity you cannot leave it there, you have to go onto the next stage, even if this wasn't covered as part of your original brief or within the 'bottom-line' questions. Your reader will not feel as if you have delivered a value adding report unless you spot this implication and follow it up.

If the implication suggests a problem you should come up with ways in which the problem may be resolved. To do this you should be as creative as possible, to identify a range of possible options. Although you record the options on the planning sheet not all of them will end up in your report, only a few will be worthy of further comment. So, having written down as many solutions as possible, we should next decide which of these options is best. To do this we need to evaluate them. As this is a different type of evaluation, we are not evaluating information but options; we therefore need a different set of criteria.

If you have identified an opportunity the process is a little easier. If it is an opportunity you do not need to solve anything, but you do need to offer some advice as to whether the option should be taken. As above we need to evaluate the option.

Example

Information	Implication	Type	What next?
1. The Operations Director has just resigned and is to go to a competitor.	Loss of a key employee. May take sensitive information to the competitor.	Problem.	**Identify potential options to solve the problem and then evaluate the options.** 1. Ask him/her to withdraw his/her resignation. 2. Ask him/her to leave immediately. 3. Look into non compete element of his/her contract. 4. Review contract of employment regarding notice periods and restrictions preventing working for a competitor.
2. A key competitor has announced they are to pull out of the UK by the end of 2010.	An opportunity to increase market share.	Opportunity.	**Evaluate the opportunity.**
3. The new data capture system has been tested and is working well.	Information being captured is reliable.	Neither.	**Include the observation in your conclusion.**

In example 1 we have the information that the Operations Director has resigned and is to go to a competitor. The implications are that we will lose a key employee and a concern that he/she may take sensitive information with them. This is clearly a problem, how big a problem depends on what we found when evaluating the information as outlined above. For example if we also knew that the Operations Director had made some significant errors, then recognising this linkage would suggest that this is not as big a problem as we may first have thought.

If however for the purposes of this example we assume that the resignation is a problem that we would like resolving, then the next step is to come up with as many solutions to the problem as possible. Here we have restricted the possible solutions or options to three but there are more. The final stage will bring us back to evaluation and is discussed in the next section, evaluating options.

Notice with example 3, there is no need to go on to the 'evaluating of options' stage, simply because there are no important implications. The implication is that the system is reliable, and comment to that effect should be made in our conclusions section if relevant given the 'bottom-line' questions our report must answer.

Evaluating options

We have seen from the example above that you get to a stage where you have some possible options and these options will need evaluating. Because this is an evaluation process you will need another set of criteria. Don't confuse this with the conclusions and recommendations stage, you are still unsure what to conclude. Until you have evaluated the merit of these options you cannot advise or pass opinion on what you think.

Criteria for evaluating options

Once again it is important to state that the criteria noted below are not exhaustive. But you may find them a useful starting point from which you can add your own thoughts and include specific criteria that is relevant to the situation.

- Is it commercial, will it improve the company's profitability either now or in the future?
- Is it practical, can it be delivered, are the resources available?
- Is it ethical, how will society judge this, is it the right thing to do?
- Is it too risky, are the rewards greater than the exposure to uncertainty.

Of course you must always be thinking of the context surrounding the information and the original brief.

In chapter 4 we have already explored what being commercial means. But we should perhaps say more about the other three criteria.

Is it practical?

An option that is not practical, where what is proposed cannot be delivered, is not worth the paper it is written on and certainly won't add any value to your report. Therefore, part of your evaluation must consider whether it would work in reality.

One way in which you can get into this practical mind set is to think what would you need to do if it were your company? You need to take responsibility.

Ask what you would do it were your company?

If it was your money would you invest it in this project? If you had to go to the bank what would you say that would convince the bank manager to lend you the money? And if it was your company what would your concerns be about expanding? Powerful, commercial and practical conclusions and recommendations come from answering these types of questions.

One of the reasons that people fail to think through an issue is because they don't think of themselves making the decision; they hide behind a corporate veil. And although you need to think about the business from many different perspectives most of the practical ideas and thoughts will come from thinking about the business as if it were yours.

Most business decisions are simple and can be translated into situations that people have to deal with every day. Do I have enough money, how much will this cost, where can I get money from, what if I can't pay it back, what is the worst thing that can happen etc? Think like this and you are beginning to think not only responsibly but also practically.

Is it ethical?

In chapter 4 we discussed the importance of being commercial and narrowed this down to two key factors: that you should have a profit motive and that you should take into account the context in which the information is set.

This is of course invaluable advice if you want to be commercial. But as also mentioned in chapter 4, having a profit motive can be viewed as being mercenary, someone who will do anything for money, who cares little about the implications of their actions as long as it adds to the profitability of the company. Companies do not operate in isolation; they are part of a greater community and so have to behave as if they are a citizen of that community. They have to be responsible for their actions and as a consequence should not simply be judged by a single measure, whether it makes profit or not. And it is for this reason that we have included ethics as one of the criteria you should use to evaluate your thoughts or ideas.

Companies are part of a greater community and so have to behave as if they are a citizen of that community

Ethics itself can be a little tricky to define but in principle it involves doing the right thing. Some of the following questions might help you decide if an option would be viewed as the right thing.

- Is what you are saying true, are you being honest?
- Is it fair to all?
- How will society view this?
- Will it build goodwill?

Is it too risky?

As with ethics, risk is hard to define. One definition is the exposure to something that is uncertain or unknown that could result in a variation from what you want or expect. It is also often subjective. For example if you were trying to identify if something is risky, the judgement by an individual will depend on the individual's attitude or experience. Some people will look at events and consider them very risky, perhaps dangerous or reckless. Yet others may consider them necessary risks to take in order to achieve a profit. In the world of finance there is a simple rule: the bigger the risk the greater the profit. If we are profit motivated we will have to take some risks. The big question is how much risk and for how much reward. This is not always easy to get right as the banks in both the UK and Europe proved!

Nevertheless, when evaluating the worth of something you must at least consider the risks and rewards involved.

Be critical of your proposals

In chapter 4 we discussed both logical and creative thinking but there are other types of thinking; one such example is to think critically, that is to think about what might go wrong. One of the reasons some people fail to think creatively and come up with new ideas is because they think critically too quickly. They try to find reasons why something will fail before they have thought about how it might succeed. But critical thinking is useful and used at the right time is valuable, and the time to use critical thinking is now, when you are evaluating your options.

Critical thinking is useful and used at the right time is valuable

You should look at what is being proposed and come up with reasons why it won't work or problems that might be met. The reason that being critical is so useful is that you get a chance to come up with solutions to those problems and develop strategies to cope should the worst scenario actually happen. If of course you can't find reasons why it might fail then your confidence that your proposal is the right one will grow.

Evaluating options – some techniques

As we saw in chapter 4, a logical structure can often assist a creative thought process, and using business models is a good example of how the two ways of thinking can be combined. Evaluating options is no different; you will need to think creatively and by applying some logical techniques you can work more efficiently. Two such techniques are outlined below.

1) Advantages and disadvantages

Not so much a business model but a useful way to structure your thoughts is to simply evaluate the idea or proposal by identifying the good points, the advantages, and the bad points, the disadvantages. It is not how many advantages compared with the disadvantages that is important, but rather the quality, relevance and significance of them. Although this on the face of it seems basic, it can, like a SWOT be a very useful way of gathering your thoughts so that you can arrive at a conclusion.

A useful way evaluate an idea or proposal is to identify the advantages, and the disadvantages

Example

Let's explore how we might evaluate some of the options presented in the previous example. Given the problem of the loss of a key employee we came up with some possible solutions that now need to be evaluated; are they good solutions or not?

Using advantages and disadvantages will help with this one. However keep in mind: is it commercial, is it ethical, is it practical and is it risky?

1. **Ask him/her to withdraw their resignation**

   The main advantage of asking the Operations Director to withdraw his/her resignation is that if it works, we retain a key member of the management team. The disadvantage is that we may have to improve pay/benefits or concede something in return.

2. **Ask him/her to leave immediately**

   The main advantage of asking the Operations Director to leave immediately is that we are making our position very clear and if it is done instantly they will have little or no time to talk to suppliers / customers or staff or take valuable commercial information away. The disadvantage is that they may already have taken the information and by asking them to leave immediately we are being too harsh, perhaps unethical for someone who may have given many years service and has simply decided to move on.

3. **Review control of employment**

   The main advantage of investigating further the legal implications of the Operations Director's contract is that we may be able to delay or even stop them going to the competitor. There is no specific disadvantage of looking into the contract itself, but should we have to go to court, the result of a legal dispute could be very expensive.

2) Suitability, Feasibility and Acceptability (SFA)

Although business models can seem complicated when you read about them in a text book, the more useful ones are easy to use in practice. The SFA model developed by Johnson, Scholes and Whittington is one of those easy to use models. Although its main purpose is to evaluate a company's strategy, it can be adapted to other situations, such as the evaluation of options. To apply the model, you should ask whether the strategy you are evaluating is:

To evaluate an option you can consider whether it is suitable, feasible and acceptable

- suitable? Is the strategy consistent both externally and internally? Does it fit with expected future changes in the environment and with existing strategic objectives and competences of the organisation?

- feasible? Can it work, does the organisation have the resources, competences and markets to deliver the strategy?

- acceptable? Is the reward acceptable given the level of risk involved? Will the key stakeholders want this to happen and does it meet their criteria for success?

Now although this applies specifically to evaluating a company's strategy, can you see the common theme between this model and our criteria for evaluating options? Suitable is a little like the commercial aspect, feasible sounds very much like our, 'is it practical', and acceptable encompasses both risk and ethics.

Example

Let's turn our attention to the second illustration in the earlier example, the announcement by a key competitor that they will pull out of the UK by the end of 2010. We identified this as an opportunity and as there are no problems to solve all we need to do is to evaluate this opportunity, the only option available.

We will assume that the competitor pulling out of the UK is thought of as a strategic opportunity. Without more detail about the organisation illustrating how the model can be used is a little difficult, so we have used some poetic licence and brought in facts that were not in the original example.

Suitable

The news that a key competitor will pull out of the UK by the end of 2010, represents a real opportunity for us to take on many of their customers and so improve both market share and profitability. We have known for some time that they have been struggling to make money in the UK market given their large fixed cost base and high salaries. Equally their pricing structure, offering cheap prices could not be sustained indefinitely. This will however need careful coordination between all departments to ensure we get as many customers as possible. One concern is that some of the accounts could have very low margins and unless these customers can be persuaded to accept price rises, we should not take them on.

Feasible

We believe that the competitor had approximately 20% of the market; with our 25% this will make us the biggest player in the UK. However, we will not win all the customers and neither should we try, (see the comments above). We are clearly going to have to recruit many new employees and make considerable investment in new office space and working capital. As a result we will need additional finance. The scale and availability of funds should be quantified as soon as possible. We will of course be able to pick up many experienced staff from our competitors, although they may have to lower their expectations of salary.

Acceptable

Not only will this increase our market share but should also help us gain significant economies, the result of us being a much larger company. This will further improve our profitability and will be attractive to the shareholders. We will need a major staff reorganisation and should go to some lengths to ensure our existing workforce see this as a great opportunity and do not feel threatened in any way. One concern is how the competition authorities will react to the announcement and our subsequent increase in size. They will of course have the power to stop us taking on many of the customers if our overall scale is perceived to be anti-competitive and not in the public's interest. Given by then we will already have spent large amounts of capital and invested many hours of management time financially we would be exposed if they were to step in.

Forming conclusions

Some people think that a conclusion is a summary of what you have already said; it is not. A conclusion is an opinion or view (something offered for consideration or acceptance) which is reached after considering the evidence, arguments or premise. It is an opinion based on reason that should have a sense of completeness, and leave the reader in no doubt as to what you think at a point in time.

A conclusion is an opinion based on reason that should have a sense of completeness, and leave the reader in no doubt as to what you think

A recommendation, on the other hand, implies an action for the reader to follow. There can be a fine line distinguishing the two; by way of illustration, consider the following sentence:

It is recommended that the Operation Director be allowed to leave.

Is this a conclusion or a recommendation? It is, in fact, a conclusion, even though the words 'it is recommended' appear at the beginning. It is stating the opinion that the Operations Director should be allowed to leave. The recommendations relating to this would be actions such as sending a letter to the Director formally accepting their resignation, getting the HR Director to prepare a job specification which should be sent to recruitment agencies in order to find a replacement etc. We'll consider recommendations in more detail in the next section but for now we're going to focus on the conclusions you form.

The process of evaluation involves moving your thoughts forward, you are getting to the point where you can express an opinion. You've gathered and processed all of the necessary information, you've evaluated your findings and you've figured out what they do mean rather than what they might mean. All of this has been done by recording each step of the process on your planning sheets.

However, before you start writing, you should be clear about the conclusions you've reached. You may find it useful to think about the following and make additional notes on your planning sheets to ensure that your conclusions can then be written in a persuasive manner.

Don't sit on the fence

Conclusions cannot be vague nor should you pose questions. At this stage you only want answers

Conclusions cannot be vague nor should you pose questions. At this stage you only want answers so your conclusions must be unequivocal. If you are still unsure of your facts then you have a number of choices:

1. Go back and investigate further. At this stage we can of course still do this, but you may be running out of time or only discover this lack of clarity whilst writing the report.

2. Make reference to your concerns in your conclusions e.g. subject to the bank lending us the necessary finance, the project should be accepted. This should be supported by recommendations to resolve the concerns e.g. that the Finance Director speaks to the bank at the earliest opportunity. Alternatively, you could put your concerns into perspective and state an opinion e.g. although we are not sure if the bank will lend us the money, given the amount involved and our credit rating, we should have little problem raising the necessary capital.

What you cannot do is suggest that there are many options available or even pass the responsibility to someone else by recommending an expert is brought in to make the decision.

Remember, your reader will be expecting you to provide the answers, so before you start writing you must make sure you have addressed every question within your planning. Make notes of any concerns you have and consider how best to resolve them. If for some reason you can't answer all of the questions, you should have very good reasons why and those reasons should be noted on your planning sheets so they can be included in your report.

Ask challenging questions

Don't be afraid to ask challenging questions, which on the whole you should have an answer to. When you write up your report this can be a very effective way of making a point e.g. the board should consider if they have the appetite for the level of risk involved in this project.

One example is to ask "what might happen in the future" as this forces you to consider the consequences and implications of what you are suggesting e.g. if you have identified a problem that the companies wage bill is too high, ask what will happen if this continues for the next six months? This might lead you to change the point you will make or at least the way you present it in the report itself.

Challenge your conclusions by asking questions such as "what might happen in the future" and "so what?"

Another example is to ask, "so what?" One reason that people fail to get to the point in a report is because they make statements of fact without thinking of the reason they are drawing the reader's attention to that fact.

> e.g. Conclusion - the company has made losses in the last two years due to the recession

> Ask "so what?" – this suggests the economic climate has proved a little more challenging than at first thought.

If, on your planning sheet you have made a statement, just scribble next to it, so what? This will help clarify the point you wish to make before you start writing.

No new information

Everything in your conclusion should be derived from your findings. The implication is that you should not have anything in your conclusion that cannot be seen to have come from your earlier analysis, interpretation and evaluation. In particular, conclusions will be all the more persuasive if accompanied by statements of fact.

On your planning sheet make sure all conclusions link back to some analysis or commentary that will eventually be included in the body of the report when you come to write it. Thinking about this before you start writing can help you decide which pieces of analysis, interpretation and evaluation you should include within your report (see chapter 7 for more detail on this).

Recommendations

The first thing to say is that not all reports require recommendations, and offering a justified opinion in the form of a conclusion can often be sufficient. But when asked to make a recommendation or where it is implied, you should do so. You should put forward an action or series of actions that tell the reader of the report what they should do, but ensure it is always thoughtful, respectful and persuasive.

A recommendation is an action or series of actions that should be followed

We should perhaps clarify that recommendations, no matter how forcefully made, are not facts. Recommendations are actions that the author 'thinks' should be taken; they may be justified using facts, but they are not facts.

As with conclusions, it is worthwhile being clear about your recommendations before you start writing. You may find it useful to think about the following and make notes on your planning sheet to help develop your recommendations further.

Look to the future

Your recommendations section should not consist of short statements, they should be well argued and as already explained will need justification. You should also look beyond where you are now and consider what will happen in the future.

Thinking of the next steps is a very useful way of exploring the practicality of a recommendation and helping you fully understand the implications of what you may have suggested. For example, if you are going to conclude that the organisation will need to raise £4m to finance a new project in the Middle East, then think what you need to do next; speak to the bank, then invest the money in the new machinery and working capital, then recruit more employees etc. This process of thinking about the future will help identify the actions that must be taken.

Short-term vs long-term

Another very useful technique for structuring recommendations is the use of short-term and long-term. When thinking about what you are going to recommend you may find that it is simply impractical for the organisation to do everything you want them to do, or to be precise impractical for them to do it all now.

It can be helpful to break your recommendations down e.g. in the **short-term** we recommend that the organisation raises £4m to finance its proposed investment in the Middle East. In the **long-term** they should build stronger relationships with other major financial institutions, so that should similar opportunities arise in the future the organisation will have more choice as to possible sources of finance. On your planning sheet identify which recommendations can be done now and which ones may need more time.

You can add depth to your recommendations by considering actions required in both the short- and long-term

Justify

Telling someone that they should do something is easy, getting them to do it is a little harder. At this point we recommend that you re-read this sentence once more.

Some people may well have re-read this sentence again, but others would have asked "why, what's the point in reading the sentence again?"

To make your recommendations convincing and persuasive you need to justify them. This means you need to support them with a reason as to why your recommendation should be followed. As with conclusions, statements of fact will add particular weight to your suggestions.

To make your recommendations convincing and persuasive you need to justify them

You can present your justification either before or after the recommendation. For example:

'Telling someone that they should do something is easy, getting them to do it is a little harder. At this point we recommend that you re-read this sentence once more, because only by re-reading it will you appreciate its importance.'

Or 'In order for you to appreciate the importance of the next sentence, can you read it twice. Telling someone that they should do something is easy, getting them to do it is a little harder.'

Be specific – include who and when

One of the ways in which you can improve the quality of your recommendations is to include a high level of detail and be specific about that detail. If you read any good news story it does not say that 'four men were found guilty today,' it will say 'four men, all in their mid-thirties, were found guilty of assault by Judge Richardson at the Old Bailey on Friday.' Although not a recommendation, this example illustrates our point well. When putting forward recommendations you will need to include specific reference to **who** should do **what** and by **when**. If you recommend that the Operations Director's resignation should be accepted, then who should accept it and when should it be accepted. So before you start writing, make sure you're clear about who should carry out your recommendations and when, and note this on your planning sheet.

When putting forward recommendations you will need to include specific reference to who should do what and by when

Jumping to conclusions

In the last three chapters we have talked through the detail of the information journey. We've shown how once gathered, information must be analysed, interpreted and then evaluated in order to form your conclusions and give recommendations.

In reality, these three steps, analysis, interpretation and evaluation are sometimes carried out simultaneously. You may not even be aware that you are working through three distinct stages, perhaps just seeing it as one seamless thought process. By separating them out you could argue that we've artificially slowed down that process.

So, why have we done that? Everyone has heard the expression 'jumping to conclusions', and this sums up nicely the dangers involved in not appreciating the separate stages.

Jumping to conclusions

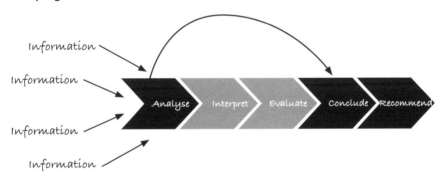

Without an appreciation of the importance of interpreting and evaluating information, it is easy to jump straight from analysing information to concluding on what it means, without considering things such as what it might mean, linkages in information and the bigger picture. Missing out these steps can ultimately lead to incorrect conclusions.

So whilst there is nothing wrong with working through the stages simultaneously, you must ensure that you don't cut corners and miss out a crucial element.

Further reading

'Exploring Corporate Strategy' by G Johnson, K Scholes, R Whittington, FT Prentice Hall; 8th Edition (2008).

The Case – a chance to practise

Using the output from your strategic analysis in chapter 4 and your financial analysis in chapter 5, apply the techniques outlined in this chapter to:

1. Evaluate the information relating to the performance of Nicelife and reach some conclusions on how the company's performance compares with Broadsword's and why they have incurred losses over the last two years.

2. Evaluate the information relating to the Competition Commission and reach some conclusions on their likely reaction to a proposed acquisition. Consider the implications of this and think creatively to identify and then evaluate the options available to Broadsword.

Add the outcome of your evaluations onto your planning sheets.

Specific applications

 ## Exam based

Although planning time may well be available it is often insufficient and so time again will cause problems for the exam based students. Exercising judgement is on the whole a thoughtful process that is better if the author can reflect on the significance of what has been found in the context of the other events and issues in the question. Exam based students will not have the luxury of this reflective process and will find themselves having to make judgements when they are not yet comfortable to do so. This problem is compounded by rushed evaluations, where the student has not explored sufficiently the many alternative solutions to problems.

Unfortunately where you have to produce a report under exam conditions most of the above is unavoidable. Having more time would be an obvious solution and yet this in itself would not entirely solve the problem. To help with judgement ideally you would want to think about the situation overnight and discuss some aspects with colleagues, challenging your initial thoughts and opening up your mind to other possibilities. But in the exam room this will not be possible and so the truth is, students may have to accept that what they produce on the day will not be their best work and will not identify nor make the more subtle points.

Students can however, go through the process, demonstrating that they are aware of what they should be doing, even if they don't have time to do it as well as they could. Concentrate instead on strong conclusions and well constructed recommendations. This is, after all, the most important part of the report and so should carry most marks.

 ## Dissertation

Many of the problems encountered by exam based students do not apply when preparing a dissertation. In fact your judgement and evaluation should be well thought through and comprehensive.

Remember that this is a far more academic report and so should explore and challenge the more accepted business concepts. One such area would be the pre-occupation that business has with profits. It is the bedrock of our argument about commerciality and is used as one of our main criteria for evaluation. Yet it is an ideal target to discuss and explore more specifically the ethical aspect and how large a part ethics should play in the evaluation process.

 Business reports

When writing reports in a business context the recommendations take on a whole new level of significance. These are not academic proposals that may challenge conventional thought but may never be implemented, as is the case when writing a dissertation. Nor are they recommendations that will score well on the day of the exam because they include elements of what the examiner thinks is important.

No, these are real recommendations that will need careful thought and solid justification. The proposals in a business report may well be implemented and so there is an added sense of importance; get them wrong and you could cost the company significant amounts of money.

Pay particular attention to the commercial elements, the impact on profits, the context and most importantly, the practical aspect - can it really be done? Asking "would you do this if it was your company?" can be particularly useful here.

In a nutshell..............

What you say in your conclusions and recommendations will probably have more impact on the reader than any other part of the report. The conclusion is your opinion, the recommendations what actions you think should be taken. Yet you will not be able to form good conclusions and recommendations without evaluating the information carefully beforehand. Evaluating, concluding and, where required, recommending is all part of the process involved in forming judgements.

Evaluation involves assessing the worth of something by comparing it with set criteria. We identified that you will need to evaluate both information and the options that evolve from considering more deeply the implications of the information.

The step by step process to exercising judgement is:

1. Evaluate the information you have and identify its worth.

   To evaluate information we suggested that the following might be helpful.

   - Go back to the 'bottom-line' questions.

   - Look for linkages between different pieces of information.

   - Be sceptical, don't believe everything.

   - Prioritise the information based on the degree of usefulness and impact.

   - Remain objective and balanced.

2. Consider more deeply the implications of the information by asking, does this information cause the organisation a problem or offer up an opportunity?

3. Evaluate the options to identify the best solutions to the problems and clarify if we should take up the opportunity. To evaluate options we should ask:

- is it commercial?

- is it practical?

- Is it ethical?

- Is it too risky?

Useful techniques to help structure the evaluation of options include Johnson, Scholes and Whittington's SFA and advantages and disadvantages

4. Plan what your conclusions will be and what recommendations you will make, and ensure you are able to fully justify both.

write

Presenting your report in an effective way

This section will contain

Chapter 7

Structuring your report

In this chapter

We begin to look at how to present your report in an effective way. The aim of the plan and think stages of the process is to find the right answer to the 'bottom-line' questions; to make sure you've undertaken a thorough investigation that's left no stone unturned. But having the right answers is only half the story. Now we need to persuade our reader that we're giving the right answer, and the secret to that is in the way you structure and write your report.

Thinking about the structure of your report allows you to build a bridge between your planning sheets and the document you ultimately deliver. Having the right structure is essential if your user is to follow the logic in your argument. You will need to find the path that is easiest to navigate in order to take your reader from A to B without them getting lost. And you'll need to decide what sights they will take in along the way to ensure their journey fulfils its potential.

After first considering why structure is important, this chapter will look at a series of steps to follow in order to discover the best structure for your report. We'll re-visit the skill of prioritisation and consider why it is so vital at this stage of the process. We'll also look at how to group information and decide on the order of your points.

We'll review some of the common sections found in many reports and explore the purpose of each. This will be followed by guidance on including a summary of your report. We'll finish by providing an illustration that pulls it all together.

Why is structure important?

Have you ever attended a meeting where no agenda has been set in advance? Did much get achieved at that meeting? Probably not! An agenda ensures that everyone knows what will be covered in the meeting, the order in which things will be discussed and ultimately what the objective of the meeting is. An agenda gives structure to a meeting.

Having said that, simply having an agenda does not mean a meeting will be successful. To be effective, an agenda must be well thought out. More important items must be given sufficient time to ensure they are properly addressed and the order of the topics must be chosen carefully to ensure the items flow logically from one another. So it's not just having a structure that's important; it's having the right structure.

It's not just having a structure that's important; it's having the right structure

Writing your report is no different. Having completed your planning and thinking, you now have a list of information, ideas and opinions to potentially include within your report, all of which are recorded in a more than likely haphazard way on your planning sheets. Whilst we know the objective of your report is to answer the 'bottom-line' questions, to be effective it must also persuade the reader that your answers are the correct ones. You will not be able to do this unless your report is structured well.

The term 'structure' in this context is referring to the flow of your report, the order in which you present your analysis and findings and the series of headings and sub-headings you use to signal to the reader what is coming next. Considering the structure of your report before you start writing is a key stage in the overall process of preparing a report. It builds a bridge between your planning sheets and your final document and ensures that your report is effective.

We've referred several times throughout this book to the need to 'construct' an argument to support your assertions; now's the point where we show you how.

What is the best structure for a report?

The simple answer is it depends. There is not one single, universal structure that will work for all situations. Factors such as who you are reporting to, your role, and precedents set by previous authors of reports facing similar situations will all have a bearing on the best structure for your report.

There are however, a number of steps, a process for adding structure, which should be followed in all circumstances. Following these steps will ensure your arguments are constructed well and are presented in a way that your reader can follow and understand.

Step 1 – Divide your report into sections

One of the most highly cited papers in psychology was published in 1956 by the cognitive psychologist, George A Miller. Frequently referred to as Miller's Law, it argues that the number of objects an average human being can hold in working memory is 7 ± 2.

By breaking your report down into discrete sections, you reduce the user's perception of the amount of information they have to absorb and process at any one time. This makes it easier for them to digest the information and consider its meaning.

Further advantages of breaking your report into sections relate to how the brain processes and stores information. On average information can only be retained for a period of about 30 seconds. This is why you'll get to the bottom of reading a page and not remember what you've just read. If you want to extend the 30 seconds, you need to help the brain form a memory.

A key step in the formation of memories is to label or compartmentalise data to allow it to be stored effectively. Think of your brain like a filing cabinet. If you just keep dropping paper in, in no particular order, you'll not be able to locate that piece of paper the next time you need to refer to it. By 'filing' the paper in a folder, clearly labelled with a topic or title, you are better able to track it down when it's needed. The section headings you use in your report act like those files and folders. They give the reader some ready-made labels to help them compartmentalise the information you're giving them.

Factors such as who you are reporting to, your role, and precedents set by previous authors of reports facing similar situations will all have a bearing on the best structure for your report

Breaking your report down into discrete sections makes it easier for your reader to digest information and consider its meaning

The section headings you use in your report help your reader compartmentalise the information you're giving them

All business reports will have standard headings; we will talk more about what the most useful headings are later in the chapter. These headings will help break the report up, making it easier to read and so absorb the content. However, by way of an overview and to give a bigger picture as to how the whole report should fit together, you should think about the beginning, the middle and the end of your report. What should you start with, what should go in the middle and how will your end contribute to the overall feel of the report. It's a little like a sandwich, with the bread being the beginning and end, and the contents the filling in the middle.

A report is like a sandwich, with the bread being the beginning and end, and the contents the filling in the middle

The report writing sandwich

Beginning
Middle
End

Beginning

Often referred to as an introduction (see later), this is where you can provide some background on the scenario, ensure your reader is aware of the context of your report and knows what your report is going to cover. Much of the content for this section will have been entered on your planning sheets at the beginning of the process of preparing your report; the stage where you formulated your initial PLAN and considered the 'bottom-line' questions.

Middle

The middle section is the largest part of your report; it is where you will present the information you've found, your analysis of that information, your interpretations of what it might mean and your evaluation of what it does mean.

For more complex reports, it may be that you have a number of 'middle' elements, each one covering a different topic or requirement or perhaps considering a different 'bottom-line' question.

Example

You've been asked to write a report on a proposal to outsource the repair centre function of a high street electronics retailer, XYZ Ltd. The retailer currently completes all repairs in on-site centres and directly employs all repair centre staff. The repair centres are thought to be a key differentiating factor as they provide reassurance for customers. The 'bottom-line' questions have been agreed as:

- Do the proposed costs look reasonable?
- Will the proposed agreement save the company money?
- What are the risks of the outsourcing arrangement?

This report would be best structured with five separate sections:

1. Introduction (Beginning)
2. Review of the proposed costs (Middle 1)
3. Evaluation of cost savings(Middle 2)
4. Assessment of risks (Middle 3)
5. Conclusion (End)

End

This is the part of the report that will have the most impact; it is where you summarise your findings and present your conclusions and recommendations. As we have said before, the objective of your report is to answer a number of 'bottom-line' questions and this is the section of the report where your reader gets their answers.

It is important to end on something powerful

It is important that you end on something powerful. You must think carefully what you want your last paragraph to be since anything at the end always has more impact than something in the middle.

There are a number of different ways in which conclusions and recommendations can be presented within a report (see later when we look in more detail at providing a summary of report) but the majority of situations will always require some kind of final summary.

The Beautiful Princess

Reports have beginnings, middles and ends; poems have beginnings, middles and ends; and stories have beginnings, middles and ends. To illustrate, consider the following short story:

"Once upon a time there was a beautiful Princess who lived in a castle with her husband, and although he loved her, she spent much of her time alone.

Saddened and often confused by her husband's lack of attention the beautiful Princess spent many of her days with the ordinary people who lived in the Kingdom. Some of these ordinary people were far less fortunate than the beautiful Princess, and through her smile and genuine need to help, she won their hearts. To them she was compassionate, caring, but most of all made their lives better by just being herself, she had become a leader.

One day her husband saw how the ordinary people looked at the beautiful Princess. Realising the error of his ways and with his love for her rekindled he asked if she would teach him what she knew.

Being such a kind and forgiving person, the Princess agreed, and they both lived happily ever after."

This shows how the beginning, middle and end structure works. Notice how the beginning starts with some background information and is relatively short, only two lines. The middle, which is the largest section, links to the beginning but explains and expands, moving the story on towards the end. The end is longer than the beginning and brings the story to a conclusion. It provides the answers to the reader's questions, which in this case were clearly, "what happened to the Princess?"

Step 2 – Prioritise

In chapter 2 we showed you how prioritisation can be used to help relieve time pressure whilst preparing your report. We also saw in chapter 6 how prioritisation is vital to exercising judgement when evaluating information. Now we're going to see the ways in which prioritisation is needed to structure your report.

What to include?

After completing the PLAN and THINK stages of the overall process, you should have some planning sheets that are bursting with notes to allow you to answer the 'bottom-line' questions. Often you can find that you actually have too much jotted down. You may find yourself restricted by the amount of time available for writing your report (this will particularly apply to those sitting an exam), or perhaps a word limit that has been imposed (usually the case for dissertations), meaning that you just can't fit everything in. In such situations you will need to prioritise the contents of your planning sheets to decide what goes into your report and what gets left out.

You will need to prioritise the contents of your planning sheets to decide what goes into your report and what gets left out. Ask yourself "would the reader want to know that?"

To do this you'll need to think about the value of each piece of information or each option to the reader of your report. Ask yourself "would they want to know that?" We need to be clear as to what we believe the most important points are. To do this sit back, look at the bigger picture, taking into account everything you have thought about and put on your planning sheet, and ask, "if I could only make three points, what would they be?" This is not because you will only make three points; it is just a way of getting you to focus on what is important and what is not.

As suggested in chapter 6, when forming your conclusions and recommendations you should think about what pieces of analysis, interpretation and evaluation have helped you make your decision. Any element that is essential for your reader to be convinced by your argument must be included.

What order?

The other key way in which prioritisation can be used to structure your report is in thinking about the order in which you should present information. It is not possible, nor desirable to have everything equal. Your report has to make a point, it has to get its message across, and it can't do that without promoting some thoughts and ideas to the detriment of others. Your reader will generally prefer to read about the most important information first, working through to the less important. This is preferable to spending time reading about more trivial matters before being hit with the crucial piece of news.

Your reader will want to read about the most important information first, working through to the less important

Criteria for prioritisation

Some of the techniques we outlined in chapter 2 on how to prioritise, and in particular the criteria we suggested you use to prioritise, are just as relevant here:

Criterion 1   Link to 'bottom-line' questions

Is the information or analysis an essential part of your path towards answering the 'bottom-line' questions? Would your answer still make sense and would the reader still have faith in your answer if this information was missing? By answering these two questions you should be able to quickly eliminate the information that is non-essential.

Criterion 2   Impact

By this we mean how significant something is or by how much it influences your analysis or your conclusions. This criteria is useful for both eliminating information and for ordering it.

When you're looking to eliminate information, you should ensure anything with a significant impact is included in your report. You can then work down your list in order of impact until you feel you will run out of time or space.

This process can also be used to consider the order in which you should cover information within your report; you should start with the information of greatest impact and work down your list.

When you assess the impact of some information, additional factors to consider are size and likelihood.

Size

The bigger an issue or the impact of a piece of information, the higher prioritisation should be given to it. But what do we mean by big? When writing a report in the area of business and finance big will often refer to monetary value but that won't always be the case, e.g. you could be referring to the number of units or people.

Likelihood

Your commercial thought processes may have identified a potential risk associated with a decision or an alternative solution. Whether you should mention that risk within your report will depend upon your assessment of the probability of that risk turning into reality. How likely is it to happen?

You must assess what is the most likely meaning of the information and ensure you focus more attention on this than any other possibility

This factor is particularly important when it comes to deciding on which potential implications or 'effects' you've identified should be included in your report. In chapter 4 we covered how the creative thinking process is the best when it comes to looking into the future and asking the question "what might this mean?" If done properly, creative thinking can lead to a multitude of ideas and suggestions, some of which are quite plausible and others slightly less so. Your reader will quickly switch off if your report simply lists out a number of things that some information might mean. Instead you must assess what is the most likely meaning of the information and ensure you focus more attention on this than any other possibility. Figuring this out will require the judgement techniques referred to in chapter 6.

Example

Using our earlier outsourcing example again. You've been asked to identify the risks associated with the proposed outsourcing agreement. Let's assume you've identified the following risks and you now want to prioritise them based on their size and likelihood. The risks are as follows.

- Confidentiality of information. The retailer would have to supply the outsourcer with details of the customers and the products bought by them. Also the data stored on any electronic device (computer, mobile etc) sent for repair would now be seen by a 3rd party and not solely by the retailer's staff.

- The retailer may lose control over the day-to-day repair work. There would be a service level agreement (SLA) in place with designated contact names.

- Many of the existing staff would have to be made redundant. Some may be redeployed to the outsourcer. Many of these staff have been with the retailer from the outset of the business. There is a risk that there may be a backlash on the company as a result of bad publicity.

- Customer confidence may be damaged. For many people the purchase of an electronic device is a worrying prospect. The existence of the on-site repair centres is a comfort blanket for customers anxious about a purchase.

The risk which should be prioritised highest is the threat to customer confidence. If the repair centres are seen as a key differentiator then this strategy could result in a fall in customer numbers and a loss of market share. The size of this could be immense although the likelihood is a little harder to assess. Further research should be advised.

The next risk to be prioritised would be the loss of control of day-to-day work. Failure to deliver on customer expectations would be a big issue. However, one of the main advantages of outsourcing is that someone else controls and plans the workload. The SLA should guarantee a level of service that satisfies customers and so the likelihood of problems is restricted to the likelihood that the provider cannot deliver the SLA. Hopefully such issues would be ironed out during the negotiation process.

The third priority is the risk of reputational damage following the announcement of redundancies. Although the situation is unfortunate for the employees involved, it would be rare to see such action result in a reduction in customer numbers, especially in the current economic climate where many companies are announcing redundancy programmes.

The final risk to be prioritised would be the confidentiality of information. This is actually a 'red herring' and would probably not even be mentioned in the report. Customers would normally be asked to sign a warranty agreement and this would contain a clause authorising the release of what is fairly non-personal information (product bought, name etc). Personal data held on the customers' devices are subject to the same legislation whether the retailers staff or an outsourcer sees the data. This risk is neither sizeable nor likely.

The third criterion we covered in chapter 2 was urgency. We'll consider this in more detail under the next step.

Step 3 – Follow a logical order

For your arguments to persuade your reader your points must be presented in a logical order. By this we mean an order that makes sense.

Reading should be a pleasurable and enlightening experience. Your reader should not feel like they have to battle to get through your report

If you wrote your report in the same order that you gathered and processed the information, it is unlikely your reader would make all the connections needed to understand your argument. Reading anything should be a pleasurable and enlightening experience. Your reader should not feel like they have to battle to get through your report. This is particularly important for those sitting an exam since the reader of your report (i.e. the marker) will be on a tight time schedule and will not be able to spend lots of time trying to follow your argument.

You should think of the order of your report like a path connecting pieces of information and analysis together. Your job as the author is to find the path from A to B that is easiest to navigate and follow.

You should think of the order of your report like a path connecting pieces of information and analysis together. Your job as the author is to find the path from A to B that is easiest to navigate and follow

1: Confusing path **2: Easy to follow path**

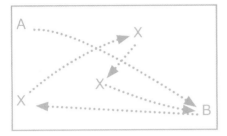 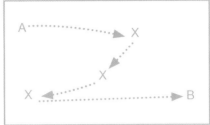

You may think that the best path will always be the shortest. In our diagrams above, the shortest, and most direct path is to go straight from A to B. However, this neglects to take in the crucial pieces of information and analysis found at each of the X spots. Without this information, your reader may not be convinced by your argument. It is therefore worth taking the slightly longer de-tour, via these pieces of information in order to ensure your report achieves its objective. Despite this de-tour though, note how in the second diagram the path linking these pieces together is still the shortest and most logical.

Now we know we need to follow the easiest path, the next question is how do we find it. Again, this will likely depend on the situation but the following are all principles that can be applied to help give a logical order to your report.

General to specific

Information that is more general in nature, that provides a background to the argument, is best presented before the more specific information needed to answer the 'bottom-line' questions.

Information that is more general in nature should be presented before the more specific information needed to answer the 'bottom-line' questions

Example

Keeping with the electronic retailer and specifically, the review of the costs associated with the proposal. Some general information on the number of repairs and the current costs incurred would provide a sound backdrop before the specific proposals are reviewed, cost savings calculated and comments made on whether they are reasonable.

Chronological order

In some reports there may be a chronological order to the information you're presenting or recommendations you're providing. If this is the case, it is best to follow this order. When reporting on historic things (generally providing information and analysis), you should start with the oldest and work towards the more recent pieces of information. When reporting on actions to be taken in the future (your recommendations), start with those that must be completed in the short-term and then work towards the longer-term recommendations.

Follow the chronological order of the information you're presenting

Urgency

This is really an extension of the chronological order principle and can easily be applied when writing any recommendations. You should aim to cover the most urgent recommendations first.

In some circumstances it can also be used when deciding on the order of different sections or sub-headings in your report (see steps 1 & 4).

Example

The CIMA Case Study examination requires students to analyse a number of issues facing a company, to evaluate a number of alternative solutions to those issues and provide recommendations. Students generally structure their report with a separate section for each issue they've identified however the order they place the sections in is determined by the impact and urgency of each issue.

You will need to be on the look-out for implicit urgency (where action must be taken quickly to avoid a problem escalating) as well as explicit urgency (where a deadline is clearly stated).

Dependency order

By this we mean that sometimes information or analysis will naturally flow on from other pieces of information i.e. one is dependent upon the other. In this situation you should follow the natural flow and explain the nature of any dependency.

Example

Using the electronic retailer again where you've been asked to review the proposed costs and evaluate whether the proposal will save the company money. You will need the output of your assessment of the reasonableness of the cost proposals to be able to evaluate whether the proposal will save money. Given this dependency, your report should address the proposed costs first before considering how much money the proposal will or won't save.

Step 4 – Group information together

Even though you've divided your report into sections, it is still possible to provide your reader with more signals of what you're covering and where you intend to go by using sub-headings.

Sub-headings will prevent you jumping around from one subject to the next in your report. This in turn will ensure your report flows well and that your argument follows a clear path.

To group information together you should review your planning sheets and identify any aspects that pieces of information have in common. It may be that there are a number of ways in which information could be grouped in which case you should choose the way that will be of most use to your user.

Example

Your report on the outsourcing proposal needs to answer the 'bottom-line' question on the risks associated with the proposal. The danger with this sort of question is that your report ends up with a scattergun of points, almost a number of bullet points listing out all of the risks. You can avoid this by grouping the risks together under some sensible sub-headings. These could be time related (short-term and long-term) or could relate to the impact on the business (strategic, financial, and operational).

Common sections in a report

Having seen the steps we should follow to ensure a logical structure, it is worth spending some time looking at the common sections that can appear within reports. Whether you include each section or not will come down to precedents but we felt it was useful to provide some guidance and illustrations.

Introduction

An introduction gives you an opportunity to set the scene and outline the context of the report

We commented earlier that all reports should have a beginning, a middle and an end. The beginning part is often referred to as an introduction and it gives the author the opportunity to set the scene and outline the context of the report. We saw in chapter 4 that context is a vital part of being commercial and so providing this context so early in the report will help your reader follow your commercial logic.

There is a fine balance between setting the context and simply outlining a number of facts that your reader will already be aware of. You must be careful not to annoy your reader in this opening section by wasting their time repeating information they already know and not adding any value. The best way to add value is to note down the implications of the facts as well as just the facts themselves.

As a suggestion, your introduction could include things such as:

- performance of the organisation to date

- future prospects

- any specific key challenges.

Example

Using our outsourcing scenario (which we've embellished with a few additional facts), an example would be:

With revenues of over £60m and year-on-year growth of nearly 12%, XYZ Ltd is clearly offering something that its competitors are not. Some believe that the key differentiating factor is the presence of on-site repair centres, which help to reassure the less experienced electronics consumer. Given this context the proposal to outsource this facility must be carefully considered to ensure this competitive advantage is not lost.

Like all first impressions, your reader will form an opinion about your competence (or otherwise) from what they read here

You should always remember that this is the first thing your user will read and, like all first impressions, they will decide a lot about your competence (or otherwise) from what you write here. This is particularly important for those sitting an exam where the user (i.e. your marker) will be marking a number of scripts in a day and will undoubtedly be under some time pressure when doing so.

Terms of reference

A terms of reference is a small section of the report where you can outline what specifically has been asked of you, note any constraints that have been placed on the report (so, for example, what it is not seeking to do), and spell out who is able to rely on the content of the report. You should also state whether you have been able to verify all of the information you've relied upon.

This section is of most importance for those writing a business report since having parties other than the intended recipient rely on your report can expose you and your employer to unnecessary risk.

Example

An example using our outsourcing scenario would be:

The purpose of this report is to evaluate the proposal to outsource the repair centre function of XYZ Ltd. Specifically it will:

- consider whether the proposed costs appear reasonable

- evaluate whether the proposal will increase XYZ's profitability

- assess the risks associated with the outsourcing proposal.

The report has been prepared by ABC Consultants for the Board of Directors of XYZ Ltd. It should not be relied upon by any other party.

It uses information provided by XYZ Ltd, which has not been independently verified.

Appendices

Any detailed information or findings should be presented in the appendices to your report

As a general rule, any detailed information or findings should be presented in the appendices to your report. As well as financial analysis, which was discussed in chapter 5, examples would include results of questionnaires or experiments, analysis of competitors or any detailed background information.

You shouldn't present anything in your appendices that isn't used and referred to within the main body of your report

The golden rule is that you shouldn't present anything in your appendices that isn't used and referred to within the main body of your report. You should always pull through the key pieces of information or findings into your main report and then refer the reader to where in the appendices they can find the detail (see chapter 8 for more details).

Your appendices should be able to be understood as a stand-alone document. This means that sources of information, assumptions taken to derive the information or anything needed to be able to understand that information must also be presented in the appendix.

Summarising your report

Providing a summary of key elements of your report can help your reader to extract key information when they need it. There are two common types of summary that you can provide.

1) A summary of conclusions and recommendations

The most valuable part of your report is the conclusions you reach and the recommendations you make. At the end of the day, these are the reason why the report was commissioned, these are the answers to the users 'bottom-line' questions. As a result, it is commonplace for the key conclusions and recommendations to be presented in a separate section of the report, as well as within the sections to which they relate. Such a summary allows the reader to easily refer to the key outcomes and be able to quickly look up what they need to do next.

Key conclusions and recommendations are often presented in a separate section of the report, as well as within the sections to which they relate

Whilst this is the easiest method of providing a summary, it does mean that your user has to read, understand and digest your full report in order to understand your arguments and appreciate the significance of your findings.

2) An executive summary

An executive summary is typically presented at the start of your report. It does exactly what it says on the tin; it provides a summary of your report for a busy executive who is perhaps too busy to read the report in full.

An executive summary provides a summary of your report for a busy executive who is too busy to read the report in full

It is therefore more than just a summary of your conclusions and recommendations. It needs to present the key pieces of information, your commercial thoughts surrounding that information and the arguments you present to support your opinions. The most important skill needed to prepare an effective executive summary is one which we've referred to many times throughout this book, prioritisation. You will need to prioritise the contents of your report, pulling out the elements that will be most important for your user to be able to understand your point.

You should view your executive summary as being like a précis of a book. You wouldn't just write about what happened in the final chapter but would instead provide a brief summary of the key things that happened in each chapter.

One common question often asked by students is "how long should my executive summary be?" The correct, but not very useful answer is as long as it needs to be. There is not a 'one size fits all' answer. Typically though, an executive summary will average about 10% of the total length of the report.

3) Which method to adopt?

Having told you about both of these common methods, the next question is how do you decide which one to go for? As we said at the start of this chapter, looking for precedents, reviewing reports produced for this user in the past or in this scenario previously will give a good indication. This will be particularly true for dissertation students where there is often a very detailed outline of how your report should be structured.

Alternatively, you may be able to discuss this with your user at the beginning of the process to discover how they would prefer to have the information presented.

If none of these options are available to you, the final deciding factor can be the length of the report. Given that the purpose of an executive summary is to save time for the busy executive, such a section would seem pointless if the total length of you report was under five pages. Anything above twenty pages and an executive summary would be strongly advised. In between these – the choice is up to you.

Putting it all together – an illustration

Although we don't want to be prescriptive about exactly how your report should be structured, we thought it important to give an illustration of what a report might look like. It contains many of the points discussed above and is the structure that we have used for our answer. Once again we have made reference to the outsourcing example by way of illustration. Please note it is only an example and does not cover every aspect covered in this chapter.

To start with, your report should have a front cover that clearly shows what the report is about, who it is to, who it is from and importantly when it was prepared. A report with no date is almost worthless.

REPORT – To evaluate the proposal to outsource the repair centre function of XYZ Ltd

To: Board of Directors of XYZ Ltd

From: ABC Consultants

Date: Today

The contents page acts as a signpost to what is included in the report. It should make reference to the page numbers and/or section numbers. It also gives some idea of the relative importance, as those chapters with more pages will be viewed as more important.

CONTENTS

The introduction is discussed above in some detail. In essence the introduction gives you the opportunity to set the scene.

1 Introduction

- Performance to date.

- Future prospects.

- Any specific key challenges.

The terms of reference is also discussed above. It is the section of the report where you can outline what specifically has been asked of you.

2 Terms of reference

- Who asked for the report and who you are.

- Have there been any constraints regarding the information you have had access to or been able to find. Have you relied on any one individual for facts, if so you may wish to say so here.

Although not always required an executive summary presents the key pieces of information, your commercial thoughts surrounding that information and the arguments you present to support your opinions. It also includes your conclusions and recommendations.

3 Executive summary (where applicable)

- What are the most important points from this report.

- What commercial issues does this raise.

- Justify why they are important.

- Conclusions and recommendations.

This is the body of the report and should contain sub-headings as appropriate but don't overdo it, keep it simple. Notice that you could conclude after each main point as shown here or conclude on all three main points at the end of the report.

4   Main point 1- review of the proposed costs

4.1   Sub-heading 1

4.2   Sub-heading 2 etc

You could present your conclusion relating to main point 1 at this stage.

If you have too many main points you may want to consider if they are all important or if in fact they should be the focus of a separate report.

5   Main point 2 - evaluation of cost savings

5.1   Sub-heading 1

5.2   Sub-heading 2 etc

You could present your conclusion relating to main point 2 at this stage.

Don't over complicate your referencing, for example 5.1.a. (i) helps no one.

6   Main point 3 - assessment of risks

6.1   Sub-heading 1

6.2   Sub-heading 2 etc

You could present your conclusion relating to main point 3 at this stage.

The conclusion could well be the last part of the report and should contain your opinion and views. You can conclude at the end of the report on all main points or at the end of each section as shown above. In this illustration we show the conclusion separate from the recommendation but there are times when they could be shown together. Don't sit on the fence; your conclusions should be unequivocal.

7   Conclusion

- State your opinion; this should be an answer to a 'bottom-line' question.

- Justify your opinion, use statements of fact where possible.

As with the executive summary, you may not be required to give recommendations; in fact you may be stepping outside your terms of reference by giving them. Remember they are the actions that you want the reader to follow, they are what, in your opinion, they should do.

8 Recommendations (where applicable)

- State your action; this should be an answer to a 'bottom-line' question.

- Justify your action, use statements of fact where possible.

- State the details, who should do something and when should they do it?

Your appendices should contain detailed calculations, information or findings .

9 Appendices

9.1 Appendix 1

9.2 Appendix 2 etc

Other business documents

Although this is a book about preparing business reports, it is worthwhile giving some brief acknowledgement to other types of business documents. The principles we've outlined for preparing a report can pretty much be applied to any other business document; the only thing that will change is the structure and the way it is written.

Having said that, very often the structure won't be as different as you might think. If you were asked to prepare an internal memorandum or some briefing notes, or even a presentation, the same steps should be followed in terms of dividing your document into sections, prioritising what you cover and working in a logical order.

Further reading

'The magical number seven, plus or minus two: Some limits on our capacity for processing information' by GA Miller, Psycological Review 63 (2): 81-97.

The Case – a chance to practise

Using all of the case information you've been supplied with so far, and working from the planning sheets you have from the last chapter, consider how best to structure your report.

Work through each of the steps outlined in this chapter and decide upon the sections, headings and sub-headings you plan to use.

Specific applications

 Exam based

When writing a report in order to pass an exam, deciding on the best structure for your report can actually be very easy. More than likely, specific guidance will be provided by the examining body or exam tutors stating how they would like your report to be laid out. Now, it may be that, if given a free hand to do as you liked, you wouldn't perhaps choose that structure. Unfortunately though, or should that be fortunately, the decision isn't in your hands.

Example

The CIMA Case study examination awards 10 marks for the consideration of ethical issues. Students are advised to have a separate section within their report dealing specifically with these ethical issues even though that perhaps isn't what you'd expect to see if this report was being written in a real life business environment.

If such guidance doesn't exist, it will most likely be given within the exam itself. When outlining the requirement, it is quite commonplace for the examiner to state particular areas your report should cover, and these can often be used as effective sub-headings.

Not only does following such guidance or direction make it easier for you, it will also make it much easier for your marker. And we all know that one of the golden rules when trying to pass an exam is to make things easy for your marker.

So, given this additional guidance, structuring your report in an exam simply focuses on deciding what pieces of information, analysis, and interpretation are going to be included and where. The final stage in the planning cycle, that of evaluation, is therefore very important (see chapter 6), along with step 2 outlined in this chapter, which looks at prioritising your points.

 Dissertation

Being a more academic report, the structure of a dissertation can be quite different, although the base principles still apply. Most universities and awarding bodies will provide some quite specific guidance on the structure your dissertation should follow. Whilst this guidance will vary from one institution to the next (and you must therefore refer specifically to the guidance provided to you), there does seem to be some common or more popular layouts that are often suggested.

The length of a dissertation is normally about 10,000 words although sometimes the word limit can be as high as 25,000. The word limits will often exclude appendices.

As with any report, a dissertation should begin with an introduction. Typically about 10% of the total words, this should cover things such as: what is your hypothesis, who will benefit from your investigation, how do you plan to solve the problem, by what methods and what are the constraints or limitations of the study? You should aim to end your introduction by stating the objectives of the dissertation.

The next section will often concentrate on reviewing relevant literature. This will act as a summary of what other people have already written and published around the theme of your research. It is very important that you acknowledge the authorship of other people's work. You should include a reference for all material to which you have made explicit reference or from which you have quoted, and this should be given at the foot of the page where the reference is made. This is often confused with a bibliography, which is usually presented at the end of your dissertation, and should include all the material to which you have referred while doing the project, even if it is not explicitly cited in the text. Entries in the bibliography are usually in alphabetical order and should typically look like this:

Robinson Z. and Pedley-Smith S. (2010) 'A Student's Guide to Preparing Business Reports' pp84-99

Depending on your topic and the amount of previous work published, the review of literature could be expected to account for up to 25% of your total word count.

The third chapter should focus on the methodology you've used, the alternatives you considered, and the reasons you selected the final version. In short, what you did, how you did it and why you did it that way? You can use this chapter to describe the scope and aims of the dissertation. This is another significant chapter as it underpins everything that follows and ensures your reader understands your processes. It can therefore be expected to be about 15% - 20% of the total length of your dissertation.

Now you can start to get into the presentation of your findings, and in particular the data you've collected; what have you observed and what was found out? This chapter should be restricted to the presentation of the data; the discussion, analysis and interpretation of the data should be left to the following chapter.

Material such as questionnaires, extensive data analysis tables etc, that would break up the flow if included in the main body of the dissertation should be included as appendices at the end of your dissertation. Make sure you only include data that adds value to the dissertation. For example, raw questionnaire responses are unlikely to have any worth if you've summarised the responses in a table.

After presenting the data, you can move on to your analysis, interpretation and evaluation of the data. You can outline the formulation of possible solutions and justify your selection of final recommendations. Given the more academic nature of the report, you should ensure that any differences between your findings and those of other people are identified and challenged. This will be key to ensuring your reader is persuaded by your argument.

The final section of your dissertation should be your conclusions. As well as summarising your main findings, you should also provide some direction for further work and critically reflect on the lessons learned from the project. This section will typically be about 10% of the length of the full dissertation.

Just to stress again, whilst this structure is typical for many dissertations, it is not the only way. Please make sure you seek and then follow guidance from the Institution you're studying at.

Business report

Those writing a business report are sometimes facing the hardest task when structuring their report. Some reports will be quite 'run-of-the-mill', something that is produced on a monthly or annual basis, and in these cases the previous version can simply be used as a template. But when a report is a one-off, something that has not been produced before, the author has little guidance when it comes to finding a structure that works.

It is this author that must draw on everything noted in this chapter. It will be important to devote sufficient time for this activity (add it in to your task plan at the start of the process) and you may have to go through a few iterations before you hit upon a structure you're happy with.

For example:

We started with an outline structure for this book that had prioritisation and time management as a single chapter, towards the end of the book. We'd taken a narrow view that both were mainly connected to the WRITE stage of the process. But, when we starting planning the detail, analysing, interpreting and evaluating our points, we realised that time management was something that was needed throughout the whole process of preparing a report. We also found that prioritisation was a fundamental skill that could be used at various stages, not just when deciding what to put in your report. This feels quite obvious to us now but at the time, we'd not been through that thought process.

This example illustrates two things. Firstly, the benefits of completing your planning and thinking before you start the WRITE stage by considering the structure of your report (unfortunately, the way the book publishing world works, you aren't always able to do this). And, secondly, that you may need to be flexible, adapting initial plans if you discover something better. More on this at the end of chapter 8.

One final point to note: when writing a report that is produced on a regular basis you should not feel confined to the structure adopted previously. As time goes by the historic structures may become outdated and it is sometimes necessary and refreshing for someone to come along and challenge the status quo.

In a nutshell..............

To persuade your reader that your answers to the 'bottom-line' questions are the right ones, your report must not only have a structure, it must have the right structure.

A clear logical structure will help your reader to understand your argument. It acts as a path, leading them from one point to the next, until they reach their ultimate destination, your conclusions and recommendations.

Deciding on the best structure for your report is like building a bridge between your planning sheets and your final report. Given all of the planning and thinking you've carried out so far, your planning sheets will be bursting with information, analysis, interpretations and evaluations. Now you've got to decide which of these are going to make the cut and appear in your report, which are fundamental to the argument you're putting forward and what order must you present them in so they make sense.

There is no one single, universal structure that will work for all reports. There are however a number of steps you can follow to find it:

Step 1 – Divide your report into sections. This helps your reader to store the information you're giving them and breaks it down into more manageable chunks. You should decide the elements that will appear at the **beginning, middle and end** of your report.

Step 2 – Prioritise. Discard the items on your planning sheet that are not essential to your argument and keep the ones that are. The usual criteria of linkage to 'bottom-line' questions, impact (including size and likelihood) and urgency are just as relevant here.

Step 3 – Follow a logical order. Such orders can include working from the general to the specific, following the chronology, considering urgency or dependency.

Step 4 – Group information together. Identifying a series of sub-headings that information can be grouped under will prevent you jumping around in your report.

171

When you are clear on the structure of your report, you must consider whether to provide a summary of the important elements of your report. As a minimum most reports will summarise all of the conclusions and recommendations in one section at the end of your report. In some circumstance, particularly where your report is quite long (say over five pages), your reader may prefer it if you included a précis as an executive summary at the start of your report.

Write

Chapter 8

Writing your report

A student's guide to
Preparing Business Reports

In this chapter

We reach the end of our journey, and consider the actual writing of the report. The time spent planning and thinking will now culminate in the words on a page and you've got to ensure that you do justice to the time you've invested preparing this report.

Your reader will be looking to extract the relevant key points from your report as quickly as possible. You can help by writing in a simplistic style, keeping everything short, punchy and to the point. You're not looking to win the Booker Prize; you just need to present your argument in a clear and concise manner.

After reviewing some of the principles behind keeping it short, we'll show you how to assess your current writing style to see if you need to make changes. The chapter will move on to look at some presentational techniques that will help to maintain your user's attention before covering the dreaded subjects of spelling and grammar.

We'll finish the chapter, and indeed the book with a quick overview of the whole process of preparing a report and a consideration of how report preparation in reality may force slight deviations from the steps outlined.

The importance of presentation

In the opening chapter of this book we observed how easily the facts in an argument can be lost if they're not constructed and presented in the correct way. Your time spent planning will hopefully ensure you have a well constructed commercial argument that is both logical and creative. But all of this time will be wasted if your argument isn't presented in a clear, unambiguous manner.

Your reader must 'tune-in' to your document quickly in order to justify spending time on it

The readers of business reports, whatever their background, will most likely be under pressure. They have too many reports, e-mails or scripts to read and therefore only have a small amount of time to devote to yours. They have developed relatively short attention spans and will be looking for answers, not more questions.

You must remember that you don't have an automatic right to their time. They need to 'tune-in' to your document quickly in order to justify spending time on it. They want to extract the relevant key points as quickly as possible.

Their ability to do this will come from a combination of the structure of your report together with the words and layout you select.

Keep it short

Most readers can take in and absorb short, punchy points more easily than long, complex points. So when we say "keep it short" we're not just referring to the total length of your report. More specifically we mean you should keep the individual elements of your report short. Let's look at these elements in more detail.

Short paragraphs

A paragraph is a group of sentences about one main idea. Ideally it should begin with a topic sentence that tells the reader what the paragraph is about. It will then have a small number of supporting sentences which add detail to the topic. It will finish with an ending sentence that concludes or finishes the topic before a new paragraph is started.

To see an example, just look at the previous paragraph. The opening sentence, the topic sentence, told you that the paragraph was about paragraphs. It then contained two further sentences which added detail to the topic before ending with a final sentence that finished the topic.

The natural tendency for most people is to read a document paragraph by paragraph. That is to say, you'll read one paragraph and then subconsciously take a break in order to process the meaning of what you've just read. If your paragraphs are too long, or focus on more than one topic, your reader will find it more difficult to process the information you've just presented.

This is particularly important for those sitting an exam. Your reader, more accurately referred to as your marker, will naturally consider how many marks to award on a paragraph by paragraph basis. If your paragraph contains more than one point or idea it is possible that the first will be lost as your marker will be concentrating more on the last point you made.

In most situations there would be little justification for a paragraph with more than say five sentences in it. Any more and you're likely to be wandering off topic.

> Most readers can take in and absorb short, punchy points more easily than long, complex points.

> Most people read a document paragraph by paragraph, subconsciously pausing to process the meaning of what they've just read after each paragraph

Short sentences

A sentence is a group of words that makes sense on its own. Most of us can recall the basics we learned at school: a sentence should start with a capital letter, end with a full stop, contain a verb (a doing word) and must have a subject (the person or thing that is doing the verb). Yet despite these basic rules, it is amazing how many people, when attempting to write professionally, end up with a string of words that do not make sense.

The problem is the misconception that in order to be professional your report must be full of long sentences. Often the extra words included in a sentence are unnecessary and have no additional value.

Example

Management accounts are produced by the chief accountant on a monthly basis in which the month's performance details and year-to-date totals are provided. Additionally, it was noted that a detailed breakdown of the income statement is also provided.

Wouldn't this be much clearer as:

The chief accountant produces monthly management accounts. These provide the month's performance details and year-to-date totals. They also give a detailed breakdown of the income statement.

The important content needed by the reader is still there. The only difference is it's presented in a more direct manner.

Remember also that the end of a sentence, together with the punctuation within, provide signals to your reader on when they should breathe. The longer your sentence, the more care you must take to ensure you punctuate the sentence correctly. More on the dangers of poor punctuation later.

To shorten your sentences you need to deflate your text.

To shorten your sentences you need to deflate your text

Example

To illustrate what we mean, look at the examples below. Each of these phrases can easily be replaced with just one word. See if you can think of the word.

1. In the event that

2. During that time

3. It is often the case that

4. Involve the necessity of

5. Affords you an opportunity to

6. Prior to the commencement of

Short words

One of the main causes of long sentences is long words. Again, there seems to be a popular misconception that a report is only professional if it includes lots of long words. This simply isn't true.

Using too many long words can actually dilute the point you're making. It becomes harder for the reader to extract the meaning and implications of what you're saying because they're too busy trying to understand the words you're using.

Using too many long words will dilute the point you're making

Another implication of using long words is poor spelling. The longer the word, the more likely you'll misspell it; surely this is no way to convey professionalism.

Answers: 1. if; 2. whilst; 3. frequently; 4. requires; 5. allows; 6. before

Example

Here are some examples of words often associated with professional language. Each could easily be replaced with a much shorter, more straightforward word. Can you think what they are?

1. Remuneration

2. Aggregate

3. Adequate

4. Endeavour

Discover your 'fog index'

This exercise, developed in 1952 by Robert Gunning, an American businessman, is designed to test whether you are writing in a simple, easy to understand way. You will need to start by writing a section of text of at least 100 words. We would perhaps suggest that you either write an introduction for the case study report or alternatively you could write a summary of one of the chapters of this book. Now you should perform the following tasks:

a. Count the number of words in the sample (do not omit any sentences).

b. Count the number of sentences in the same sample.

c. Divide the number of words by the number of sentences to get the average number of words per sentence (for professional writers, the average sentence length is about eighteen words per sentence. In speech it is about twenty).

d. Count the number of complex words (defined as words with three or more syllables).

e. Calculate the percentage of complex words by dividing the number of complex words, by the total number of words and multiply by 100.

f. Add the average words per sentence to the percentage of complex words.

g. Multiply this by 0.4.

h. The result is your fog index.

Answers: 1. pay; 2. total; 3. enough; 4. try

The fog index gives a rough estimate of the number of years of formal education that a person requires to understand your text on a first reading. It is generally used by people who want their writing to be read easily by a large segment of the population. The average person will read at an index of 9. Anything above 15 will be difficult for a university graduate to comprehend on a first read.

A change is as good as a rest

There can be nothing more off-putting than turning over the front cover of a report to be faced with a whole page of closed typed text. We talked in chapter 4 about your inner voice, and the important role it plays in determining how you feel. What do you think your reader's inner voice is saying to them when they see that page? BORING, BORING, BORING is what it's screaming at them!

The way you write a report is about a lot more than just the words you use. Much is to do with the layout or presentation of your report. By layout we mean the appearance of your page, and it's worth noting that this is a very different thing to the structure of your report. We're no longer considering the flow and order of your report, we're now thinking about the way it looks to your reader, and the way that look makes them feel. If your reader is bored before they even start reading, your report will have to contain some pretty scintillating stuff to re-ignite their interest.

> The way you write a report is about a lot more than just the words you use. Much is to do with the layout or presentation of your report

We've already considered one aspect that will help with your presentation; the use of sub-headings within your report will serve to break up the text and make it appear more manageable. There are, however, a number of other things you can do that will help make the action of reading your report more pleasurable, and will help to keep your reader's interest for longer.

White space

White space is a real weapon in the fight against distractions and boredom. It serves to break up your sections and paragraphs so your reader knows when you're moving from one point to the next. It also helps to make the task of reading your report less daunting.

> White space is a real weapon in the fight against distractions and boredom

For those sitting a written exam, it also means that if you do miss out a point there will likely be some space where you can go back and squeeze it in.

Bullet points

Used effectively bullet points can be a very powerful way to convey information. However, if they're overdone their impact is significantly reduced and they can border on being annoying. Bullet points are best used when you're listing or stating a number of facts that require little explanation.

Example

Tips on the effective use of bullet points include:

- keep lists brief
- begin with action verbs when possible
- make verb tenses and forms consistent
- limit your list to three to six items - if possible.

Numbered points

Very similar to bullet points, these are best used when there is a precise order to the points you are making.

Numbered sections

A clear way to signal to your reader how sections relate to one another is to number each section of your report

In chapter 7 we talked about the benefits of dividing your report into sections and grouping information under sub-headings. One clear way to signal to your reader how sections relate to one another is to number each section of your report. Main sections can be given core numbers (1, 2 etc) and subsections can be numbered as 1.1, 1.2 etc. This approach makes it much clearer to your reader when they are starting a new section or when they are reading about another facet of the same section. Be careful not to get carried away though: reports with a section numbered 1.4.3.8 will do nothing but confuse.

Integrating analysis: using tables, charts and graphs

As noted in chapter 7, detailed information or findings are best presented within the appendices of your report. However, you will be expected to refer to this information in the body of your report (or else what is the point of including the information in an appendix) and an integrated approach is best for this. By this we mean directing your reader to the appendix where they can see the detail but also including the key points or a summary within the main body of your report.

So, for example, an appendix for financial statement analysis may calculate a number of different ratios and show the workings behind the calculations. In the main body of your report, you could select the most relevant ratios, the ones that tell the most important story, and summarise these in a table like this:

Revenue growth (09-10)	12.1%
Gross profit margin	22.3%
Operating profit margin	6.4%

If you don't provide a summary within the main body of your report your reader will be forced to stop reading and turn to the appendix in order to follow your argument. It is therefore not good enough to simply say "a valuation of the business has been given in Appendix 1". Instead you should say, "the business has been valued at between £1 million - £1.2 million based on the calculations performed in Appendix 1."

In addition to tables, other presentation methods that can be used to summarise the information provided in an appendix include charts and graphs. Not only are these easier to digest but they help to 'mix it up' in terms of presentation and keep your reader interested for longer.

Findings from your analysis are best presented within some kind of table or chart that summarises the key figures

Choosing the right words and presenting them properly

As we've already noted, writing a professional report does not mean it has to be full of long words. What it does have to include is the right words. The professionalism of your report will reduce if it is full of words being misused, misspelt or being put in an order that doesn't make sense. How can your reader be expected to have faith in your conclusions and recommendations when faced with such carelessness?

The following are some quotes from students' exam scripts:

'Things are bad, but would be much worse if they weren't getting better'.

'Mr Simpson should sell all his shares, also his wife'.

'Finance could be raised by equity or debt, but a mixture of either would not be as good as a mixture of both'.

'The auditor should not be having a relationship with anyone'.

'The chickens are coming home to roost by the busload'.

Whilst we can all have a little chuckle when reading these, unfortunately quotes of this type are becoming more and more frequent within reports. To avoid extracts from your reports being used as illustrations of what not to do, here are some common areas to watch out for:

Spelling

As more reports are typed rather than handwritten, the likelihood of discovering spelling mistakes within reports increases. Typographical errors (or typos as most people call them) are easy to make but most should hopefully be detected by standard spell-checking software. The first rule, when writing a typed report, is to always spell-check your documents.

But typos can't be blamed for everything. Many people struggle with spelling, with the greatest issues being caused by homophones (words that sound like each other but are spelt differently). Examples of homophones that are often confused include your and you're, there and their, principle and principal and been and being. Spelling errors of this type are exactly that: errors and not mistakes; that is to say they are borne out of carelessness (or some would go so far as to say ignorance) rather than accident. As such, they will detract from the professionalism of your report.

To avoid such errors you need to recognise your weaknesses. Identify words that you often struggle with and find ways to remember the correct spelling. Many problem words have little sayings that can help you remember. Examples are:

Identify words that you often struggle with and find ways to remember the correct spelling

- Big elephants can't always use small exits (because)

- 2 sugars in my coffee are necessary (i.e. necessary has one c yet two s')

- E for envelope reminds us that stationery (paper etc) is spelt with an e and then stationary (not moving) must be with an a.

- Separate – means to keep apart so we can remember the correct spelling is sep<u>a</u>rate and not sep<u>e</u>rate.

Grammar and punctuation

The golden rule here is to keep it simple. Some people view punctuation as a way of adding theatrical effect, almost like a series of props. But remember, you're not looking to win any literary prizes; you simply want your report to be effective, and as such, theatrics have no place in a business report. Having said that, poor grammar and punctuation will affect how your report is perceived. It's therefore worthwhile spending some time revising the basics and having a look at some common mistakes that are made; we'll start with punctuation:

The comma (,) has two main purposes: they separate things in a list and are used to mark out the less important part of a sentence. They can also be used to indicate where the reader can pause. Perhaps the most common mistake is to overuse the comma or to use it instead of a full-stop.

The apostrophe (') is used to show that some letters have been taken out of words to shorten them, or you can use apostrophes to show that something belongs to something else. Perhaps the most common error is incorrectly distinguishing between something belonging to a singular noun (the boy's hat) and something belonging to a plural noun (the directors' report).

The colon(:) is used before an explanation about something or to introduce a list.

The semi-colon (;) is sometimes used instead of a full-stop to balance two sentences or clauses which are closely related in meaning. Perhaps the most common error is mixing up colons and semi-colons.

Dashes and brackets (-) perform similar functions. They are useful for separating off parts of a sentence which introduce subordinate information that could be omitted. Again, they can be overused and this can distract the reader (you're effectively telling your reader that they're reading something that isn't that important).

Finally, the exclamation mark (!) can be used when someone is excited or shouting or if they are saying something that's strange or surprising. It generally has little place in a business report and should not be used to indicate that the author has just made a joke.

When it comes to grammar, mistakes most commonly arise from inconsistencies in the narrative mode, and in particular from whose point of view the report is written and the tense (or sense of time) of the report.

It is more professional to write your report from the third person view

It is generally regarded as more professional to write your report from the third person view. This means you should avoid the use of 'I' or 'we' in your report. An example would be to say 'it is recommended that...' rather than 'I recommend...' This is particularly true when writing a business report on behalf of the company or firm for which you work (or if you were assuming this role within an exam scenario).

Where a report is required to analyse some historical facts and comment on their implications for the future of the company, it would be expected that the report will need to use combinations of the past, present and future tense. This is, in itself, not a problem. However, care is needed to match the tense of a verb with the singular or plural noun. So, for example, in the present tense we would have 'I am', 'we are', 'it is', but this would change to 'I was', 'we were', 'it was' in the past tense. A common mix up would be the incorrect 'it were' or 'we was'.

Consider the meaning of your words

Carefully consider the meaning of the words you choose to ensure they reflect what you're trying to say and won't lead to misunderstandings

Sometimes you will need to carefully consider the meaning of the words you choose to ensure they reflect what you're trying to say and won't lead to misunderstandings.

A good example of this is the distinction between 'could' and 'should'. When writing about possibilities or options, you should use the word 'could' (e.g. the company could do x or it could do y). But when giving your recommendations, you must use the word 'should' (e.g. the company should do x). If you inadvertently used the word 'could' in your recommendation, it would put some doubt in the mind of your reader. This point was touched on in chapter 6 when we noted that you shouldn't sit on the fence with your conclusions and recommendations.

A further point under this heading is the use of emotion or emotive language in your report. This should be avoided as once again, it isn't regarded as very professional. No director would want to read a report whose opening line was 'The outlook for the company is bleak'.

Plan, think, write – an overview

We're virtually at the end of our journey now. We've guided you through the three stages of preparing an effective report: plan, think and write.

We've shown you that by identifying your user's 'bottom-line' questions you can be clear about what information you'll need to gather and the tasks you'll need to complete. We've demonstrated that by populating a series of planning sheets with the information you've gathered, and your thoughts on that information, you're better able to evaluate that information as you can see everything in one place. We've explored how to think commercially about the information you gather but also to generate ideas of future actions that might be taken. And then we've seen how to evaluate that information and those ideas, how to exercise judgement in order reach your conclusions and recommendations. Finally we've looked at how to present your report; how to structure it so that your argument seems logical and how to write in a professional manner.

Is that it? Will every report you write from now on fall into these neat stages? The reality is that there is often a blurring between the stages, sometimes even a complete overlap, which means you can't complete these stages in isolation. Often this is borne out of time restrictions, which force you to compromise and cut corners. You may have to start writing your report before you have finished thinking commercially about the information or exercising judgement by evaluating everything you have. This means that during the WRITE stage, you will often still be mulling over the argument you're presenting, still thinking through the message you're delivering. The words on the page are little more than the crystallised thoughts of the author that form throughout the whole process of preparing the report.

The reality is that there is often a blurring between the stages, sometimes even a complete overlap

Words on a page are little more than the crystallised thoughts of the author

Preparing your report in this way is not wrong; it might even be preferred by some. But we wanted to finish by alerting you to some of the problems this can bring and ensuring you know how to overcome them.

Consistency

If you change your mind, you must go back to the earlier parts of your report and ensure your arguments are consistent

Thinking as you write can lead to you changing your mind, and this in turn can damage the flow of your report. We're not saying you should never change your mind; if you're genuinely convinced that your initial beliefs were wrong then of course you should not continue on that path. But if you do change your mind, you must go back to the earlier parts of your report and ensure your arguments are consistent.

When preparing your report on a computer this isn't too much of any issue. When hand-writing a report, it can be a little trickier.

The dangers of multi-tasking

Thinking and writing at the same time is asking a lot from your brain. Like any situation when you try to do more than one task at once, you rarely do a great job of either. You're unlikely to be as creative as you could be if you devoted specific time to that activity. Your written word will not be as eloquent or considered as it might be if you were just writing from your plan.

You can clearly see evidence of this when you re-read what you've written. You might find that you've missed a word out of your sentence, or maybe repeated a word, or even substituted a completely different word in its place. These all happen because your fingers intuitively typed or wrote what your brain was thinking about at that time, not what was required in the sentence.

Now there's not a lot you can do about this other than be aware of it. If you're preparing a report where you know you're going to need to be exceptionally creative, try to avoid thinking and writing at the same time. Invest more time into your planning and thinking stages. If however, this is a more standard, run-of-the-mill report, thinking and writing at the same time probably won't be an issue.

Do make sure you thoroughly proof read your report to pick up on any errors. Don't assume that a spell-check program will detect them all.

Do make sure you thoroughly proof read your report to pick up on any errors. Don't assume that a spell-check program will detect them all.

Further reading

'The technique of clear writing' by R Gunning, McGraw-Hill International Book Co; New York (1952).

The Case – a final chance to practise

This is what we've been working towards. Now is your chance to put everything you've learned into practice by writing your report to the Corporate Development Director on the potential acquisition of Nicelife by Broadsword. Remember, the agreed 'bottom-line' questions are:

- how does Nicelife's performance compare with Broadsword's over the last two years? Why has Nicelife incurred losses over that period?

- what will be the likely reaction of the Competition Commission to an acquisition?

In a nutshell..............

The effective presentation of your report is about more than just having the right structure. The layout you adopt and the words you use will be crucial to ensuring your reader stays 'tuned-in' to your report from start to finish.

The golden rule when writing your report is to keep it short. This means:

- short paragraphs
- short sentences
- short words.

Calculating your fog index can help to reveal how your writing style might need to adapt to keep it 'fog free'.

In terms of layout, make sure your report contains plenty of white space, uses bullet points where appropriate and incorporates a combination of text, charts, diagrams and images.

Choosing the right words and presenting them correctly is essential. This includes spelling, grammar and punctuation, so if you know these are not your strengths make sure you build in plenty of time for spell-checking and proof-reading your document.

If we put all of the above together, we're able to produce a writing skills checklist that can be used to ensure you stay on track.

1. Split any long sentences – one main point per sentence.

2. Simplify the language – change long, complex words into shorter words.

3. Keep it 'fog free'.

4. Add a variety of presentation styles to your toolkit and include plenty of white space.

5. Choose the right words and be careful to avoid poor spelling and punctuation.

answers

Answers to case study exercises

This section will contain

Chapter 9

Answers to case study exercises

A student's guide to
Preparing Business Reports

In this chapter

We have provided some suggested answers to the case study exercises set throughout the book.

It is important to note that these are suggested answers and not the right answer. In the context of preparing a report in the business and finance arena, it is rare for one single, correct answer to exist. As you've seen in earlier chapters, the content of your report is the result of your specific thought processes.

Having said all of this, it is possible to be wrong, or at least to be un-commercial. So, if your answers contain something different to ours, take some time to stand back from what you've written and review the foundations of your arguments.

Chapter 1 – The objective of your report

Identification of 'bottom-line' questions

You have been asked to prepare a report on the potential acquisition of Nicelife by Broadsword. Consider how the 'bottom-line' questions addressed by your report would differ if you were reporting to:

- the shareholders of Broadsword

- the shareholders of Nicelife

- the Competition Commission

- the employees of both companies

- your boss in the Corporate Development Department.

In chapter 1, we outlined the importance of identifying the 'bottom-line' questions your report must answer. Indeed, this exercise is an excellent example of how the 'original brief' can be vague and unclear; being asked for a report on 'the potential acquisition of Nicelife by Broadsword' does not provide sufficient detail to enable the outline content or direction of the report to be decided.

It is therefore necessary to funnel down, through the aim of the report, on to the factors affecting the specific purpose of the report in order to reach the 'bottom-line' questions. Here's how each of these would alter depending on who the report was directed at.

The shareholders of Broadsword

Broadsword shares are owned as follows:

- 43% - public ownership (of which 9% are owned by a leading institutional investor)

- 40% - original founders (all retired)

- 17% - current and former employees

The primary concern of all groups will be the maximisation of their wealth (in the form of future dividends and growth in share price). However, the specific objectives of the different groups may vary. The institutional investor may be willing to take a longer-term view, and may be less concerned about the short-term pattern of dividend payments. The original founders may however rely upon the dividend payments to supplement their income (since all are now retired).

The likely 'bottom-line' questions of a report to shareholder would therefore be:

1. Will the acquisition lead to an increase in the value of Broadsword shares?

2. How will the acquisition be funded and will this result in a reduction in dividend payments or a dilution in control?

3. Will the acquisition lead to the long-term increase in shareholder wealth?

The shareholders of Nicelife

30% of Nicelife shares are owned by the senior management team and the remaining 70% by a venture capitalist.

Given the recent performance, the venture capitalist (VC) will be particularly concerned about the return on their investment. We're told they increased their level of investment in 2008, meaning they presumably have faith in the ability of the company to turn it around. Despite this, the VC will be keen to ensure they have a clear exit strategy.

Whilst the senior management team will be concerned about the value of their shares, they will also be focused on their future role in the business and the security of their jobs.

The 'bottom-line' questions are therefore likely to be:

1. Will the future of Nicelife be more secure and prosperous under Broadsword or as an independent company?

2. Does any offer from Broadsword enable shareholder wealth to be maximised?

3. What roles, if any, will the Nicelife senior management team be offered within any combined entity?

The Competition Commission

The objective of the Competition Commission is to encourage healthy competition between companies to ensure a fair price for consumers. They will therefore be concerned with the ability of a combined entity to distort the market and act against consumers best interests. Such distortions may arise if the combined entity was felt to be too powerful or had too great a market share. Their 'bottom-line' questions will therefore be:

1. How is it best to define the market(s)?

2. What is the size of the market(s)?

3. What level of market share will the combined entity have?

4. Will the combined entity wield enough power to be able to distort the market?

The employees of both companies

The primary focus areas for all employees will be job security, rates of pay and terms of employment, and working conditions. They would therefore be interested in the impact of any acquisition on these things.

Since this is being viewed as an acquisition (and not a merger), and given the recent redundancy programme seen in the company, Nicelife employees may have greater concerns surrounding job security. It is possible that they may view the acquisition as improving job security considering the recent financial performance of the company. The 'bottom-line' questions are likely to be:

1. Will the acquisition result in redundancies?

2. Will employees be forced to change their current roles?

3. Will employees be forced to move locations?

4. What will be the impact on levels of pay and the terms of employment?

Your boss in the Corporate Development Department

Although the primary objective of any director should be seen as the maximisation of shareholder wealth, successful directors are those who acknowledge the needs of all stakeholders and who seek to balance these needs and minimise conflicts.

Any report to a director may therefore need to address the implications of any acquisition for all stakeholders, consider what opposition there may be to the action as well as the benefits that could be realised.

The 'bottom-line' questions will therefore be:

1. How does Nicelife's performance compare with Broadsword's over the last two years and what has led to the losses incurred over that period?

2. What synergies will arise from any acquisition and how are they best realised?

3. How much will Broadsword need to pay to acquire Nicelife and will this price be low enough to enable the wealth of Broadsword shareholders to increase given the likely future performance of the combined entity?

4. What will be the likely reaction of the Competition Commission to an acquisition?

Chapter 2 – Your content plan

Gathering information

Prepare a shopping list of information you will need to answer the 'bottom-line' questions. Then populate your planning sheets with the information you've already been given in the introduction to this book.

Next, review the new information provided, using speed reading techniques, and make a note of any relevant facts. You should also identify any further information that you will require to complete your report.

Document your answer on a planning sheet

Having set the 'bottom-line' questions we're now able to start the planning process. This chapter introduced you to the planning cycle, where you first gather information, then process it before finally evaluating it. At the heart of the cycle is the need to document your findings at each stage. This should be done on a series of planning sheets, typically one for each 'bottom-line' question the report needs to answer. To start our planning process for the case report, we will therefore have two planning sheets; one for each of the 'bottom-line' questions.

Within the 'gather' stage of the cycle we should start by populating our planning sheets with a 'shopping list' of information we would like to have. In the suggested answer below, these items have been shown in green. Next we should add on any information we already know. For the purposes of this exercise, we've gone back to the initial case information presented in the introduction of this book, and picked out any information we feel might be relevant to the objective of this report. This, together with the information provided in this chapter have been added in blue. Within the planning cycle we should now process that information but since we haven't yet shown you how, it would seem a little unfair to do that now.

Instead we've started the repeat of the cycle, by allowing you to handle some new information, as presented in the chapter, and the suggested solution shows what key pieces of information you should have found there (in black). Finally, we've noted down further pieces of information we'd like to know (effectively adding to our shopping list) as a result of our findings so far. These have been shown in red.

Planning sheet 1 – How does performance compare to Broadsword and why has Nicelife incurred losses?

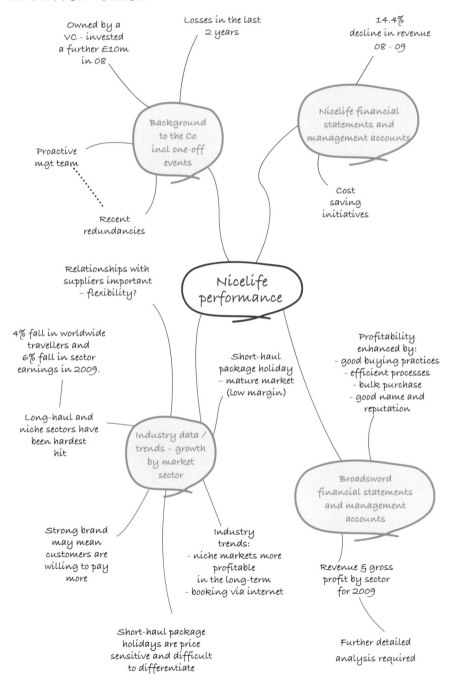

Owned by a VC – invested a further £10m in 08

Losses in the last 2 years

14.4% decline in revenue 08 - 09

Background to the Co incl one-off events

Nicelife financial statements and management accounts

Proactive mgt team

Recent redundancies

Cost saving initiatives

Relationships with suppliers important – flexibility?

Nicelife performance

4% fall in worldwide travellers and 6% fall in sector earnings in 2009.

Short-haul package holiday – mature market (low margin)

Profitability enhanced by:
- good buying practices
- efficient processes
- bulk purchase
- good name and reputation

Long-haul and niche sectors have been hardest hit

Industry data / trends – growth by market sector

Broadsword financial statements and management accounts

Strong brand may mean customers are willing to pay more

Industry trends:
- niche markets more profitable in the long-term
- booking via internet

Revenue & gross profit by sector for 2009

Short-haul package holidays are price sensitive and difficult to differentiate

Further detailed analysis required

Planning sheet 2 – Likely reaction of the
Competition Commission.

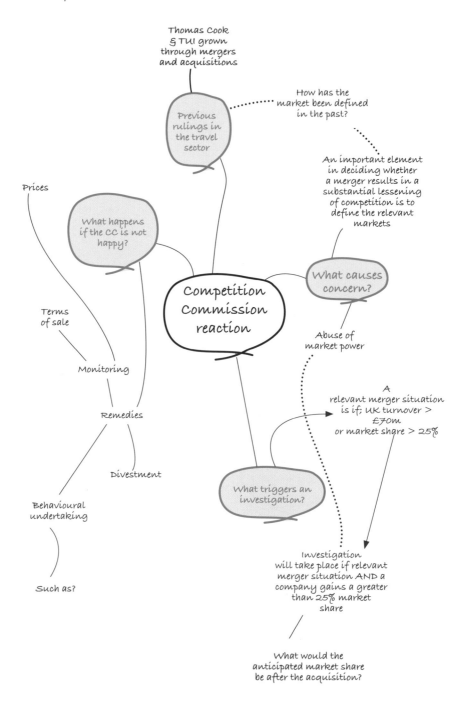

Chapter 3 – Your time plan

Building a time schedule

Prepare a list of further tasks or activities you will need to complete in order to answer these questions and consider how those tasks should be prioritised.

This chapter looked at the importance of planning your time when preparing a report, before introducing the four steps to scheduling success. Step 2 is to consider what tasks need to be completed, effectively what this exercise was asking you to consider.

How does Nicelife's performance compare with Broadsword's over the last two years and why have they incurred losses over that period?

A list of initial tasks to be completed, might include:

- analyse the external environment in which Nicelife operates to consider what impact this might have had on the company

- analyse the industry and obtain some industry data to enable an effective benchmark

- obtain more information on Nicelife, including its history and operations. Analyse the current position of the company

- obtain the financial statements for Nicelife for the period under consideration

- perform financial analysis on the accounts of both Nicelife and Broadsword in order to identify similarities and differences

- contrast performance with industry data.

What will be the likely reaction of the Competition Commission to any acquisition?

A list of initial tasks might include:

- consider the definition of the market that could be used by the Commission and research what definitions have been applied in other merger situations in the travel sector

- estimate the combined market share held if Broadsword was to acquire Nicelife

- identify and assess any potential remedies if an objection was felt likely, especially behavioural undertakings.

In terms of the prioritisation of these activities; obtaining the information from Nicelife (financial statements and overview of business) would have to be given the highest priority. This information may take some time to arrive and so a request should be made as soon as possible.

Whilst waiting for the information, further research can be done on the market definitions likely to be applied by the Competition Commission. Broadsword's financial information can also be analysed so as to provide a benchmark and some research can be performed on industry trends. The analysis of the environment and the industry can be completed.

When the information is received, a meeting should be scheduled with Nicelife management in order to discuss your findings. The date for this meeting should be set based on how long you estimate it will take you to perform your analysis.

Chapter 4 – Thinking commercially

Strategic analysis

Why has Nicelife incurred losses in the last two years?

Carry out a strategic analysis by preparing the following:

1. a PEST analysis

2. a Porter's Five Forces analysis

3. a SWOT analysis.

Don't forget to interpret your analysis by thinking about what each point might mean.

This chapter explored what it is to think commercially and showed how using a logical structure to help guide your creative thinking can often be the most efficient and effective approach. We showed that processing information involves both analysis and interpretation, and each aspect is presented below.

1. PEST analysis

This looks at the environment in which the business operates in order to identify factors that will influence the company. This can then be used to identify external opportunities and threats for the business.

Analysis	Interpretation – what might this mean
Political	
• Consumer protection schemes (ATOL)/Trade Associations (ABTA) • Competition Commission • Legislation on children being out of school in term time	• Regulation although in the public's or industry's interest could restrict opportunities for expansion and increased profitability. • The legislation regarding school holidays and the subsequent price increases during those holidays creates a perception in the public's mind that travel companies are being exploitative.
Economic	
• Very sensitive to the economic cycle (especially interest rates and unemployment levels) • Price elastic – low margins • Exchange risk if £ receipt and payments in local currency • High oil prices • A seasonal industry	• Economic climate in 2009 / 2010 might mean volumes will decline due to lower disposal income. Travel companies will often lag any economic decline by up to one year as travellers have already made reservations for the following year. • Low margins could have been further squeezed due to high oil price and the collapse of the £ against the $ and €. • The seasonal nature of the industry may affect resourcing and the management of working capital.

Social	
• More travellers now de-packaging and seeking different types of holiday e.g adventure • Shift in destinations away from traditional favourites • Greater awareness of health risks e.g. flu pandemics, DVT etc • Greater awareness of & concern over the environmental impact of flying (carbon footprint)	• Could well indicate potential growth areas. • High growth areas more likely to be in the niche sectors (adventure / group), although demand in this area will be tempered by economic conditions. • Need to ensure customers are well informed and not responding to media headlines as to health risks. Perhaps the idea of "keeping customers informed" about potential health risks could be used as a way of differentiating. • Although long-haul destinations have increased in popularity, concern over carbon footprint, and rising oil prices could mean short-haul holidays or even staying in the UK might see a resurgence.
Technological	
• Internet companies such as Expedia make de-packaging a lot simpler for consumers • Greater price transparency • Technology in the home and particular the availability of broadband makes buying online attractive to more people	• Internet companies may represent a key threat to traditional package holiday tour operators. In addition to focusing on the sector of the market with significant growth (de-packaging) they have lower overheads and so can compete more effectively. • Price transparency can further reduce margins as customers choose to buy what appears to be the same, but cheaper products. • This explosion in the use of technology in the home could result in traditional outlets/shops becoming underutilised and inefficient. Might be time to move more business online or look to enhance the high street offering. It needs to offer more, perhaps personal service, friendly staff, reliable reviews from experts etc.

2. Porter's 5 forces

A useful business model for understanding more about the industry context is Porter's Five Forces. Michael Porter argued that the long-term profitability of companies within an industry is reduced by the presence of one or more strong forces or threats that affect their ability to compete. The profitability and survival of any company in the industry will depend on countering these five forces.

Analysis	Interpretation – what might this mean
Threat from potential new entrants	
• Increasing due to removal of the barrier to have outlets, as firms can now sell directly via the internet. Reduces capital investment • Relationships with hoteliers (distribution channels) makes a strong barrier for new entrants as most/all decent accommodation is already allocated to tour operators • Short-haul package holidays are difficult to differentiate	• Without a strong brand and good buying, companies are threatened by potential new entrants, especially those trading on the internet. This threat will force companies to keep prices (and more importantly margins) low to avoid attracting new players into the market as they see a chance to earn healthy profits. • Perhaps an opportunity exists to further develop the relationships with hoteliers so as to ensure the good hotels do not become available to others. • Although short-haul business is difficult to differentiate, high levels of repeat business and customer loyalty can help create a strong brand and large volumes lead to cost advantages in both travel and accommodation (economies of scale).

Threat from substitutes	
• De-packaging of holidays by more and more consumers • Competing with other leisure activities	• These threats are particularly high when viewed alongside the global economic recession and that consumers have less money to spend on leisure activities.
Threats from the power of suppliers	
• Tour operators tend to book hotels for the whole season giving power over each provider • Commitments are made over a year in advance • Vertical integration is commonplace	• The legal commitment means suppliers do not have power if they wish to withdraw supply. However, they do have power to ensure the tour operators stick to their commitment. When the economic cycle is in decline this poses a significant threat to tour operators as they are left with spare capacity which they are unable to fill unless they discount their holidays. This causes dramatic falls in margins. In the current climate perhaps different deals could be structured e.g. 3 months in advance instead of 12 months. • Perhaps consideration should be given to the vertical acquisition of a hotel chain.

Threats from the power of customers	
• Holidays account for large proportion of consumers disposable income therefore high price sensitivity • Low switching costs • More price visibility via internet • Customer loyalty reduces the competitive pressure	• To counteract this threat a tour operator needs a strong brand in order to encourage customer loyalty. Anything that might damage the reputation of a tour operator can therefore be expected to have a big impact on bookings, revenue and margins. • Regarding the low switching costs, consideration should be given to larger and earlier payment of deposits. This could of course further impact on margins. • Once again, if cost leadership is not the answer, price visibility can only be offset by a powerful brand. The brand may be enhanced if it can be shown that other travel companies are not so reliable e.g. any news stories of 'cheap' providers failing to deliver on their promises.
Threats from competitive rivalry	
• Short-haul is very price sensitive meaning that a lot of competition tends to be price led • Market dominated by some large players who benefit from significant economies of scale	• Getting the balance right between cost leadership and differentiation is critical.

3. SWOT analysis

A SWOT analysis helps us position the company by considering its strengths, weaknesses, opportunities and threats. Strengths give the organisation an advantage and so should be used to create opportunities. The weaknesses put the organisation at a disadvantage and so should be minimised; they are areas on which management time should be invested. The opportunities should be exploited and investment made. The threats should be assessed and avoided wherever possible.

Analysis	Interpretation – what might this mean
Strengths	
• Proactive management team • Trading for over 40 years • Broad range of geographic destinations and sectors served • Nicelife have continued to operate well despite the redundancies	• Less likely to wait too long to find a solution and will probably react quickly when one is found. Responded quickly to the decline in revenue when it arose. • A long history is often good for the brand and should lead to more customer loyalty. The impact of the 'near misses' on the brand however cannot be ignored. • A broad range of geographic destinations should help to reduce overall risk since company is not overly reliant on any one sector. However the recent global recession and the impact on long-haul travel will probably have hit Nicelife harder than other tour operators who may specialise in European package holidays. • Although the ability to continue to provide a service despite staff cuts is a strength, it could point to a more broader concern, that they were over staffed in the first place.

Weaknesses	
• Possible low staff morale following the redundancies	• Low staff morale could be reflected in poor customer service which could further damage reputation.
• Loss making in each of the past two years and although cost cutting has taken place, management don't appear to have resolved the situation	• Although the 'near-miss' incidents and current economic environment must be contributory factors, further financial analysis is needed to establish if these are the only reasons for Nicelife's recent losses. Comparison with Broadsword's financials will help.
• Does not have a strong relationship with some hotels	• The lack of a strong relationship and ultimate flexibility with some of the hotels could mean that Nicelife find themselves incurring costs that could be avoided if they could pick up the phone and ask for a favour.

Opportunities	
• Investment of a further £10m by the venture capital owner, Judo	• Potentially this demonstrates confidence by the owners and provides cash to both invest and survive at least in the short run should the problems continue.
• Customers de-packaging and seeking different types of holiday e.g. adventure	• This offers Nicelife further growth potential. At present only 53% of revenue comes from these types of holiday.
• Increase of online buying could provide Nicelife with new customers	• Selling holidays via the internet could help Nicelife further reduce its costs as well as being able to offer holidays on a more global scale.

Threats	
• Two 'near misses' within the space of three weeks involving aircraft carrying Nicelife passengers	• This probably has had an impact on Nicelife's reputation and brand. It has possibly resulted in a fall in bookings; the question is, will this continue in 2010 and beyond?
• Continuing global economic recession	• Many businesses will find it hard to increase profits if the global recession continues. Nicelife however is not well positioned. It has made losses for the last two years and although further analysis is needed to identify exactly why these losses have arisen it is hard to imagine a continuation of the recession will help.

Chapter 4 – Thinking commercially

Analysis and interpretation

Likely reaction of the Competition Commission

In chapter 2 you read about the UK Competition Authorities and how they work, and noted a number of facts on your planning sheet that you thought might be relevant to your report.

Use the techniques outlined in this chapter to analyse and interpret these facts in order to identify what each might mean.

Remember, analysis involves taking the information and breaking it into parts in order to examine it before you can interpret what it might mean for the reader of your report. During both steps you should be logical, creative and commercial, paying particular attention to the context of the information.

Facts / Information	Analysis and interpretation
Investigation will take place if a company gains a greater than 25% market share	How will the market be defined and how will the 25% be measured?
	If the combined Nicelife and Broadsword business was to have a greater than 25% market share then an investigation would be likely.
An important element in deciding whether a merger results in a substantial lessening of competition is to define the relevant markets	Market could be defined by:
	• the market as a whole
	• the tourist market
	• by geographic destination
	• by type of holiday.
	25% could be based on revenue or passenger numbers and could be calculated using historic or forecast figures. We will need further analysis to clarify exactly what the market share is within these market sectors. (see chapter 5).
	Whatever definition is selected by the Commission will have implications on their assessment of market share. Broadsword may be able to influence the decision of how the market will be defined / measured in order to suit its own position.

A relevant merger situation arises if one of two thresholds are met; UK turnover > £70m or market share > 25%	We need to gather further information on the turnover of Nicelife, to see if it is greater than £70m. If so then regardless of the market size a relevant merger will arise.(see chapter 5).
	It may be required to structure the deal in such a way that it becomes possible to argue that there are several different businesses; and that these businesses should not be treated as part of the group in order to get around the regulations. This of course may not be considered ethical.
A typical remedy involves the divestment of assets or business units or sectors	A combined entity may have to sell off some sectors of the business. This could impact on the future profitability of the business and must be incorporated into any review of the financial viability of the acquisition.
Another remedy could involve behavioural undertakings	No details are provided on this although one potential would be to partially withdraw or downsize in a particular market. This may not be a preferred remedy for the Commission as it is easily reversed.
A further remedy may be 'monitoring'	Broadsword may have to supply specified information (say on prices or terms of sale) to prove that it is not acting against the interests of consumers.
	It may become more difficult to compete as information required as part of the monitoring is disclosed. This information may be valuable to competitors, so giving them an unfair advantage.

Note:

For ease of presentation we are not showing how the output from either of these chapter 4 exercises would be added to your planning sheets. We will defer this until the end of chapter 6, once we have evaluated the information in more depth. In reality, you may decide to take a similar approach. If you've followed the suggestions in this chapter properly and explored your creative side, you could well have far too many thoughts that you'd prefer to filter down to the more relevant ones before adding them in to your final planning.

Chapter 5 – Dealing with numbers

Financial statement analysis

Use the financial information on both Broadsword and Nicelife, along with the other case information provided in previous chapters to compare and contrast the financial performance and position of Broadsword with Nicelife.

You will need to think commercially in order to analyse and interpret your findings.

As noted in chapter 5, the key elements when analysing performance will be to consider revenue growth, gross profit margins and operating profit margins. However, we will need to flex this depending on the circumstances. So, in this instance:

- you have the ability to look at changes in revenue by market sector and this could be key to identifying the drivers behind movements in total revenue (this was identified from our analysis and interpretation of the external environment (PEST) in chapter 4)

- reviewing the cash position of the company may help to reveal reasons for changes in profitability or give indications of future issues that could affect how the company performs.

When reviewing financial information you should always make reference to benchmarks. This can either be prior year, a competitor or market averages. In this situation, our 'bottom-line' question clearly steers us towards using Broadsword as the benchmark.

Your analysis will then focus on breaking down your calculation and examining the impact that each of the variables has had on your answer (remember, you must do more than just explain the maths). Your interpretation should involve thinking commercially about what this might mean for the business. Is there anything that should be of concern, anything that means the business might fail to hit targets or may suffer a decline in profitability? Might action be needed to prevent problems in the future? Remember, this commercial thought process is where the real value lies in your report.

	Broadsword	Working	Nicelife	Working
Revenue growth	(3.1%)	(877.3-905.4) ÷ 905.4	(14.4%)	(726.0 – 848.1)÷ 848.1

Analysis	Interpretation
The reputational damage following the two 'near miss' incidents at the end of 2008 will undoubtedly have contributed to Nicelife's reduction. Further detailed analysis of the segmental revenue may reveal further reasons since we believe that long-haul travel has been affected more than short-haul and that the more premium niche sectors have been hardest hit (see chapter 4 answer). What is not apparent from these headline numbers is whether the decline in revenue is driven by volume or price. We've identified that some operators may have been forced to discount quite heavily due to over-commitments (chapter 4). We'll be able to tell more when we review the gross margins.	Given the worldwide decline in receipts from tourism of 6%, Nicelife's performance might be viewed as disappointing.

	Broadsword	Nicelife
Segmental analysis of revenue	Total short-haul = 72.2% Total long-haul = 27.8%. This can be further analysed as: Short-haul package: 59.1% Long-haul package: 7.7% Winter: 6.9% Group: 8.6% Cruises: 7.6% Adventure: 8.9% Flights: 1.2%	Total short-haul = 64.9% Total long-haul = 35.1%. This can be further analysed as: Short-haul package: 18.7% Long-haul package: 12.2% Winter: 15.1% Group: 38.3% Adventure: 15.4% Flights: 0.3%

Analysis	Interpretation
In 2009 over 35% of Nicelife's revenue related to long-haul destinations. Whilst this doesn't appear to be much higher than Broadsword's 28%, it doesn't quite tell the full story. In 2008, over half of Nicelife's revenue related to long-haul destinations. This potentially indicates how significantly the economic conditions have impacted the company. It isn't just the destination, but also the type of holiday they offer as over 50% of the long-haul holidays supplied were in the niche sectors of group / charter and adventure / specialist holidays. These holidays would be regarded as luxury or premium products and will most likely have been hardest hit by the economic climate.	The more balanced portfolio of Nicelife might actually present less long-term risk since the exposure to any one market is reduced. It appears to have acted against them in the current economic environment but they may be well placed to improve performance significantly when the global economy does recover.

	Broadsword	Working	Nicelife	Working
Gross profit margins	2009: 10.0% 2008: 13.2%	2009: 87.4 ÷ 877.3 2008: 119.2 ÷ 905.4	2009: 5.7% 2008: 6.4%	2009: 41.7 ÷ 726 2008: 54.6 ÷ 848.1

Analysis	Interpretation
Although Nicelife's gross margin has declined between 2008 and 2009, the fall is not as significant as that seen in Broadsword. Nicelife's gross margin is still significantly lower than Broadsword's, even after the recent redundancies. To identify the cause of this, it is necessary to compare the margins within each individual sector with Broadswords (see below).	This could suggest that Broadsword has found itself having to discount last-minute holidays more than Nicelife have. The results could be masked by other cost saving initiatives – we know that Nicelife has shed around 20% of its non-seasonal staff. The lower gross margin overall could indicate poor buying practices or inefficient processes.

	Broadsword 2009 Margin %	Nicelife 2009 Margin %
Short-haul (UK & Europe)	6.3	1.0
Long-haul	11.2	2.9
Total package	6.9	1.8
Winter	5.1	2.2
Group/Charter	16.7	7.4
Cruise	15.9	–
Adventure / specialist	25.2	13.1
Flight / hotel booking	10.9	4.0
Total	**10.0**	**5.7**
Short-haul	7.5	5.9
Long-haul	16.4	5.5

Analysis	Interpretation
Broadsword attribute their profit levels to four main things: bulk purchasing; good buying practices; efficient business processes; and its good name and reputation. The margins earned in short-haul package holidays are significantly lower, most likely due to the absence of bulk purchase deals. However, this explanation cannot be the case in other areas where Nicelife actually seem to be bigger than Broadsword. In total, there is not a significant difference in the sizes of the two businesses. Given that Nicelife has only been operating in the niche sectors since the late 1990's, their brand is unlikely to command the premium prices that Broadsword are able to charge. Equally, they won't have had the time to foster such long-term trusting relationships with hoteliers. These could be two potential explanations for the lower margins. It is also possible that the company suffered from some inefficient processes.	It is to be hoped that the recent round of cost-cutting exercises will have eliminated some of the inefficient processes within the company. The key question will be to what extent Broadsword management could improve the buying practices and streamline the processes to increase the margins. Process re-engineering should be easily achieved but establishing better relations with suppliers may take time. Although Broadsword have a good name and reputation, it is more closely associated with the package holiday market. Market research will need to be undertaken to determine whether the Broadsword brand would benefit the existing Nicelife niche business.

	Broadsword	Working	Nicelife	Working
Admin expenses as a % of revenue	2009: 7.8% 2008: 10.9%	2009: 68.6 ÷ 877.3 2008: 98.9 ÷ 905.4	2009: 7.1% 2008: 7.6%	2009: 51.7 ÷ 726.0 2008: 64.2 ÷ 848.1
Analysis			**Interpretation**	
Both companies have experienced a drop in admin expenses both in absolute terms and as a percentage of revenue. It is unclear to what extent these costs are affected by the volume of business but it would be sensible to assume they are a combination of fixed and variable costs. We know Nicelife have implemented a redundancy programme during 2009 and this may have been part of the reduction seen.			That Nicelife's admin expenses as a proportion of revenue are lower than Broadsword's suggests that Broadsword may be able to learn from some of the practices at Nicelife in order to streamline their operations.	

	Broadsword	Working	Nicelife	Working
Operating profit margins	2009: 2.1% 2008: 2.2%	2009: 18.8 ÷ 877.3 2008: 20.3 ÷ 905.4	2009: (1.4%) 2008: (1.1%)	2009: (10.0) ÷ 726.0 2008: (9.6) ÷ 848.1
Analysis			**Interpretation**	
The losses incurred in Nicelife appear to be caused by the lower gross profit margins rather than lack of control of overhead costs.			If the root causes of the problems are brand image, inefficient processes and lack of economies of scale (discussed above) many of these could be avoided if an acquisition were to go ahead.	

	Broadsword	Working	Nicelife	Working
Cash management	Cash balance: 2009: £239.9m 2008: £191.6m Movement: £48.3m		Cash balance: 2009: £279.3m 2008: £310.2m Movement: (£30.9m)	
Analysis			**Interpretation**	
Although the absolute cash balance in Nicelife is higher than in Broadsword, the company has suffered a net cash outflow in each of the last two years. Although part of this will have resulted from the operating losses, this cannot be the sole reason since the outflow is greater than the losses incurred.			Given the nature of the travel sector, much of the companies cash balance can be expected to relate to deposits paid by customers for holidays not yet taken. This decline in cash could therefore be a reflection of lower (and / or later) bookings. If bookings are lower for 2010 this may not bode well for their performance in the next financial year.	

You might want to re-visit your SWOT at this stage to populate it with your findings from your financial analysis. The things we would add following our analysis are: Strengths – low admin costs as a percentage of revenue may suggest processes operate efficiently; weaknesses – low gross profit margins could be lack of brand reputation or economies of scale; opportunities – to improve relationships with key suppliers; threats – low bookings in 2010 due to economic conditions.

Chapter 5 – Dealing with numbers

Financial data analysis

Use the information on Broadsword's estimated market share, along with information provided earlier to estimate the size of each market and to make an assessment of the total market share held if the proposed acquisition of Nicelife by Broadsword went ahead.

Some of the general rules we covered regarding financial data analysis included acknowledging the subjective areas, recognising that interpretation is the most important part and that you must clearly present your calculations to ensure they are understood. All of these are demonstrated below.

Given the information provided on revenues for both Broadsword and Nicelife, together with the estimate of Broadsword's market share in 2009, the following combined entity market shares can be estimated:

	Broadsword's estimated market share in 2009 A	Broadsword's revenue in 2009 £m B	Estimate of total market size £m (C = B ÷ A)	Nicelife's revenue in 2009 £m D	Estimate of combined entity revenue £m (E = B + D)	Estimate of combined entity market share (E ÷ C)
Package holidays - Short-haul (UK & Europe)	2%[1]	518.5	25,925	135.7	654.2	2.5%
Package holidays - Long-haul	3%	67.7	2,257	88.4	156.1	6.9%
Winter holidays	10%	60.7	607	109.6	170.3	28.0%
Group / charter	9%	75.0	833	277.8	352.8	42.3%
Cruises	7%	66.8	954	–	66.8	7.0%
Adventure / specialist	9%	78.5	872	112.0	190.5	21.8%
Flight / hotel booking	5%[2]	10.1	202	2.5	12.6	6.2%

1. Stated market share was below 2%. 2% has been used for prudence.
2. Stated market share was 3% - 12%. The overall average figure of 5% has been used.

Analysis

These calculations suggest that if the acquisition were to go ahead, the new combined entity would breach the 25% market share test in two of the seven markets in which it operates: winter holidays and group / charter. At an estimated 21.8% market share, there may also be some concern within the adventure / specialist market, especially given that Broadsword's market share in some destinations is already 60%.

Interpretation

Assuming that the Competition Commission were to use this method to define the market, it would most likely have concerns about the potential for a substantial lessening of competition in at least two or possibly three of the market sectors.

Chapter 6 – Exercising judgement

Evaluating information and options

Using the output from your strategic analysis in chapter 4 and your financial analysis in chapter 5, apply the techniques outlined in this chapter to:

1. Evaluate the information relating to the performance of Nicelife and reach some conclusions on how the company's performance compares with Broadsword's and why they have incurred losses over the last two years.

2. Evaluate the information relating to the Competition Commission and reach some conclusions on their likely reaction to a proposed acquisition. Consider the implications of this and think creatively to identify and then evaluate the options available to Broadsword.

Add the outcome of your evaluations on to your planning sheets.

In chapter 6 we continued with our information journey and introduced the next steps of evaluating (both information and options), forming conclusions and making recommendations. These steps set out the process involved in exercising judgement.

We now find ourselves with the analysis all done, and with the interpretations as to what that analysis might mean. The next stage is to evaluate not what it might mean, but what it does mean for Broadsword in the context of its potential acquisition of Nicelife. To do this we need to evaluate how useful the information is, the implications of the information, solve any problems, evaluate solutions and put forward our conclusions and recommendations. And when we have done all that, we will be ready start the 'write' stage of the process.

1. Compare the performance of Nicelife with Broadsword and identify the cause of Nicelife's losses

In chapter 4 in response to the question, why has Nicelife incurred losses in the last two years, we were asked for a PEST, a Porter's Five Forces and a SWOT analysis. These methods of analysis have helped us look at Nicelife differently and creatively, yet within a logical framework. This analysis was interpreted to identify what it might mean, but some of the comments suggested that we needed to gather and process more information. In chapter 5 we did just that, concentrating our analysis and interpretation on the financial statements.

We are not going to take every single piece of information from chapter 4 and 5 and evaluate it. Instead we will be selective, picking on examples from the analysis in both chapters to illustrate key points. At some point we need to hand over the reins to you and allow you to have a go, and this would seem an excellent point to do that. Also, remember there are many different ways of getting to an answer, not just the way we have done it.

Evaluate the information

In chapter 6 we suggested that a useful criteria to assess the worth of information is to:

- go back to the 'bottom-line' questions
- be sceptical
- be objective
- look for linkages
- prioritise.

Remember, each of these is a point to consider. They are not steps to be followed and so can be tackled in any order. Below we've given examples of each of these criteria in turn to illustrate the technique. For each example, we'll repeat the analysis and interpretation given in either chapter 4 or 5 and then note down our evaluation.

Go back to the 'bottom-line' questions

Eliminating information or thoughts that don't relate to the 'bottom-line' question is often the most efficient place to start.

From the PEST	Evaluation
Legislation on children being out of school in term time. The legislation regarding school holidays and the subsequent price increases during those holidays creates a perception in the public's mind that travel companies are being exploitative.	Although this may be true, as a piece of information it is not relevant to the bottom line question and so will be ignored.
From Porter's 5 forces	**Evaluation**
Relationships with hoteliers makes a strong barrier for new entrants. Perhaps consideration should be given to the vertical acquisition of a hotel chain.	This is certainly an option but not one that relates to our 'bottom-line' question.

Be sceptical

From the PEST	Evaluation
Greater awareness of & concern over the environmental impact of flying. Although long-haul destinations have increased in popularity, concern over carbon footprint, and rising oil prices could mean short-haul holidays or even staying in the UK might see a resurgence.	Maybe the buying public are not as green or environmentally concerned as we might think. As long as holidays are cheap do they really care?

Be objective

From the financial analysis	Evaluation
The reputational damage will undoubtedly have contributed to this reduction. These luxury products will most likely have been hardest hit by the economic climate. Given the worldwide decline in receipts from tourism of 6%, Nicelife's performance might be viewed as disappointing.	It is perhaps easy to draw a conclusion that Nicelife's losses were the result of the 'near miss' incidents and economic conditions. However the 'near misses' happened in late 2008 and, given the lag often seen in the travel industry, it is unlikely that the effects of the recession will have been felt to any significant level until 2009. Neither of these are therefore likely to have had a significant impact on the 2008 performance. This would suggest that Nicelife's losses, although not helped by these factors, are the result of a more fundamental problem.

Look for linkages

From the PEST	From the financial analysis	Evaluation
Very sensitive to the economic cycle. Economic climate in 2009 / 2010 might mean volumes will decline due to lower disposal income. Travel companies will often lag any economic decline by up to one year as travellers have already made reservations for the following year.	In 2008, over half of Nicelife's revenue related to long-haul destinations. And by 2009 Nicelife's long-haul revenue had reduced to 35%. This potentially indicates how significantly the economic conditions have impacted the company.	It seems reasonable to conclude that the suggestion put forward in the financial analysis about the impact of the economic environment on Nicelife's long-haul revenue is true.
From the PEST	**From the financial analysis**	**Evaluation**
Shift in destinations away from traditional favourites. High growth areas are more likely to be in the niche sectors (adventure / group), although demand in this area will be tempered by economic conditions.	Over 50% of the long-haul holidays supplied were in the niche sectors of group / charter and adventure / specialist holidays. These holidays would be regarded as luxury or premium products and will most likely have been hardest hit by the economic climate.	The idea that niche sectors represent high growth areas on the face of it is true and may deliver growth in the future. But as suggested here they have been hardest hit by the poor economic climate and have contributed to Nicelife's falling revenue.

From Porter's 5 forces	From the financial analysis	Evaluation
Holidays account for large proportion of consumers disposable income. To counteract this threat a tour operator needs a strong brand in order to encourage customer loyalty. Anything that might damage the reputation of a tour operator can therefore be expected to have a big impact on bookings, revenue and margins.	The reputational damage following the two 'near miss' incidents at the end of 2008 will undoubtedly have contributed to this reduction.	The comment in the financial analysis column is referring to the fall in revenue in Nicelife in 2009. And although it is not the whole story, see earlier comment under be objective, Nicelife's revenue has clearly been affected and as a result the brand reputation seems to have been damaged.
Tour operators tend to book hotels for the whole season giving power over each provider. The legal commitment means suppliers do not have power if they wish to withdraw supply. However, they do have power to ensure the tour operators stick to their commitment. When the economic cycle is in decline this poses a significant threat to tour operators as they are left with spare capacity which they are unable to fill unless they discount their holidays. This causes dramatic falls in margins.	Equally, they won't have had the time to foster such long-term trusting relationships with hoteliers. This could be a potential explanation for the lower margins.	The fact that Nicelife has not been in the market long enough to foster these long-term relationships is a logical explanation as to why their margins are not as strong as Broadsword's.
From the SWOT	**From the financial analysis**	**Evaluation**
Trading for over 40 years. A long history is often good for the brand and should lead to more customer loyalty.	Given that Nicelife has only been operating in the niche sectors since the late 1990's, their brand is unlikely to command the premium prices that Broadsword are able to charge.	Although Nicelife has been trading for over 40 years, as highlighted in the financial analysis this loyalty is not in all business sectors. The businesses in these niche sectors have not yet had time to establish themselves. This is yet another reason that Broadsword has a higher margin.

Prioritise

As a result of linking together the information we have begun to understand more about the reasons that Nicelife has incurred losses. There are still more thoughts to add and observations to make; this is not yet the answer. Before we complete our evaluation we should look to organise some of these thoughts; we need to put them in order of importance and prioritise in the context of the 'bottom-line' questions.

- The economic environment has had an impact on Nicelife's performance; it has reduced turnover specifically for long-haul and in the luxury niche sectors, and this has contributed to its losses. But is this the most important reason for the poor performance?

- The 'near misses' have had a negative impact on turnover and the brand. This would also have contributed to the poor performance, but is this the most important reason for the poor performance?

- Nicelife's brand is not as strong a negative Broadsword's and so they have been unable to charge a premium. This would have impacted on the margins and so would also have contributed to the poor performance, but is this the most important reason for the poor performance?

The answer is of course, they have all contributed to the poor performance as have some other factors not mentioned above (we'll leave it up to you to spot these) and all should be referred to in the conclusion. But if we had only the information above and needed to prioritise them, we should think about the bigger picture. We are only looking at the financial performance of Nicelife because Broadsword are considering buying it. So how big a problem are some of these in that context?

- Economic climate – the product mix that has resulted in Nicelife being more exposed to the economic down turn was not an error as such. The broader product offering in the long run should be an advantage, so in some ways Nicelife have just been a victim of timing.

- 'Near miss' incidents – although the 'near misses' may point to some operational issues that need investigation, there is no suggestion this is an ongoing problem and so within time confidence should return.

- The brand – the fact that Nicelife's brand is not so strong (the 'near misses' will not have helped) is of greater concern and for this reason would be considered more important. It has implications for Broadsword as to how the business should be operated in the future (if we keep the Nicelife brand) should the acquisition go ahead. This may be referred to in the conclusion to this report but you must be careful not to take this much further as it is outside the scope of what you have been asked to do.

The implications

One way of spotting implications is to ask, does this cause the company a problem or does it offer up opportunities? In this instance it is neither. There is nothing within the information we have gathered, processed and evaluated that suggests any further opportunities or problems beyond what were known when the report was commissioned. Since evaluating whether Broadsword should acquire Nicelife (an opportunity) or how Broadsword could turn the business around (a problem) was not within the original scope, they should not be included within your report.

Although we did identify opportunities from the analysis e.g. from the SWOT it was suggested that an increase in online buying could provide Nicelife with new customers, this is clearly outside the scope of this report which is to identify why Nicelife has incurred losses. Since it is not relevant to the 'bottom-line' questions it should be ignored.

As the information does not reveal either a problem nor an opportunity we will not have any options to evaluate. We look at how you might do this in the section below. If there are no relevant opportunities and problems we can move on from our evaluation to conclusions.

Forming conclusions

The actual conclusions will appear in our answer later on in this chapter but remember what we said about forming conclusions. Don't sit on the fence; your reader is looking for answers, not more questions. Ask challenging questions, for example, will we ever be entirely happy buying a company that has been associated with 'near misses'? And don't start bringing in new information that has not been identified and discussed in earlier sections of your report.

On the next page is an example of what your planning sheet could look like after evaluating the information, considering the implications and forming your conclusions. It has been presented for illustration purposes only to help you appreciate what a full planning sheet may look like and how it can be used.

Planning sheet 1 – How does performance compare to Broadsword and why has Nicelife incurred losses?

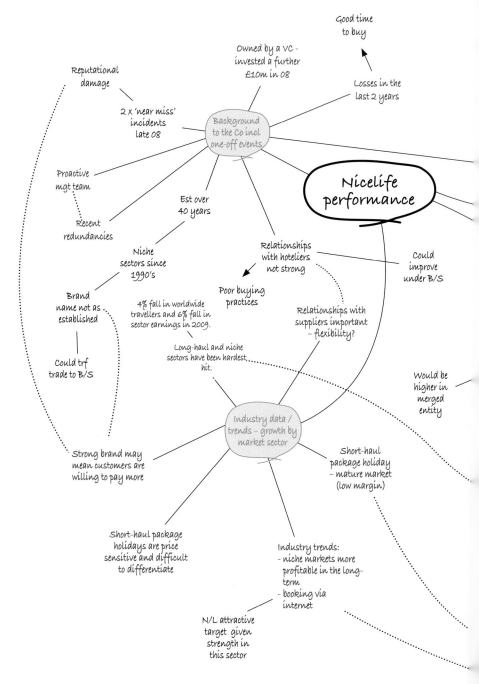

Good time to buy

Owned by a VC – invested a further £10m in 08

Losses in the last 2 years

Reputational damage

2 x 'near miss' incidents late 08

Background to the Co incl one-off events

Nicelife performance

Proactive mgt team

Est over 40 years

Relationships with hoteliers not strong

Could improve under B/S

Recent redundancies

Niche sectors since 1990's

Poor buying practices

Brand name not as established

4% fall in worldwide travellers and 6% fall in sector earnings in 2009.

Relationships with suppliers important – flexibility?

Long-haul and niche sectors have been hardest hit.

Could trf trade to B/S

Would be higher in merged entity

Strong brand may mean customers are willing to pay more

Industry data / trends – growth by market sector

Short-haul package holiday – mature market (low margin)

Short-haul package holidays are price sensitive and difficult to differentiate

Industry trends:
- niche markets more profitable in the long-term
- booking via internet

N/L attractive target given strength in this sector

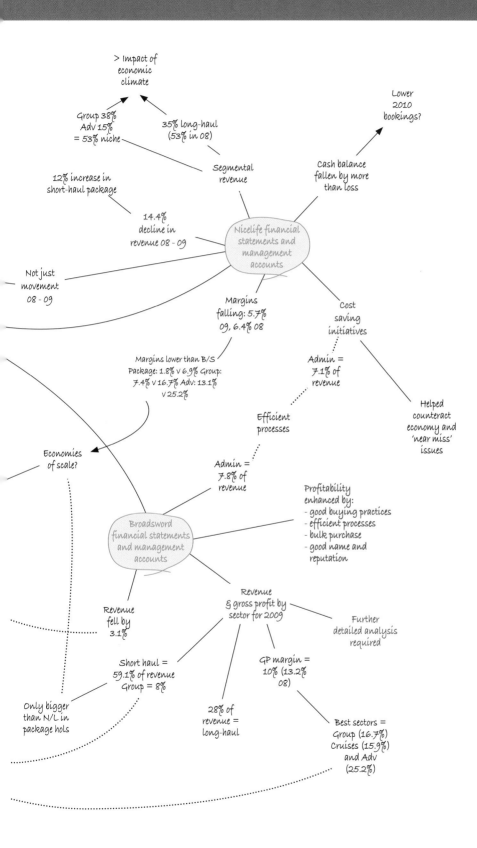

> Impact of economic climate

Group 38% Adv 15% = 53% niche

35% long-haul (53% in 08)

Lower 2010 bookings?

12% increase in short-haul package

Segmental revenue

Cash balance fallen by more than loss

14.4% decline in revenue 08 - 09

Nicelife financial statements and management accounts

Not just movement 08 - 09

Margins falling: 5.7% 09, 6.4% 08

Cost saving initiatives

Margins lower than B/S Package: 1.8% v 6.9% Group: 7.4% v 16.7% Adv: 13.1% v 25.2%

Admin = 7.1% of revenue

Helped counteract economy and 'near miss' issues

Efficient processes

Economies of scale?

Admin = 7.8% of revenue

Broadsword financial statements and management accounts

Profitability enhanced by:
- good buying practices
- efficient processes
- bulk purchase
- good name and reputation

Revenue & gross profit by sector for 2009

Revenue fell by 3.1%

Further detailed analysis required

Short haul = 59.1% of revenue Group = 8%

GP margin = 10% (13.2% 08)

Only bigger than N/L in package hols

28% of revenue = long-haul

Best sectors = Group (16.7%) Cruises (15.9%) and Adv (25.2%)

2. What is the likely reaction of the Competition Commission

Evaluate the information

Having demonstrated how to evaluate information using the 'why have Nicelife incurred losses' example we will use the Competition Commission example to illustrate how you should evaluate options. To do this it may be helpful to summarise what we have discovered so far from chapter 4 and chapter 5, and provide some indication of our evaluation of this information.

From chapter 2 we know that the Competition Commission will be asked to investigate if there is a relevant merger and a relevant merger exists if;

- the value of the UK turnover of the enterprise acquired exceeds £70m; or

- the share of supply of goods or services in the UK by the merged enterprise is at least 25%.

Recognising linkages – from the financials we can see that Nicelife's turnover is greater than £70m and so a relevant merger does exist.

Again, from chapter 2 we know that the second stage of the Competition Commission's process is to consider if the merger could result in a substantial lessening of competition. This will be the case if the relevant market share is at least 25%.

Recognising linkages – from chapter 5 it was established that for Winter holidays we have a 28.0% potential market share and for Group / charter 42.3%. In fact we may have a further problem with Adventure / specialist holidays, for this example we will ignore this possibility.

Be objective – this is of course is all on the assumption that the Competition Commission calculates the market share as we have done in chapter 4. We must acknowledge this in our report and briefly discuss how their definition could differ; particularly given the length of time any investigation could take.

The implications

The implications of this should be considered. Remember, one way of spotting implications is to ask, "does this cause the company a problem or does it offer up opportunities?"

This is clearly a problem and so we should come up with potential solutions to this problem. Please note that the 'bottom-line' question didn't originally specify that you should provide recommendations; it was simply to outline what the likely reaction of the Competition Commission would be. However, given their reaction is likely to be negative, your reader would not be happy is your report did not provide some guidance on how the problem could be resolved. In effect, you have re-stated your 'bottom-line' question to "what will be the likely reaction of the Competition Commission to an acquisition and what remedies should be suggested if they were to object?"

What can we do to solve this problem? – remember you'll need to think creatively:

1. Don't go ahead with the acquisition of Nicelife.

2. Relocate abroad where such regulations don't exist.

3. The combined entity could divest of all or part of the trade in the Winter and / or Group / charter.

4. Downsize operations in the affected parts of the business.

5. Look to manipulate the data so that the 25% rule is not breached.

6. Lobby government to change the rules on what is considered a relevant merger or the 25% rule.

7. Give behavioural undertaking s and accept some degree of monitoring.

Some of these might be unrealistic or in fact not practical, but remember at this stage we are thinking as widely as we can. You will get chance to rule some of these ideas in or out in the next section when we come to evaluate the options.

Evaluating options

We should now consider which of these should feature as realistic options that will ultimately appear in our report. The criteria we identified in this chapter were:

- Is it commercial, will it improve the company's profitability either now or in the future?

- Is it practical, can it be delivered, are the resources available?

- Is it ethical, how will society judge this, is it the right thing to do?

- Is it too risky, are the rewards greater than the exposure to uncertainty?

Let's consider some of the above options against these.

- Options 1 and 2. Not to go ahead with the acquisition of Nicelife simply because it breaches the Competition Commission rules is neither practical nor commercial. Remember there are only two or possibly three sectors where there might be a problem and we should not dismiss what might be a very sound commercial opportunity just because we may have regulatory problems. And so for these reasons this option should be ruled out. Equally relocating abroad seems an over-reaction to the scale of the problem; it is also incredibly risky.

- Options 3 and 4. Divestment of part of the business has commercial implications. We would not for example want to sell off the most profitable part of the business simply to comply with the rules. This would negate any value in the proposed acquisition. And from a practical point of view, what exactly would you be selling? There's unlikely to be any value unless either the Nicelife or Broadsword brand was sold as part of the transaction. Downsizing should be questioned on similar commercial grounds, together with the possible risks involved that downsizing brings, such as potential redundancies and the poor staff morale that may ensue.

- Option 5. It may of course be the word manipulation, but the idea that we might change the way information is presented to get what we want should be ruled out on ethical grounds. Most people would consider doing that as just wrong.

- Option 6. Lobbying government might be a good idea but is probably not that practical given the timescale it would take the government to make the changes and the speed in which we need to decide on whether to acquire of Nicelife. Many companies have attempted this in the past and none have succeeded.

- Option 7. The behavioural undertakings could result in the merged company being in a worse commercial situation so should be looked at carefully.

Advantages and disadvantages or SFA

In order to evaluate these further we could use either the heading of advantages and disadvantages or suitable, feasible and acceptable (SFA). Both models would help to structure our thoughts. Given the nature of these options a simple advantages and disadvantages approach would probably be best.

Some of the options outlined will survive the evaluation process better than others and will emerge as excellent suggestions that should go forward into your conclusions and recommendations.

Forming conclusions

You should ensure that you have thought about how you will present your opinions using the guidance above and in chapter 6.

Recommendations

In order to complete this part of the report we need to make recommendations as to which of these options we think are best. As with conclusions you will find our recommendations in the answer later on in this chapter. But don't forget, when finalising your planning sheets to be clear about your justifications and be specific about when something will be done and by whom.

In order to give your recommendations a realistic feel, ask yourself what is the next step. If we recommend that we should divest the winter holidays for example, how would you go about doing this?

And finally a really good way of structuring recommendations is to think of what you would recommend in the short run compared to what you would recommend in the long run. A good example of this is the suggestion to lobby government to change the rules under which the Competition Commission operate. In the short run this is not practical but in the long run it could be a great idea.

Planning sheet 2 – Likely reaction of the Competition Commission.

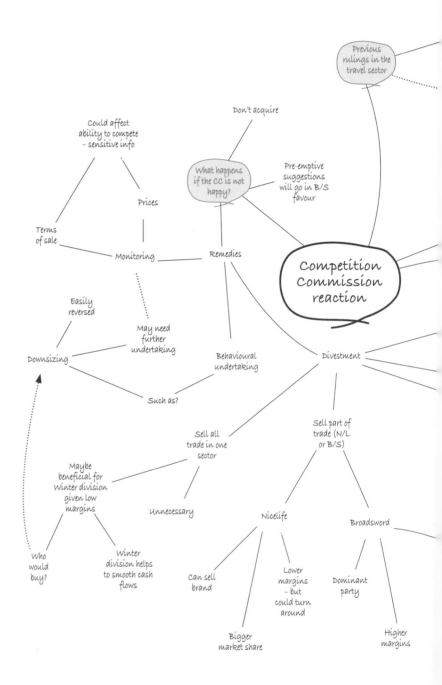

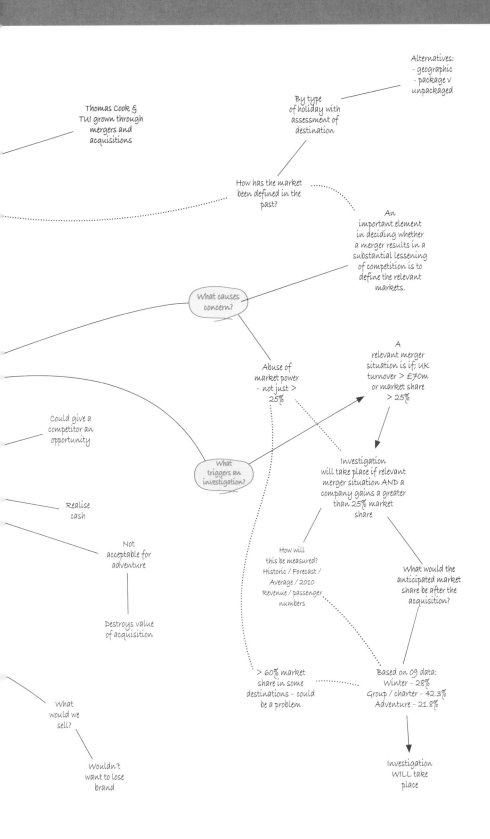

Alternatives:
- geographic
- package v unpackaged

By type of holiday with assessment of destination

Thomas Cook & TUI grown through mergers and acquisitions

How has the market been defined in the past?

An important element in deciding whether a merger results in a substantial lessening of competition is to define the relevant markets.

What causes concern?

A relevant merger situation is if; UK turnover > £70m or market share > 25%

Abuse of market power – not just > 25%

Could give a competitor an opportunity

What triggers an investigation?

Investigation will take place if relevant merger situation AND a company gains a greater than 25% market share

Realise cash

Not acceptable for adventure

How will this be measured? Historic / Forecast / Average / 2010 Revenue / passenger numbers

What would the anticipated market share be after the acquisition?

Destroys value of acquisition

What would we sell?

> 60% market share in some destinations - could be a problem

Based on 09 data:
Winter – 28%
Group / charter – 42.3%
Adventure – 21.8%

Wouldn't want to lose brand

Investigation WILL take place

Chapter 7 – Structuring your report

Grouping information

Using all of the case information you've been supplied with so far, and working from the planning sheets you have from the last chapter, consider how best to structure your report.

Work through each of the steps outlined in this chapter and decide upon the sections, headings and sub-headings you plan to use.

In order for your arguments to be clear to your reader it is important that your report has a good, logical structure. This chapter showed you how information can be grouped together and then presented under a number of sections and sub-headings in order to help your reader understand and follow the points you're making.

On the next two pages we've re-printed the planning sheets that appeared within the previous chapter answers. This time we've shown how you can build a bridge between these planning sheets and what will ultimately appear within your report by considering the sections and sub-headings you will use, and the information you'll put in each.

Planning sheet 1 – How does performance compare to Broadsword and why has Nicelife incurred losses?

You will often have a number of options open to you and it is important to take a decision and stick to it. A good example can be seen on this planning sheet. The comparison of margins by sector between Nicelife and Broadsword could appear within a section reviewing margins. However, since this information tells us a lot about why Nicelife incurred losses, it is thought more important to include this within the section explaining these causes.

Prioritising is one of the key steps in structuring your report. Note how some items have been excluded from our final plan (the trend of booking online, and the proactive management team and good examples). This is because, although relevant, they are not felt to have as much impact on the conclusions in our report.

The key to the colour coding on our planning sheet is:

Introduction
Revenue growth including segmental analysis
Gross profit margins
Operating profit margins
Cash management
Why has Nicelife incurred losses?

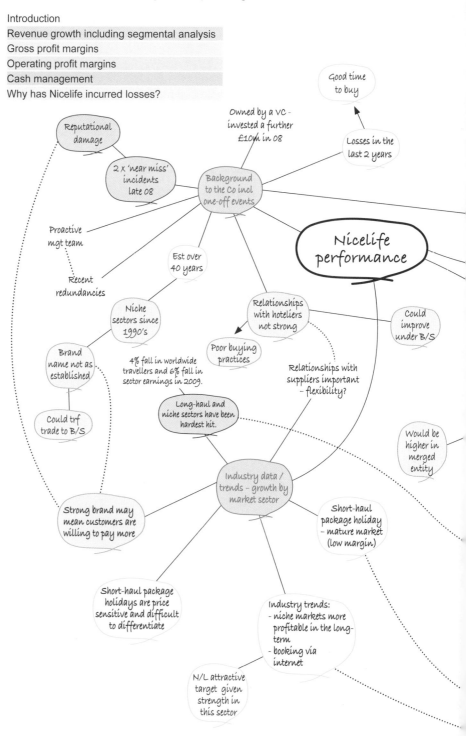

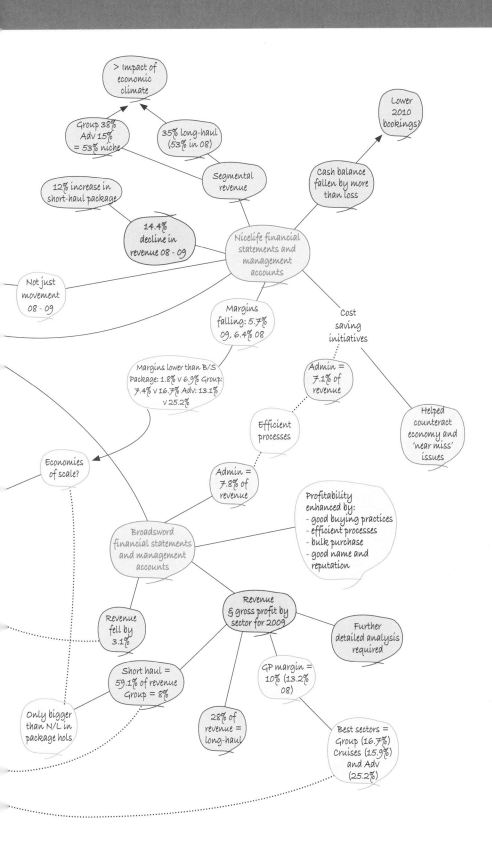

> Impact of economic climate

Group 38% Adv 15% = 53% niche

35% long-haul (53% in 08)

Lower 2010 bookings?

Segmental revenue

Cash balance fallen by more than loss

12% increase in short-haul package

14.4% decline in revenue 08 - 09

Nicelife financial statements and management accounts

Not just movement 08 - 09

Margins falling: 5.7% 09, 6.4% 08

Cost saving initiatives

Margins lower than B/S Package: 1.8% v 6.9% Group: 7.4% v 16.7% Adv: 13.1% v 25.2%

Admin = 7.1% of revenue

Efficient processes

Helped counteract economy and 'near miss' issues

Economies of scale?

Admin = 7.8% of revenue

Profitability enhanced by:
- good buying practices
- efficient processes
- bulk purchase
- good name and reputation

Broadsword financial statements and management accounts

Revenue & gross profit by sector for 2009

Revenue fell by 3.1%

Further detailed analysis required

Short haul = 59.1% of revenue Group = 8%

GP margin = 10% (13.2% 08)

Only bigger than N/L in package hols

28% of revenue = long-haul

Best sectors = Group (16.7%) Cruises (15.9%) and Adv (25.2%)

Planning sheet 2 – Likely reaction of the Competition Commission.

Key to colour coding:
Investigation
Findings
Divest
Downsize
Monitoring

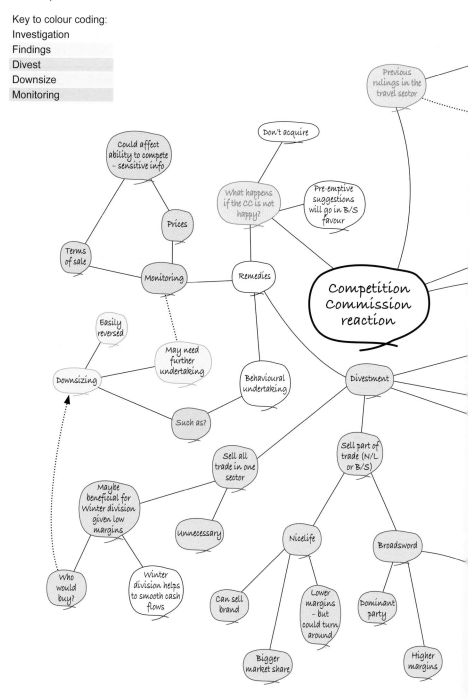

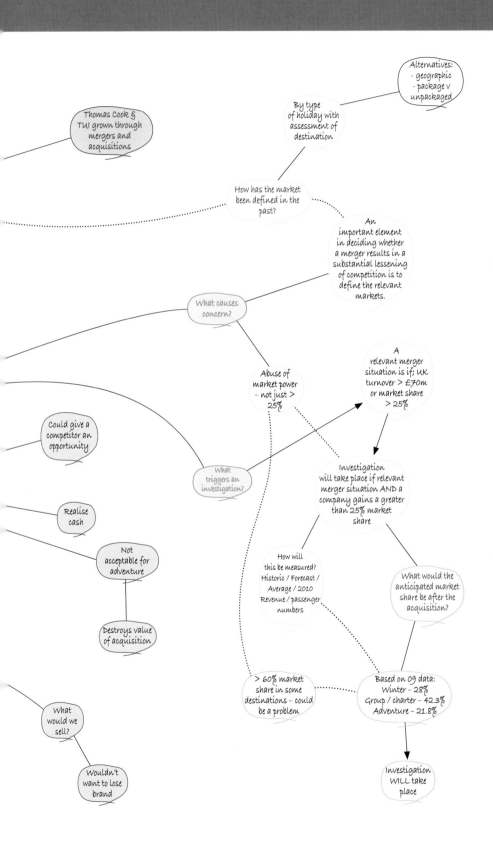

Thomas Cook & TUI grown through mergers and acquisitions

By type of holiday with assessment of destination

Alternatives:
- geographic
- package v unpackaged

How has the market been defined in the past?

An important element in deciding whether a merger results in a substantial lessening of competition is to define the relevant markets.

What causes concern?

Abuse of market power – not just > 25%

A relevant merger situation is if; UK turnover > £70m or market share > 25%

Could give a competitor an opportunity

What triggers an investigation?

Investigation will take place if relevant merger situation AND a company gains a greater than 25% market share

Realise cash

Not acceptable for adventure

How will this be measured? Historic / Forecast / Average / 2010 Revenue / passenger numbers

What would the anticipated market share be after the acquisition?

Destroys value of acquisition

> 60% market share in some destinations – could be a problem

Based on 09 data:
Winter – 28%
Group / charter – 42.3%
Adventure – 21.8%

What would we sell?

Wouldn't want to lose brand

Investigation WILL take place

Chapter 8 – Writing your report

A complete illustration

Write your report to the Corporate Development Director on the potential acquisition of Nicelife by Broadsword.

The following represents an answer to this case study exercise. It is not the only answer; you may have reached different conclusions or have suggested alternative recommendations that may be equally as valid. Remember the objective of your report is to answer the 'bottom-line' questions, but more importantly, to do so in a way that persuades your reader that your answers are correct. Given the total length of the report is fairly short, we have decided not to provide an executive summary.

REPORT ON THE POTENTIAL ACQUISITION OF NICELIFE BY BROADSWORD

To: The Corporate Development Director, Broadsword

From: A N Executive

Date: Today

Contents		**Page**
1	Introduction	1
2	Terms of Reference	1
3	Comparison of Nicelife performance with Broadsword to identify the cause of the losses	2
4	Reaction of Competition Commission to an acquisition	3
5	Conclusions	4
6	Recommendations	5
7	Appendices	6

1. Introduction

   With nearly 60% of revenue generated from short-haul package holidays, Broadsword is facing a very mature, highly price-sensitive market that offers little opportunity to differentiate.

   Organic growth post-recession seems unlikely, meaning that expansion via acquisition may represent the best opportunity to deliver improved shareholder wealth. Risk could also be reduced by further diversifying into other, more profitable, high growth areas such as adventure and specialist holidays. A potential target has been identified. Nicelife have operated in the travel industry for just over 40 years. Although they operate across all sectors, over 50% of their revenue is earned in the group / charter and adventure / specialist sectors.

   Over the past two years they have reported operating losses meaning this could be an excellent time for Broadsword to make an approach. Before doing so, it is important that Broadsword understand the nature of these losses, and consider the likely reaction of the Competition Commission to a proposed acquisition.

2. Terms of reference

   This report has been prepared by A N Executive for the Corporate Development Director of Broadsword. Specifically it will determine:

   - Why Nicelife has incurred losses in each of the past two years by comparing the performance of the company with that of Broadsword over the period.

   - What the likely reaction of the Competition Commission would be to any proposed acquisition.

3. Comparison of Nicelife performance with Broadsword to identify the cause of the losses

   To determine why Nicelife has reported operating losses in each of the past two years their financial statements must be compared and contrasted with Broadsword's to reveal similarities and differences. The performance over this period must also be viewed in the context of the global recession and the two 'near miss' incidents in 2008.

3.1   Revenue growth

Nicelife's revenue has fallen by 14.4% from £848.1m to £726.0m. This compares to the reduction in Broadsword of 3.1% from £905.4m to £877.3m.

Undoubtedly this greater reduction will have resulted from the reputational damage caused by the two 'near misses' as well as the greater exposure of Nicelife to long-haul business (see below).

3.2   Segmental analysis

Appendix 1 shows the geographical analysis of revenue for Nicelife compared to Broadsword for 2009. This shows that Nicelife operates a more diversified portfolio of products with 35% of their revenue relating to long-haul destinations outside of Europe (Broadsword: 28%). This is a significantly lower proportion than was seen in 2008 when just over half of Nicelife's revenue related to long-haul destinations.

This greater diversification is also seen when looking at the type of holiday, where Nicelife's largest sector is Group / charter accounting for just over 38% of total revenue. By way of contrast, this sector only accounts for just over 8% of Broadsword revenue.

This exposure to the more expensive or niche holiday market has meant the company has been more affected by the economic downturn. Revenue from the short-haul package holiday market actually increased by 12% (from £120.7m to £135.7m) and given that this sector accounts for nearly 60% of Broadsword's turnover, it is easy to see why each company has fared so differently.

3.3   Gross profit margins

Although Nicelife's gross margin has declined between 2008 and 2009 (from 6.4% to 5.7%), the fall is not as significant as that seen in Broadsword (from 13.2% to 10.0%). This suggests that the cost saving initiatives undertaken in 2009 have been successful.

However, the level of Nicelife's gross margin is still lower than Broadsword's in every sector (see appendix 2). The sectors where the difference is most pronounced are:

Sector		
	Broadsword margin	Nicelife margin
Total package	6.9%	1.8%
Group / charter	16.7%	7.4%
Adventure / specialist	25.2%	13.1%

3.4 Operating profit margins

That Nicelife's admin expenses as a proportion of revenue are lower than Broadsword's (7.1% v 7.8% in 2009) indicates that the business processes are fairly efficient. In fact, Broadsword may be able to learn from some of the practices at Nicelife in order to streamline their operations.

The damage to Nicelife's reputation caused by the two 'near miss' incidents, together with the economic climate in 2009 have served to make matters worse. However a radical programme of cost cutting has helped to prevent too much slippage at the operating profit level.

3.5 Cash management

Although the absolute cash balance in Nicelife is higher than in Broadsword, the company has suffered a net cash outflow in each of the last two years. Although part of this will have resulted from the operating losses, this cannot be the sole reason since the outflow is greater than the losses incurred.

Given the nature of the travel sector, much of the companies cash balance relates to deposits paid by customers for holidays not yet taken. This decline in cash could therefore be a reflection of lower (and / or later) bookings.

If bookings are still lower for 2010 this does not bode well for their performance in the next financial year. Action must be taken now to avoid over-committing on hotel and flight bookings to prevent large scale discounting and further losses.

3.6.   The cause of Nicelife's losses

Although both the current economic climate and the recent 'near-miss' incidents have both led to reductions in revenue in 2009, they do not help to explain why Nicelife incurred losses in 2008. This indicates something more fundamental about the way the business is run is leading to the losses. In order to reveal why Nicelife has made losses over the past two years, the focus should not simply be on the movement between the two years, but more on the underlying cause.

Given the comparison between the two companies, the lower gross margin in Nicelife helps to reveal the range of potential causes.

Broadsword attribute their high profit levels to four main things:

- bulk purchasing

- good buying practices

- efficient business processes

- its good name and reputation.

By reviewing each of these we can identify areas of concern for Nicelife.

The lower margins earned in short-haul package holidays (see appendix 2) are most likely caused by the absence of bulk purchase deals. If the acquisition was to proceed, these margins would be expected to increase to the level currently seen in Broadsword.

However, this explanation cannot be the case in other areas where Nicelife earn more revenue than Broadsword so an alternative explanation must be sought.

Given that Nicelife has only been operating in the niche sectors since the late 1990's, their brand is unlikely to command the premium prices that Broadsword can charge. This will not have been helped by the recent 'near miss' incidents. Although Broadsword's brand is primarily associated with the short-haul package holiday market, the margins earned in the niche sectors shows that customers are willing to pay a premium for the comfort of a name they can trust.

Nicelife's relationships with key suppliers (and in particular hoteliers) are not as strong. This lack of good buying practices will mean they're less likely to be able to flex their hotel and flight commitments when required. Without this flexibility Nicelife may have been forced to discount holidays, possibly to below cost, in an attempt to rescue something from the situation. By utilising Broadsword's buying practices in Nicelife it may be possible to improve these relationships over time.

The final attribute noted was efficient processes. That 20% of non-seasonal staff can be made redundant with no apparent impact on operations suggests that there were some historic inefficiencies. However, the cost cutting programme will have eliminated many of these.

4. Reaction of Competition Commission to an acquisition

The objective of the Competition Commission (CC) is to encourage healthy competition between companies to ensure a fair price for consumers. Any investigation will focus on the ability of a combined entity to abuse their power and act against consumers best interests; something they refer to as a 'substantial lessening of competition'.

4.1   The investigation

The CC will undertake investigations in situations where the value of the UK turnover of the company being acquired exceeds £70m and where the combined market share of the new merged entity exceeds 25%. Given that Nicelife's revenue already exceeds £70m, investigation will take place if the combined market share in any sector breaches the 25% limit.

The key aspect in assessing whether anti-competitive behaviour is possible is to define the market. Previous rulings in the travel sector suggest that the market will most likely be segmented by type of holiday, with some broad assessment of destination (short-haul v long-haul). This is to say, the way in which Broadsword currently present their segmental analysis. However, this is a subjective area, and it is possible the CC could decide to segment based purely on geographic destination, on package v unpackaged holidays or perhaps on other non-financial bases.

A second consideration is which data will be used to assess market share. Any investigation will take time and the revenue generated by each company could be very different in 2010 compared with 2009.

4.2   The findings

Assuming that the market is segmented in the expected way, appendix 3 shows that a combined Broadsword / Nicelife business, based on historic results, would have a greater than 25% market share in the Winter holiday sector and the Group / charter sector.

This will mean investigation is likely. The market share criteria will act as an initial guide although a market share of greater than 25% does not mean the CC will automatically conclude that anti-competitive behaviour is possible. They will have regard for the other operators in the market, and will consider the way in which they are able to compete against each other.

Given this, the CC may also have some concerns about the Adventure / specialist sector where the combined entity would have a market share of 21.8%, especially since Broadsword's market share for certain destinations exceeds 60%.

It must be noted that an investigation by the CC could take many months. The market shares of both entities could change considerably in the meantime, particularly given the significant decline in trade seen in Nicelife's long-haul business between 2008 and 2009, and the uncertainties regarding economic prospects over the next few years.

4.3   The remedies

If indeed the CC did conclude that there would be a substantial lessening of competition in these sectors, they will seek to find some remedies. Potential remedies include:

4.3.1 Divestment

Divesting of a division would have the advantage of realising some cash, which could be used to further grow the business.

However, by selling part of the business you are giving other competitors an opportunity to grow. Depending on who bought the trade this could lead to a significant threat. However, Nicelife already has a greater than 25% market share in the Group / charter market meaning any acquisition of this trade will lead to further CC investigations. This may help to reduce the scale of this threat.

The combined entity could divest of all or part of the trade in the Winter and/or Group / charter.

Option 1 – Divest all of the winter holiday and / or group/charter business

Disposal of the whole trade would seem unnecessary as the CC will not object to the combined entity having some trade in these sectors.

However, this may be the most appropriate solution for the winter holidays sector. Although the winter holiday trade does at least make a positive contribution to fixed costs in both businesses, the margins are so low it is entirely feasible that they do not cover the incremental fixed costs associated with operating these holidays. If this was the case it may be difficult to find a buyer for this part of the business.

Option 2 – Divest of part of the trade

Assuming the CC will be satisfied if the market share is below 25%, one option is to divest either the Nicelife division or the Broadsword division of the Winter and/or Group / charter sector. Since the Nicelife divisions have the lower profit margins, this may be the preferable option. It would also ensure that Broadsword was the dominant party in the enlarged entity.

However, Nicelife does have the larger market share in both sectors so if Broadsword could turn around Nicelife's profit margins, divesting the original Broadsword business may represent the best long-term opportunity.

It must also be considered what exactly is being sold. The only real value would be attached to the brand yet the Broadsword brand is crucial to the success of the company; disposing of that is not a viable alternative.

4.3.2   Behavioural undertaking - downsizing of operations in the affected parts of the business.

If it is not possible to sell part of the business, the combined entity could look to downsize in the affected sectors. This is unlikely to be the preferred option as far as the CC is concerned as it can easily be reversed. They would therefore require greater undertakings with more on-going monitoring and review. This may be the only option in the winter holidays sector given the current low margins.

4.3.3   Monitoring

Given the main motivation for this acquisition is to gain a greater presence in the Adventure / specialist sector, any CC concerns in this area must be fought. Neither of the options presented above would be acceptable to Broadsword as they would result in a significant de-valuing of the acquisition. A remedy of monitoring could however lead to a beneficial outcome for everyone. The key question is what sort of evidence the CC would require to be satisfied that no anti-competitive behaviour is occurring, and whether providing this information could mean competitors are able to access valuable information regarding Broadsword's competitive strategy.

5. Conclusions

5.1. The losses incurred in Nicelife have been caused by the lower gross profit margins which in turn arise from fewer economies of scale, less power over suppliers and the lack of a strong brand. The impact of the economic climate and the two 'near-miss' incidents have served to make matters worse in 2009 although the cost-cutting initiatives have improved the efficiency of processes.

The key question is to what extent Broadsword management could improve the buying practices and leverage their brand. Establishing better relations with suppliers will take time, especially in the sectors where Broadsword currently has little presence. Furthermore, whilst Broadsword does have a good name and reputation, it is more closely associated with the package holiday market.

5.2 Since a relevant merger situation would exist, and the combined entity would have a greater than 25% market share in some sectors, the acquisition will be investigated. However, just because the share exceeds 25% does not mean the CC will conclude that anti-competitive behaviour would be possible.

Key to this conclusion is how the market has been defined, although based on previous rulings in the industry, the assumptions taken appear to be realistic.

If the CC did conclude that the acquisition could result in a substantial lessening of competition, it would only be allowed to proceed if effective remedies were put in place.

6. Recommendations

    It is recommended that, should the acquisition proceed, the Nicelife division of the winter holiday market is downsized or even closed down altogether. Given the financial performance of this division, it is unlikely that anyone would be interested in buying it. The division operates at very low gross profit margins which are unlikely to cover the directly attributable fixed costs, although this should be verified prior to action being taken. The Finance Director of Broadsword should determine whether the Broadsword Winter holidays division generates an operating profit. Assuming it does, this should be retained.

    Regarding the Group / charter sector, it is recommended that a buyer is sought for the Nicelife division. With a 33% market share, this is the sector for which Nicelife has the greatest reputation, and selling the brand as part of the deal will help to realise the greatest value. The additional cash can then be used to invest in the Adventure / specialist sector until the economic recovery firmly kicks in. As this remedy will most likely be required by the CC, the search for potential buyers should begin as soon as the terms of the acquisition are agreed.

    Given the significant market share being sold, it is unlikely that the CC would approve any acquisition by a key competitor. This minimises the threat of giving an advantage to a close rival.

    If the CC did express concern over the Adventure / specialist sector, Broadsword should pursue a remedy of behavioural undertakings and monitoring. Any insistence of divestment must trigger a re-review of the benefits of the acquisition.

Appendix 1 – Segmental analysis of revenue

	Broadsword 2009 £m	Mix %	Nicelife 2009 £m	Mix %
Short-haul package (UK & Europe)	518.5	59.1	135.7	18.7
Long-haul package	67.7	7.7	88.4	12.2
Total package	586.2	66.8	224.1	30.9
Winter holidays	60.7	6.9	109.6	15.1
Group / charter	75.0	8.5	277.8	38.3
Cruises	66.8	7.6		
Adventure / specialist	78.5	9.0	112.0	15.4
Flight / hotel booking	10.1	1.2	2.5	0.3
TOTAL	**877.3**	**100.0**	**726.0**	**100.0**
Short-haul	633.4	72.2	471.2	64.9
Long-haul	243.9	27.8	254.8	35.1

Appendix 2 – Analysis of gross profit

	Broadsword 2009 £m	% gross profit margin	Nicelife 2009 £m	% gross profit margin
Short-haul package (UK & Europe)	32.7	6.3	1.4	1.0
Long-haul package	7.6	11.2	2.6	2.9
Total package	40.3	6.9	4.0	1.8
Winter holidays	3.1	5.1	2.4	2.2
Group / charter	12.5	16.7	20.5	7.4
Cruises	10.6	15.9	–	–
Adventure / specialist	19.8	25.2	14.7	13.1
Flight / hotel booking	1.1	10.9	0.1	4.0
TOTAL	**87.4**	**10.0**	**41.7**	**5.7**
Short-haul	47.5	7.5	27.6	5.9
Long-haul	39.9	16.4	14.1	5.5

Appendix 3 – Estimated market share post acquisition

	Broadsword's estimated market share in 2009 A	Broadsword's revenue in 2009 £m B	Estimate of total market size £m (C = B ÷ A)	Nicelife's revenue in 2009 £m D	Estimate of combined entity revenue £m (E = B + D)	Estimate of combined entity market share (E ÷ C)
Package holidays - Short-haul (UK & Europe)	2%[1]	518.5	25,925	135.7	654.2	2.5%
Package holidays - Long-haul	3%	67.7	2,257	88.4	156.1	6.9%
Winter holidays	10%	60.7	607	109.6	170.3	28.0%
Group / charter	9%	75.0	833	277.8	352.8	42.3%
Cruises	7%	66.8	954	–	66.8	7.0%
Adventure / specialist	9%	78.5	872	112.0	190.5	21.8%
Flight / hotel booking	5%[2]	10.1	202	2.5	12.6	6.2%

CW00734802

Why
REVIVAL
Waits

'If my people, who are called by my name ...'

Why

REVIVAL

'If my people, who are called by my name ...'

Waits

Selwyn Hughes

CONTENTS

CHAPTER 1

What really is
REVIVAL?

There is, I believe, no greater issue facing the Church of Jesus Christ at this time than the subject of Holy Spirit revival. And there is no greater passage in the whole of Scripture that shows the way to revival than 2 Chronicles 7:14 – a statement so seemingly simple yet so positively staggering in its implications:

> ' ... *if my people, who are called by my name, will humble themselves and pray and seek my face and turn from their wicked ways, then will I hear from heaven and will forgive their sin and will heal their land.*'

The great Welsh revivalist preachers of past centuries used to refer to this verse regularly in their preaching. Many Christians can recite it at the drop of a hat. It is God's final and finished formula on the subject of revival; His recipe for a spiritual awakening.

Before we focus in detail on this remarkable text we must take a little time to establish what we mean by revival. The word is used loosely in many circles and there is a tendency to describe as revival a great weekend in which a church sees more numbers than usual coming to know the Lord. The vague way in which the word is thrown around is unhelpful, to say the least.

Jim Packer, Professor of Historical and Systematic Theology at Regent College, Vancouver, says on this point: 'It seems that any new outburst of activity in the Church, any cloud of dust raised by the stamping of excited feet, will be hailed by somebody as revival.'[1]

In the truest sense of the word *revival* is an unusual and extraordinary movement of God's Spirit that marks it off as being **Revival** *is an unusual and extraordinary movement of God's Spirit.* vastly different to the normal sense of God's presence in the Church. It is not just a spiritual trickle, a rivulet or even a river; it is an awesome flood of God's Spirit, a mighty Niagara that sweeps everything before it.

Sometimes in attempting to define what something is, it is useful to begin by defining what it is not. So, in seeking to understand revival, let's start by looking at it first from that perspective.

Revival is not a great evangelistic thrust

When Billy Graham came to Britain in the 1950s, thousands of people were converted and committed their lives to Jesus Christ. Some of the Christian newspapers at that time stated: 'Revival has come to Britain', but wonderful though those days were, it was not revival – at least not in the real sense of the word. It was a demonstration of God-anointed and effective evangelism, but did not deserve the description of real revival.

Evangelism and revival are quite different. Evangelism is the expression of the Church; revival is an experience in the Church.

In evangelism the preacher calls on people to get saved; in revival people often call on the preacher to tell them how they can be saved. In Wales during the 1904 revival it *'What must we do to be saved?'* was not unusual for people to interrupt whoever was preaching by shouting out from the congregation: 'What must we do to be saved?' or 'I need to find peace for my heart ... help me please.'

My grandfather, who witnessed the Welsh revival, reported to me an account of a meeting he was at in the little town of Merthyr Tydfil, Mid Glamorgan, during the year 1904. A preacher, well known for his style of focusing in the first part of his sermon on the law of God before turning in the second part to the subject of grace, noticed after the first 20 minutes of his sermon a number of people leaving the church in tears. He asked one of the deacons to find out what was the matter with them and when the deacon went outside he found them leaning against the walls of the church in great distress.

'What is wrong?' he asked. One of them replied, 'We just couldn't sit through any more preaching on the law of God and we are waiting until the preacher turns from the law to grace – then we will go in and hope to find salvation for our souls.' Through powerful evangelistic preaching people can come under great conviction of sin at any time but where the Spirit is present in awesome power as in revival, then the conviction of sin and the desire for righteousness is deeper than it is sometimes possible to imagine.

Revival is not the restoration of large numbers of backslidden Christians

It's wonderful to see the thawing of the frost of indifference in the hearts of God's people, when the grave clothes of decorum are changed for the garments of praise, when voices seldom heard in testimony tell of God's wondrous grace and when lips long sealed begin to speak or sing His praises, but again this *in itself* is not revival.

I preached in a church some years ago which, according to its pastor, had been in the spiritual doldrums for well over a decade. Prior to the week-long meetings which I conducted the pastor said, 'I have to say that most of the congregation here are thoroughly backslidden, they rarely read their Bibles, no more than two or three come to the weekly prayer meetings, they appear like one of the churches in the book of Revelation to have lapsed into nominalism, having a name that they live but showing little evidence of spiritual life.'

One night during that week the Holy Spirit swept through the congregation in a powerful way and hundreds recommitted themselves to Jesus Christ, staying at the church to pray until well past midnight. The following night the whole atmosphere in the church was so different that the pastor said, 'This feels like revival.' Re-dedications to Christ numbered during that week came close to 500. It was indeed a wonderful and remarkable move of the Holy Spirit but, again, it could not truly be classified as revival.

Revival is not even unusually powerful and exciting meetings

Powerful and exciting meetings give us a taste of revival of course. In the almost 60 years I have been a Christian I have seen some wonderful things happen and sat through some thrilling meetings. The most memorable of these was in Pusan, South Korea, in the late 1970s. I was conducting a crusade there and was invited to speak at a 5 a.m. prayer meeting where I was told 5,000 Christians met to spend time with God before setting out on their day's work.

Just after the meeting began the Holy Spirit fell in a way I have not experienced before or since. You might remember in the Acts of the Apostles there was an occasion where the place in which Christians had gathered to pray was shaken (Acts 4:31). I cannot vouch for the fact that the building in which we met that mid-week morning to pray was literally shaken, but it seemed to almost everyone present that such was the case.

There was such a tremendous atmosphere of God's presence in the place that it was impossible for me to get up and preach. The Koreans have a wonderful way of what they call 'praying in concert', when everyone prays out loud asking God for whatever is on their hearts. Then after they have prayed they lift their voices in powerful praise.

A tremendous atmosphere of God's presence in the place.

ℬ

It was during this prolonged time of praise that I heard a Korean woman who was standing near me speaking words of praise to God in the Welsh language. Although I am not a fluent Welsh speaker I clearly understood what she was saying. In perfect Welsh she was praising God in words that when translated said this: 'Thank You, Lord, for the gift of Your salvation ... for giving Your Son for us on the cross of Calvary ... For the gift of Your Holy Spirit ...' and so on.

The effect on me was so great that I felt goose bumps coming up on my flesh as I stood surrounded by these thousands of worshipping

Koreans, praising God in their own language – and some, no doubt, in other languages inspired by the Spirit as well.

I consider the weeks I spent in Korea to be the closest I have ever come in my life to real revival.

In corresponding later with those who had invited me to Korea they reported that though God continued to bless them in a wonderful way, they had not experienced anything similar to the level we had encountered that particular morning. It was a taste of revival, but it was not sustained enough to be called the real thing.

What then is revival?

If the situations I have mentioned are not revival then what is? Although I have been talking and writing about revival for most of my Christian life, when it comes to defining it I come up against the same difficulty as an old friend of mine who said, 'Revival in a definition is like David in Saul's armour; it just doesn't seem to fit.' When we have said all we can say about revival it remains one of heaven's greatest mysteries.

Revival remains one of heaven's greatest mysteries.

ℬ

However, as a start, let's look at the dictionary definition of the word. My *Encarta* dictionary says revival 'is the process of bringing back something to life, to full consciousness or full strength', suggesting that something is alive but is about to die.

Years ago, when I was a pastor in Llandeilo, West Wales, I visited an old lady, a member of my church, who was very ill and appeared to be at death's door. Her sister who was looking after her said, 'I doubt whether she has long for this world.' Although she was semi-conscious I prayed for her and the family and as I left I remember thinking to myself that maybe that would be the last time I would see her alive.

Imagine my surprise a week later when she skipped up behind me in a local shop, tapped me on the shoulder and said, 'They tell me I have been at death's door but two days ago something wonderful happened and now I feel as good if not better than I have ever felt.' She had revived!

It is inappropriate I believe (as we said earlier), to apply the word 'revival' to people being converted. Those who come to Christ for conversion don't experience revival; they experience resurrection. Revival refers to the flaming forth once again of love for the Lord in those who, having known the truth and experienced the life of God in their souls, had grown cold.

'Revival' is one of those 'concertina' words which, in use, keep alternating between a narrower and broader sense. In its narrowest sense it can be applied to the personal quickening of the life of an individual when he or she has an unusual and extraordinary encounter with the Holy Spirit. In its broadest sense it can be applied to a community of believers who have been supernaturally revitalised at every level of their corporate existence – their inner life and the way they relate to one another and the outside world. It is with corporate revival that I am mainly concerned in this book.

While it was necessary to begin with a dictionary *definition* of the word revival (for communication breaks down when we give meanings to words that are not consistent with their true definitions) we must look outside the dictionary for a true *description* of spiritual revival. Some of my favourite descriptions I have come across in my time are these:

> *Revival is the inrush of divine life into a body threatening to become a corpse.*   D.M. Panton

Revival is God bending down to the dying embers of a fire just about to go out and breathing into it until it bursts again into flame.   Christmas Evans

Revival is waking up to the fact that you are asleep.
                                        David Thomas

My most favourite description of revival however is the simple but sublime statement given by Dr Martyn Lloyd-Jones:

Revival is the Church returning to Pentecost.

Whenever I think of the Church returning to Pentecost there comes to mind the story of Billy Graham who, as a young Youth for Christ evangelist, held a city-wide tent crusade in Los Angeles, California, somewhere around the middle of last century. Thousands of people came to Christ during that crusade, many of them Hollywood film stars.

A minister who belonged to a liberal church in the city (liberalism is the mindset that puts human thoughts above God's thoughts) wrote in the local paper, 'Billy Graham has put the church in Los Angeles back 100 years.' When he heard that, Billy is said to have responded, 'Oh dear – I was really trying to put it back 2,000 years.'

At Pentecost, a high-voltage burst of spiritual energy and supernatural power flowed into the

A high-voltage burst of spiritual energy and supernatural power.

℘

midst of those early disciples such as had never been known before. In a comparatively short time it affected the whole nation, spilling over eventually to other nations, even as far as Europe. When the Church witnesses the same degree of power that was present at Pentecost and that power spreads to whole communities, even to a nation as it did in Wales, then and only then can it be said to be revival.

Wales (of which I am a native), has often been described as the land of revivals as there have been repeated stirrings of the Spirit in the nation, especially between the seventeenth and early twentieth century. It would be wrong in my view, and limiting to the Holy Spirit, for the Church to expect any future revival to have the exact historical precedents of the past but there are several elements of revival that have to be present in order for it to be classified as true revival.

Our Welsh theologians used to say the three great characteristics of classic revival are these:

1. An intense palpable and extraordinary sense of God's presence.
2. A deep desire to be rid of all sin.
3. A powerful impact on the wider community.

When revival came to Wales in 1904, all three were in evidence.

There was an intense, palpable and extraordinary sense of God's presence throughout almost the whole of the Principality during that astonishing year and it lingered for some time afterwards. People would become aware of God's presence even deep down in the mines and cry out to be saved. There are stories of blaspheming miners struck down by God's power and then after surrendering their lives to Christ rising to find that so deep was the work of the Spirit in their hearts they no longer wanted to swear.

This sometimes created problems for those who directed the pit ponies that hauled the tiny trucks of coal from the coal face to the cages that came down to the pit bottom, for their instructions to the ponies were often given through swear words. Many of those who were converted in this way tell how, following their conversion, they had to teach their horses a new language. As one wag put it, 'On such occasions down there in the bowels of the earth even the horses knew there was revival!'

'Even the horses knew there was revival!'

There was also a great desire in people's hearts to be rid of sin. *'Ysbryd Glan'* is the Welsh term for the Holy Spirit which translated literally means 'Clean or Pure Spirit'. During the days of revival people could be heard crying out again and again in their native language, 'O God make me clean.' To quote Jim Packer again:

> No upsurge of religious interest or excitement merits the name ... if there is no deep sense of sin at its heart. God's coming and the consequent impact of His Word makes Christians more sensitive to sin than they previously were; consciences become tender and a profound humbling takes place.[2]

The conviction of sin was very much part of the early Christian Church. In Acts 2:37–41, for example, we read that those who listened to the apostle Peter were 'cut (pierced) in their heart' with a sense of guilt for Jesus' death.

Then the impact on the wider community was such that a community conscience informed by Christian values emerged. Revival wherever it happens usually has an ethical overspill into the world. There was a respect for law and order. In the Welsh valleys throughout 1904 crime figures dropped and for some months many magistrates found they had no cases to consider. They were presented with white gloves as a symbol of the 'clean' communities.

Most of those who have studied the subject of revival, or indeed who have experienced it, appear to agree with this analysis of the Welsh theologians. Duncan Campbell who was greatly used by God in the Hebrides revival in the early 1950s, when asked 'What have been the outstanding features of the Hebrides revival?' answered, 'Three things stand out clearly. First, an awareness of God ... The second main feature has been deep conviction of sin ... Physical manifestations and prostrations have been a further feature.' He also commented on the fact that there was a tremendous impact on the community, revival leaping the boundaries of the parish bringing refreshing and spiritual life to many all over the island.[3]

In relation to a powerful awareness of God, he said:

I have known men out on the fields, others at their weaving looms, so overcome by the sense of God that they were found prostrate on the ground. Here are the words of one who felt the hand of God upon him: 'The grass beneath my feet and the rocks around me seem to cry, "flee to Christ for refuge".' This supernatural illumination of the Holy Spirit led many in this revival to a saving knowledge of the Lord Jesus Christ before they came near to any meeting connected with the movement. I have no hesitation in saying that this awareness of God is the crying need of the Church today; 'the fear of the Lord is the beginning of wisdom'; but this cannot be worked up by any human effort, it must come down.[4]

Many critics claim that the reports of past revivals are often exaggerated and idealised and there is no doubt that in some cases this is true. However, as a number of people in my family were impacted greatly by the 1904 revival and were first-hand observers of the great things that God did, I have been able to check with these reliable sources in relation to some of the stories I have reported above.

You may wonder why I have spent so much time focusing on the meaning of revival. It is for this reason:

I am concerned that unless we have a clear understanding of what revival is and what it is all about we may easily settle for less than God wants to give us.

Why do we need revival?

The history of the Christian Church is not one long uninterrupted scene of manifest divine power. Even in the days of the Early Church six out of the seven churches in the book of Revelation had quenched the Spirit so that they had to be severely reprimanded by the Lord Jesus Christ.

Look around at the state of the contemporary Christian Church here in Great Britain. Yes, there are some good things happening, but the fact is Christianity in the mainstream churches is declining. According to Peter Brierley, a reliable research expert, we are losing about 1,000 young people a week. The level of spiritual energy in the contemporary Christian Church seems no match for the fast developing agnosticism of this postmodern generation. And while Christianity appears to be declining, non-Christian religions are growing and developing at an astonishing rate.

We may easily settle for less than God wants to give us.

In today's Britain there are more Muslims than Methodists, and the way Buddhism is growing who knows but one day there may be more Buddhists than Baptists. And this is what was once called a Christian country. While we must be thankful for the good things that are happening such as Spring Harvest, Alpha and the large summer conferences that draw thousands of Christians, we have to confess that, generally speaking, after several decades of charismatic renewal we are making about as much impact on the nation as a peashooter on the rock of Gibraltar.

Something much bigger and more powerful is needed if the spiritual situation is to be redeemed. It is going to take something much more than our methods and techniques to turn things around spiritually. As I see it, revival is the only answer.

CHAPTER 2

Why then does it
NOT COME?

I think I see something of the answer in the text I introduced to you at the start – 2 Chronicles 7:14. For years after coming into the ministry I looked at this text wishing I had enough nerve to preach on it. I used to think that to try and expound it would spoil it – like picking to pieces a rose to show off its beauty.

My two favourite verses in the whole of Scripture are John 3:16 and 2 Chronicles 7:14. John 3:16 says almost everything that needs to be said about the way to salvation and 2 Chronicles 7:14 says almost everything that needs to be said about the way to revival.

David Thomas, one of my spiritual mentors, an eloquent preacher (and also an uncle of mine) used to say of 2 Chronicles 7:14: 'This great text, lying like a diamond on a velvet couch never ceases to glisten and glitter as the light of the Holy Spirit falls upon it.' Ever since I heard him say that, every time I look at or think about this text that is the picture I have in my mind – a spiritual diamond which, under the light of the Holy Spirit, sparkles with truths that if heeded show us the way to a deeper relationship with God. If we do not see it in that way perhaps the reason is our eyes are more dazzled by the glare of this world than with the 'precious stone' itself.

Permit me to stay with this image of a diamond for a moment. Years ago one could see in a shop window in Regent Street, London, an exact replica of all the great diamonds of the world before they were cut. They looked like dull misshapen lumps of glass. How different, however, after the expert (called a lapidary) goes to work on a diamond and begins to cut faces on it so that its beauty might be better seen. Cutting faces on a diamond is called 'faceting' and it is true to say that apart from this highly-skilled work the beauty and loveliness of the stone would never be seen by the human eye. Someone who has observed the work of diamond cutting first hand has written this:

When a lapidary cuts a stone he always cuts to a pattern. It needs hardly to be said that he does not take the stone rough and cut three or four facets unrelated to one another. There is a design in his mind. The cutting itself is a work of art. The light that shoots out from the several faces when his work is done dazzles and delights the eye of all who really look.[1]

What I want to do now is not so much expound 2 Chronicles 7:14 but turn it word by word and phrase by phrase so that 'the light shoots out from its several faces'. My prayer is that this great text will do for you what it has done for me – set your heart on fire for revival.

It begins with the preposition: 'If'.

'IF'

A preposition, it has been said, can alter a proposition. And nowhere is that more evident than in the opening word of this illustrious text. Just as great doors swing open on small hinges so this word unfolds for us the truth that whatever part God plays in a spiritual re-awakening, we have a part to play too.

Set your heart on fire for revival.

ℬ

In the main there are two opposing schools of thought in relation to revival. There are those who say revival is a sovereign act of God and cannot be predicted or procured through any human means.

Others say the Church can enter into revival anytime it wants to – providing it is prepared to pay the price. Charles Finney, one of the strongest proponents of the latter view, claimed that self-examination and earnest prayer on the part of a congregation would always secure a divine visitation. 'Revival,' he said on one occasion, 'is no more a miracle than a crop of wheat ... a farmer sows and wheat comes up.'

As with most opposing theories the truth usually lies somewhere in the middle. When I was a student of theology I learned this: 'There are two rails laid down in Scripture – one is God's sovereignty and the other is human responsibility. If you do away with human responsibility you have nothing to save; if you do away with God's sovereignty you have nothing to save with. The Bible will not make sense to you unless you are prepared to run on both of those rails.'

What does it mean when we talk about the sovereignty of God and human responsibility in relation to the subject of revival? We mean by God's sovereignty that He takes action when He sees fit and answers our prayers at His own speed and in His own good time. In every revival throughout history men and women have stood back and said words similar to these: 'This is the Lord's doing and it is marvellous in our eyes.'

However, divine sovereignty does not relieve us of our human responsibility. There are things that we need to do to bring revival closer. Christmas Evans, one of our Welsh revivalists, put it well when he said, 'Revival comes from God but it is borne to earth on the wings of fervent, believing prayer.' Duncan Campbell said something similar when he wrote, 'God is the God of revival but men and women are the agents through whom revival is made possible.' The Almighty delights to team up with His people. We could not experience revival without Him and He won't bring it about without us.

The word 'if' is clearly a word of condition. 'If anyone is thirsty,' said Jesus on one occasion, 'let him come to me and drink' (John 7:37). And again, 'But if you do not forgive men their sins, your Father will not forgive your sins' (Matt. 6:15). The Bible fairly bulges with texts in which God implies that if we will do this He will do that. So, clearly, right at the start, some responsibility is placed at our door.

We are bidden over and over again in Scripture that whenever we find ourselves in need of spiritual re-awakening we are to admit our lapsed condition, repent of it and open ourselves up to God for Him to restore us to where we should be.

This brief selection of scriptures put the truth most clearly:

> *Sow for yourselves righteousness, reap the fruit of unfailing love, and break up your unploughed ground; for it is time to seek the LORD, until he comes and showers righteousness on you.* Hos. 10:12

> *'Yet I hold this against you: You have forsaken your first love. Remember the height from which you have fallen! Repent and do the things you did at first. If you do not repent, I will come to you and remove your lampstand from its place.'* Rev. 2:4–5

> *'Call to me and I will answer you and tell you great and unsearchable things you do not know.'* Jer. 33:3

> *'Return, faithless people; I will cure you of backsliding.'* Jer. 3:22

> *Take words with you and return to the Lord. Say to him: 'Forgive all our sins and receive us graciously, that we may offer the fruit of our lips.'* Hos. 14:2

But to whom is God speaking when He says 'If'? Listen carefully.

If MY PEOPLE

The message of revival is not for everyone; it is aimed specifically at the people of God. The responsibility for facing up to the challenge of revival is not on those outside the Church, but those *inside* the Church. That is you and me – if you are a believing Christian.

One of the things I have observed among those with an interest in revival is a tendency with some to focus more on the desperate spiritual state of the nation than the low spiritual state of the Church. Now every Christian ought to have a deep concern about the moral condition of our nation. We ought to lament the fact that Britain is in a bad way spiritually and morally.

Every year we kill millions of babies in the womb, we treat the Ten Commandments as if they were a joke, we consider education to be the means of our salvation, we allow our airwaves to carry the most poisonous and pernicious images, we make it possible for homosexuals to go through a form of marriage, there is corruption in high places, our courts are slow to punish evildoers, teenage pregnancies are the highest in Europe, things are happening in our nation – terrible things – that cry out to high heaven.

And while we lament the spiritual state of our land we must surely be aware that there is a worldwide epidemic of corruption, sleaze and moral deterioration that covers the earth. Selflessness has given way to an epidemic of 'what's in it for me' and self-interest seems part and parcel of life – particularly political life.

I heard the other day of a commentator in the USA by the name of Paul Harvey who read out the following statement on his radio programme:

> *There is an organisation in the USA consisting of 600 people.*
> *20 have been accused of spousal abuse*
> *7 have been arrested for fraud*
> *10 for writing bad cheques*
> *17 bankrupted for 2 businesses – at least*
> *3 arrested for assault*
> *71 couldn't get a credit card*
> *14 arrested on drug-related charges*
> *8 arrested for shoplifting*
> *21 involved in law suits*
> *84 stopped for being over the limit drink driving.*
> *The name of that organisation? The House of Congress.*

I wonder what a similar survey of other governments would reveal? Surely in the light of these things we Christians must carry a prayerful concern for the state of our nation and the world, but before we get carried away with the need for greater character qualities in the lives of those who lead our nation, let us not miss the point that when it comes to revival that is not where we should start.

Our strongest criticism and our deepest concern must be reserved for ourselves. God is concerned with the state of our nation, but He has an equal if not greater concern for His people. You and me.

To start by lamenting the deplorable spiritual state of our nation is to begin at the wrong end. The initial focus should be on *ourselves*, what kind of people we are and what kind of people we should be. We are quick to point out the sins of non-Christians, but not so quick to look at our own sins.

Revival starts then with the people of God.

But is God talking to all men and women who call themselves Christians when he says 'My people'? No. For there are many who call themselves 'Christians' but have never had a *personal* encounter with Jesus Christ. God puts this matter beyond all doubt when He says:

> *Revival starts then with the people of God.*
>
> ℬ

If my people **WHO ARE CALLED BY MY NAME**

And who are those who are called by His name? Those who have first called *on* His name. Scripture says, 'And everyone who calls on the name of the Lord will be saved' (Acts 2:21). If you haven't called on the name of the Lord in a personal way then, lovingly I say, you cannot claim to be one of His people. You can go to church, live a life that is well within the law, be religious, even take Holy Communion, but if you have not called on Him personally then you are not part of the family of God.

You see, going to church does not make you a Christian any more than going to the theatre makes you an actor. God chooses to begin with His own Church when He offers revival and that puts upon us an enormous responsibility. Not one person, but *all* His people.

His true people that is.

It is a tremendous responsibility to belong to the people of God. Every one of us carries a responsibility for the honour of God's name. As one London preacher from a past generation put it:

People judge the church by the impression that we make

upon them. If a Christian lapses and fails, people don't say to themselves, 'That person is an exception'; they judge everyone by the one individual they know who failed. They don't see us as one of hundreds of millions. They observe our ways and they say to themselves ... if that is what Christianity is all about then I want nothing to do with it. I'm missing nothing. If on the other hand when we are unselfish and loving then they are affected in this way and think of others like that also.[2]

Many Christians are not very wise in the way they relate to others. I spent a weekend preaching in a church in the south-west of England some time ago. I stayed with a very friendly couple and on the Sunday morning the man said, 'It's such a nice day, let's not bother with the car, we'll walk to church.'

As we set out, he said, 'You might be interested to see what will happen as we walk to church this morning. Because I am a Christian many of my neighbours go out of their way to avoid me.' He pointed to one up ahead who had just come out of a newsagent's shop obviously buying his Sunday paper and said, 'Now watch what he will do as soon as he catches sight of me.'

Sure enough, as soon as the neighbour spotted my friend, he went back inside the shop. A few minutes later we came across another neighbour who when he caught sight of us crossed to the other side of the road. At this point my curiosity got the better of me and I said, 'How has all this come about?'

'It's simply because when I first moved here I witnessed to my neighbours that I was a Christian.'

'And how did you do that?' I asked.

He replied, 'I began my witness by saying to them: Good morning, do you know you are going to hell?'

It is one thing when we are ostracised because of Christ; it is another thing when Christ is ostracised because of us. I say again: it is a tremendous responsibility to belong to the people of God. It is not surprising when we consider how foolish are the ways of God's people that the Almighty chooses to begin with His own Church when He focuses on revival.

Before we go any further let me deal with a difficulty that may be in some people's minds concerning the application of this Old Testament scripture to New Testament times. I have heard it said: 'You can't take a verse like this which was meant for the nation of Israel and apply it to the Church of the present day.' My answer to that objection is that while it is true that it is sometimes inappropriate to apply some Old Testament texts to New Testament situations, that does not apply in this case.

Take, for example, the concept of 'the people of God' which we have just been discussing. That's a concept that is found everywhere in Scripture. God had a redeemed people in the Old Testament whom He called Israel and He has a redeemed people in the New Testament called the Church. And take the other concepts found in the text which we shall look at in more detail in a moment – concepts such as humility, prayer, intercession and repentance – these are all truths that are enunciated most clearly in the New Testament and apply to every generation of God's people.

I believe 2 Chronicles 7:14 has as much application to the Church of the New Testament as it did to God's people in the Old Testament.

CHAPTER 3

Managing without
GOD

Wwe turn the jewel again to let the light fall on yet another phrase from 2 Chronicles 7:14:

> *If my people who are called by my name* **SHALL HUMBLE THEMSELVES …**

How do we humble ourselves? Well, first let's think about what exactly humility is for there are many fallacies in the Christian Church as to what constitutes this important spiritual quality. Some think, for example, that humility is self-effacement, but self-effacement can be a way of gaining face, like Uriah Heep in Charles Dickens' novel *David Copperfield* who approached David Copperfield, wringing his hands and saying, 'I am so very 'umble, Master Copperfield … so very 'umble.'

In a church of which I was once the pastor I remember giving an address on the subject of humility and afterwards a woman came up to me and said, 'I did so much enjoy your address.

Humility has always been a favourite topic of mine. In fact I regard it to be one of my best qualities.'

Humility has several characteristics. First, it is a right estimation of yourself. You are not God but you are not a worm either. Humble people see themselves as they really are. Humility also has within it the fact of self-forgetfulness. The humble turn their attention from themselves to God; they rarely think about themselves at all. Again, humility recognises that without God we can do nothing. Those who are not humble foolishly believe that without them God can do nothing.

Humility recognises that without God we can do nothing.

Often what we think is humility is really, when put under critical examination, nothing more than self-belittlement. People, I have found, will often express derogatory opinions of themselves hoping they are being seen as humble, while deep down in their hearts is the half-conscious hope that someone will contradict them. In the days when I used to conduct evangelistic crusades in different cities and countries, I had a friend who played the piano for me; he suffered from a strong inferiority complex. He used to persuade himself that this was in fact humility and I tried several times to disabuse him of this erroneous idea.

I made some strides one evening when after a particularly effective meeting I turned to him and said, 'That was wonderful playing tonight.'

He thought for a moment and said, 'No, not really, it wasn't all that good.'

'Come on now,' I said, 'it was tremendous playing – really brilliant.'

He said again, 'No, I don't think so, not really.' After we had repeated these same sentences to each other a few times I realised what he was doing – he was deliberately putting himself down so that I would lift him up. He thought he was being humble but in actual fact he was simply belittling himself. I waited for an opportunity to point that out to him and it came when he said, 'Well, it wasn't me, it was the Lord.'

'Now come on,' I said, 'it wasn't that good.' He got the point.

Humility, I believe, is best understood when we look at its opposite – pride. I am indebted to C.S. Lewis for this powerful statement concerning pride:

If you want to know how much pride you have ask yourself how much you dislike it in others. If you think you're not conceited, it means that you are very conceited indeed; first step toward acquiring humility is to realize that one is proud. We are all full of pride but we can't see it. It blinds us to our own condition. So it is wise to admit it even though you do not see it or feel it. There can be no surer proof of a confirmed pride than a belief that one is sufficiently humble. [1]

I consider this to be one of the most significant statements I have ever come across in relation to the matter of pride. Did you know that pride was the first sin ever to be seen in the universe? That's how the devil came into being. Once he was an angel of beauty and delight but he became puffed up by pride. Daniel Rowlands, another famous Welsh revivalist, said, 'We most resemble the devil when we are proud and we most resemble Christ when we are humble.'

'God who thrust out a proud angel from heaven,' said Spurgeon to his students, 'will not tolerate a proud preacher either. God hides from the proud, you won't even feel Him near you.' He drew the attention of his students to this verse:

Though the Lord is on high, he looks upon the lowly, but the proud he knows from afar. Psa. 138:6

Is it possible that that there could be more pride

in the church you attend than in a comparable group of non-Christians? Pride in the fact you are saved and others are not, pride in your knowledge of the Bible, your ability to pray or preach?

Pride or the lack of humility is one of the roots of sin. After all what is sin? Chop off the first and last letters and what are you left with? 'I' – the perpendicular pronoun as someone has called it. See it standing there on the page, 'I', tall and starched and stiff. Sin is really the ego standing up to its full height in the place which God has reserved for Himself – the centre of the soul.

Pride or the lack of humility is one of the roots of sin.

What does God mean when, in talking about humility, He commands us to humble ourselves? I believe that what He has in mind primarily is a willingness to judge and evaluate ourselves, not by the standards of others, but by the standards of God's Word, the Bible, to come under its authority and submit to its truths. It is not possible to understand what humility is unless we are prepared to lay our lives alongside the Bible.

One of the alarming trends in today's Christian society is the disappearance of the truly biblical

Christian. I refer not so much to respecting the Bible as God's Book, or even carrying a Bible to church. I am thinking of those who fail to bring their lives under its authority, to see it for what it is – God's infallible Word – and live by its standards, eager to obey its commands. Such Christians are fast disappearing. We need the attitude that will not stand in judgment over the Scriptures but will sit under them in humility.

Listen to what God, speaking through Isaiah, says:

> *'This is the one I esteem: he who is humble and contrite in spirit, and trembles at my word.'*   Isa. 66:2

What does it mean to tremble at God's Word? I remember in a counselling session many years ago talking to a young man – a Christian – who had come to me for some spiritual advice over a certain issue but seemed to resist every scriptural principle I presented to him. After an hour or two of this I said, 'Look, on your way out of here today I am going to put my Bible down and invite you to walk over it, to wipe your feet on it.' He was quite shocked and asked me to explain what I meant.

'Well,' I said, 'you seem to be unwilling to act on the principles of God's Word which you asked me to show to you, and so you might as well demonstrate your contempt for it by wiping your feet on it.' When I said that he began to tremble physically.

I do not usually resort to such melodramatic statements when I am counselling, but in this case it seemed appropriate. I can tell you the counselling session took a decidedly different direction from that moment and I am glad to say the young man came to a place where he decided to put God's Word into action as it related to his difficulties.

I am not suggesting that the phrase to tremble at God's Word means a literal physical trembling. It means, I believe, that we allow the Word which is alive to penetrate our lives to such a degree that enables us as we come up against Scripture, to feel the inner vibrations of truth in our soul that point out some violation in our life. How many of us can honestly say that we value the Word of God so highly that when we realise we are in violation of it our soul trembles within us?

It is here then when we talk about pride and the need to step down from it in true humility that we come face to face with the first reason why revival waits.

I have no hesitation in saying that pride or lack of humility is the biggest single impediment to revival. Theologians in the past have listed what they call the seven most deadly sins and the first to head that list? Not lust, not cruelty, not even murder. Pride.

Pride is the implacable enemy of God and He gives some stern warnings in Scripture concerning it – none more sober than this:

'God opposes the proud but gives grace to the humble.'
James 4:6

There is a fecundity about pride which appears in no other sin. It is so vile and loathsome that it makes other sins more vile and loathsome. If pride is the biggest impediment to revival then it begs the question: what are we going to do about it? How willing are we to bring our lives under the authority of Scripture and face the first of the divine challenges laid out in 2 Chronicles 7:14?

Charles Swindoll in one of his books tells the story of a medical doctor, Evan O'Neill of Kane Summit Hospital in New York City, who operated on himself and removed his appendix while under local anaesthesia. Apparently the operation was a success and his recovery progressed faster than that usually expected of patients who were given general anaesthesia.[2]

It is clear from what God is telling us in 2 Chronicles 7:14 that He is looking to us to operate on ourselves. Let's call it 'self-exploratory surgery of the soul'. While you are fully conscious, fully aware, I invite you to allow the Holy Spirit to assist you, handing you the only instrument you need to do soul surgery – the germ-free scalpel of Scripture. For what we come to now is this – Hebrews 4:12 tells us that:

> ... *the word of God is living and active. Sharper than any double-edged sword, it penetrates even to dividing soul and spirit, joints and marrow; it judges the thoughts and attitudes of the heart. Nothing in all creation is hidden from God's sight. Everything is uncovered and laid bare before the eyes of him to whom we must give account.*

With this reliable instrument, the Word of God, in your hand take an honest look into your soul and consider how much pride still lies within you.

For some it will be your first ever look, for others not the first, but perhaps one long overdue.

Self-exploratory surgery should always be conducted in the presence of God and with the Word of God, in the realisation that God is not against us for our sin but for us against our sin. And remember C.S. Lewis's words, that if you think you are not proud then most likely you are.

So why does revival tarry? The primary reason is this: we are unwilling to humble ourselves. During the Welsh revival, one of the songs that was sung over and over again, sometimes moving people to deep emotion was this:

Bend me lower, bend me lower, bend me lower,
Lower down at Jesus' feet.

We provide the willingness; He provides the power.

℘

Why did they ask God to bend them lower (in other words to humble them) when the Almighty told them in 2 Chronicles 7:14 to humble themselves? Were they going against Scripture here? I think not. They were recognising that the development of humility is not a mere matter of will power. In all things spiritual there is a merging of the divine and human. We provide the willingness; He provides the power.

Keep that in mind always whenever you conduct any self-exploratory surgery. You need another will working alongside your own. We must come to God with willingness but not depending only on our willingness. We must link ourselves also to His power. The psalmist understood this when he prayed in Psalm 139:23:

> *Search me, O God, and know my heart;*
> *test me and know my anxious thoughts.*

CHAPTER 4

Call me when the
FIRE FALLS

The text of 2 Chronicles 7:14 continues:

> If my people who are called by my name shall humble themselves and PRAY ...

You may be feeling somewhat relieved as we move away from the subject of pride and you may think to yourself: Well I may have some pride in me but here is a test I can pass – I do pray.

Do you?

How much?

How sincerely?

When, for example, did you last stay up late just to pray? When did you rise early simply to pray?

It is prayer that opens us to God's power. All around us the power of God is flowing and it comes in at the place of prayer. A little prayer and a little of that power gets through. A lot of prayer and a lot comes through. Fervent believing prayer causes it to come in like a flood.

It is prayer that opens us to God's power.

How selfish sometimes are our prayer lives? It's interesting how when our family is in trouble or our needs cry out to be met we can develop a passion in prayer that is not there for those who may be outside our small circle. A lot of our praying is shot through with self-interest, our concerns, our needs, and so often everything that comes up has a self axis. Me! Me! Me!

I have quoted elsewhere the story of the chief librarian in Dagenham in Essex who discovered this prayer among the papers of John Ward, MP for Hackney during the eighteenth century:

O Lord, Thou knowest I have mine estates in the City of London and likewise that I have lately purchased an estate in the County of Essex. I beseech Thee to preserve the two counties of Middlesex and Essex from fire and earthquake, and, as I have a mortgage in Hertfordshire, I beg Thee likewise to have an eye of compassion on that county. For the rest of the counties, Thou mayest deal with them as Thou art pleased ... [1]

It's surprising the strange ideas that some Christians have in relation to prayer. I have met many who view it as nothing more than just reciting what we call the Lord's Prayer. Although it is an important framework for understanding what prayer is all about and has been a blessing to the Church universal when said corporately, if we think that when we have recited the Lord's Prayer that is the end of the matter then we are just fooling ourselves.

Some Christians have the idea also that it is no good praying unless you 'feel like it'. The precise opposite is nearer the truth. Our prayers are often more effective when we pray even though we don't feel like praying. And it is not difficult to understand why. When we pray because we feel like it there is often a degree of pleasure that we give ourselves. It feels good to hear our own voice putting together words that address the Almighty God, to sense a flexibility of language as our tongue becomes like 'the pen of a ready writer'. We can feel good about ourselves when we pray like that.

When, however, we pray though we do not feel like it, we bring to God not only the content of our prayer but the evidence of a disciplined spirit. We have gone to Him against our natural inclination. We have displeased ourselves in order to please Him. Prayer is too important to depend on the vagary of feelings. Feelings fluctuate with our health, the weather, the news, circumstances, what we eat and whom we met last. Our commerce with heaven cannot be conducted on things so fortuitous as that.

Forbes Robinson, himself a man of prayer, said: 'Do not mind about feelings. You may have beautiful feelings. Thank God if you have. He sends them. You may have none. Thank God if you have not, for He has kept them back. We do not want to *feel* better and stronger; we want to *be* better and stronger.'[2]

If in times past you have prayed only when you felt like it then pause once more for a moment of self-exploratory surgery. Determine to go to God whether you feel like it or not. You would not fail to keep an appointment with an important fellow human being because the inclination had ebbed when the appointed hour came. Courtesy would carry you there if desire didn't. Can you be less courteous with God?

But what kind of praying is it that God is thinking about when He bids us pray for revival? When I was in Sunday school I was taught a chorus about prayer that went like this: 'A little talk with Jesus makes it right, all right.' I do not mean to belittle those brief quiet moments that we spend with Jesus at any time during the day but that is not the kind of praying that ushers in revival.

Revival praying is intensive praying; passionate praying, prolonged praying – praying that holds on to God like Jacob when he prayed: 'I will not let you go until you bless me.'

'I will not let you go until you bless me.'

The prophet Isaiah gives us a picture of watchmen standing on the walls of Jerusalem crying out to God and reminding Him of His promises concerning the Holy City.

℞

> *I have posted watchmen on your walls, O Jerusalem; they will never be silent day or night. You who call on the Lord, give yourselves no rest, and give him no rest till he establishes Jerusalem and makes her the praise of the earth.* Isa. 62:6-7

The picture here is of men determined to give God no rest until Jerusalem is restored to its former glory. Revival praying is not just ordinary praying. It is unhurried praying, not just saying words with a breathless eagerness to get it finished. It is passionate praying – prayer that is not afraid to draw upon one's emotions, to cry out to God, with tears if that is the way one feels. Far too often our prayers run along these lines: 'Please excuse me from the Upper Room but call me when the fire falls.'

I heard one preacher say that this kind of praying (what I am calling revival praying) reminded him of his mother who had a habit of losing her keys – when this happened she would turn the house upside down until she found them. He said, 'There would be intense searching until they were found, everything else stopped in the house and everyone was enlisted in the task. Nothing else mattered at that moment other than finding those keys.' Someone has said that 'we will not see revival until we can't live without it'.

God goes further in this matter of prayer by saying:

> If my people who are called by my name
> shall humble themselves and pray and
> SEEK MY FACE …

If we are honest we are often more interested in seeing the hand of God at work than we are in seeing His face. We want to see the sick healed, we want to see supernatural events taking place, a desire for which of course is perfectly right and proper, but revival praying puts as its priority a new vision of God, a new understanding of Him; to know God for Himself, who He is, and not just for what He can give. Revival praying is where we are drawn into a new relationship with Him, where intimacy with God becomes the most important thing.

When did you last get down before God and pray with fervour and passion? And with a desire not simply to see a spiritual renaissance but to know God more deeply, to see His face. That's the kind of praying that brings revival.

Thus, the second reason why revival tarries is:

We do not pray enough, we do not pray passionately enough, not perseveringly enough, not persistently enough.

Is there a prayer group for revival in your church? If not, join one that might be in the area, or you could start one.

CHAPTER 5

Blocks to
REVIVAL

Our text continues:

If my people who are called by my name shall humble themselves and pray and seek my face **AND TURN FROM THEIR WICKED WAYS ...**

We said earlier when we talked about divine sovereignty that God takes action to answer prayer when He sees fit, at His own pace and in His own good time. Yet as we have seen there are things we can do at the present moment to bring revival nearer, such as humbling ourselves, praying more sincerely, specifically and passionately. But now God has a further challenge for us – He asks us to turn from our wicked ways.

The people of God with wicked ways? Surely it means silly ways, careless ways perhaps. The Bible says *wicked* ways and wicked, I imagine, is not a word we like applied to ourselves. The word 'ways' suggests behaviour that has become settled and established.

Young people nowadays tend to use the word 'wicked' in quite a different way from its dictionary meaning. A great film or an exciting event can be 'wicked', but I assure you when God uses the word He means it to be understood in its original sense – 'sinful and iniquitous'.

What are these wicked ways, these Spirit-quenching things that block the path to revival? Well, God is not specific about them so we are left to some degree of speculation in regard to their precise nature. Permit me to give you some examples based on Scripture of what I think can be listed as the wicked ways of the people of God.

When we allow our spiritual condition to remain lukewarm and complacent – that is a wicked way. Jesus had some searing words to say to the church in Laodicea about their lukewarm condition. 'I know your deeds, that you are neither cold nor hot. I wish you were either one or the other! So, because you are lukewarm – neither hot nor cold – I am about to spit you out of my mouth' (Rev. 3:15–16).

When we hold bitterness and resentment against a group or an individual and refuse to offer the same degree of forgiveness that Christ has given to us – that is a wicked way. Unforgiveness kills the spiritual life; it is like drinking poison and expecting the other person to die. Jesus said those who will not forgive will not be forgiven (Matt. 6:14).

When by our disunity we present to the world a fragmented picture of the face of Christ – that is a wicked way. How snobbish one church can be with another. Some churches would rather die in separation than live in fellowship. Denominationalism – believing your denomination or group is better than another – that is an impediment to the spiritual life. God doesn't necessarily want to take you out of your denomination, but I believe He does want to take the denomination out of you. (See our Lord's prayer in John 17.)

When we neglect the reading and study of the Scriptures – that is a wicked way. God has given us just one book – the Bible. It is His one and only published work. How much time do we spend in it? And do we really believe it? Do you know that the majority of Christians admit that they have not read every word in God's Book, while readily admitting to reading every word in other books they peruse.

When we withhold our tithes and offerings from God – that is a wicked way. One of the most sobering truths in the Bible is that when God's people do that they are guilty of robbing God. It's hypocritical to describe a thief or a robber as 'wicked' when we ourselves may be in that same category spiritually speaking. 'Will a man rob God?' (Mal. 3:8).

Nor is this all! What about such things as continued moral failure, lying, low expectations of holiness in oneself and others, indifference to the winning of others to Christ, loss of temper, idolatry, gossip, hypocrisy, pretence ... the list could go on and on. Is it any wonder why revival does not come when there are so many wicked things amongst us. Charles Finney once said, 'Christians are more to blame for not being revived than sinners are for not being converted.'

The world has a right to expect us to be different.

Some of the things listed above might not be seen as serious in worldly people. But God's own people – people claiming to have the life of Christ in them, to be new creatures? If we are in Christ and Christ is in us then the world has a right to expect us to be different.

What are we to do about our 'wicked ways'?

God says we are to *turn* from them. What does that mean? A synonym for the word 'turn' is 'repent'. Some Christians may feel that deciding to discontinue what God calls 'wicked ways' is enough. It is not. Once we admit that we are in need of change in our lives there must be a moment of deep repentance before we can move on in our relationship with God.

To recognise something as wrong and resolving not to do it again is good but not good enough. We must take care of past violations by repenting of them. There can be no deep ongoing relationship with the Lord until we know how to act over the wrongs of the past.

When our Lord spoke to the church at Ephesus, He reprimanded them because they had left their first love (Rev. 2:4). How was the situation to be corrected? They were to *remember* from where they had fallen, *repent* and *return*. Someone has described this as the Three Rs of Relationship. They were to look back to the position from which they had fallen, repent of it and return to God in deep humility of heart.

The Bible is replete with texts that stress the importance of repentance. These for example:

'If you repent, I will restore you that you may serve me ...'   Jer. 15:19

'Therefore say to the house of Israel, "This is what the Sovereign LORD says: Repent! Turn from your idols and renounce all your detestable practices!"'   Ezek. 14:6

From that time on Jesus began to preach, 'Repent, for the kingdom of heaven is near.'   Matt. 4:17

They went out and preached that people should repent. They drove out many demons and anointed many sick people with oil and healed them.   Mark 6:12

Peter replied, 'Repent and be baptised, every one of you, in the name of Jesus Christ for the forgiveness of your sins. And you will receive the gift of the Holy Spirit. The promise is for you and your children and for all who are far off – for all whom the Lord our God will call.'   Acts 2:38

'In the past God overlooked such ignorance, but now he commands all people everywhere to repent. For he has set a day when he will judge the world with justice by the man he has appointed. He has given proof of this to all men by raising him from the dead.'   Acts 17:30

Repentance, however, is one of the most misunderstood words in the Christian vocabulary. People think repentance is feeling sorry for your sins. But that is not what the word is about. The Greek word for repentance is *'metanoia'* which means a change of mind. It is good when we feel sorry for our 'wicked ways' but that is the outcome of repentance not the beginning of it. Repentance is seeing that the direction in which you are going is wrong then turning in a new direction with your thoughts, changing your mind, for example, about where your life is found.

The biggest mistake people make about repentance is that they expect to feel sorry about their sin before they repent. Repentance begins not by waiting to feel sorry about our sin but seeing how wrong it is and making up our mind to turn in a new direction. It begins with a change of mind and when the mind is changed then – *then* our feelings feel the impact of that, for our feelings follow our thoughts in the same way that ducklings follow their mother on a pond.

So don't think that because you don't have any deep feelings of sorrow or any guilty feelings that you are not required to repent.

Don't wait for your feelings to be stirred. What we think about affects the way we feel. You take

Take the first step and the feelings will follow.

ॐ

the first step and the feelings will follow – don't worry about them. Do what is right and the rest will follow on as night follows day.

But what if we do what God asks? Listen once again:

> If my people who are called by my name shall humble themselves and pray and seek my face and turn from their wicked ways THEN WILL I HEAR FROM HEAVEN WILL FORGIVE THEIR SIN AND HEAL THEIR LAND …

What a promise! God will hear, forgive and heal. Go over every word carefully.

He will *hear*. He *listens* to us when we pray. C.H. Spurgeon used to say that prayer is like pulling on the ropes here on earth which causes a bell to ring in heaven. Do you believe God hears us praying for revival? I mean *really* believe? Well, not to believe it is to make God a liar.

He will hear *from heaven*. We need to be reminded over and over again that it is from heaven that true revival comes. It is beyond our power to usher in revival by our human methods, much as we would like to do so. Only God Himself by His own quickening visitation can renew.

He will *forgive our sin.* Isn't this a most amazing thing? Even though we have impeded His grace and quenched His Spirit for years, the moment we turn and ask for His forgiveness He gives it to us, fully and freely.

He will *heal our land.* The reference here is clearly to the physical land as can be seen from the verse preceding this where God says that in judgment on His people's sins He will shut up the heavens and send locusts to devour the land. The 'land' that we possess as Christians, however, is not a physical inheritance but a spiritual one. Neglect ravages it and causes it to rot, but God can restore what has been lost in ways above and beyond our thinking.

Well, there it is.

The reason why revival tarries (from the human side at least) is because:

- We are stuck in our pride.
- We do not pray enough, passionately enough and sincerely enough.
- We are reluctant to turn from our wicked ways and genuinely repent.

Now what are you going to do about it?

It is a lot to believe that we can witness a turn of the spiritual tide in our land when we see

Christianity declining and thousands drifting away from the mainline churches, but we must put our whole weight upon it. We must humble ourselves before God, pray more in private and in groups, claim the help of God to cut out everything in our lives of which He disapproves, plead for His grace and ask Him to flood our churches with His power.

Are you willing to pray more and join a group praying for revival, or to start a prayer meeting? You can be sure of this: God would not call us to pray if our situation were unredeemable.

It would be wonderful if the whole Church in the United Kingdom would heed this message but the history of revival shows that when a proportion of God's people meet His conditions He moves in answer to their prayers. In Wales it was a small praying group who were used by God to usher in revival. You could be the vanguard of a mighty move of the Holy Spirit if you are willing to pay the price.

Drawing closer to God in the way I have described may not guarantee we see corporate revival (that must be left to God's sovereignty) but one thing is sure *you yourself will be revived.* And your action along with others will bring us closer to the great outpouring of the Holy Spirit for which so many are longing.

CHAPTER 6

A revived
CHURCH

What can we expect a revived Church to look like?

The Church of Jesus Christ will shine with a new light when revival comes. Denominationalism – already beginning to be broken down – will in the flow of revival power be broken down completely. In revival people are not inclined to say 'I am an Anglican', 'I am a Baptist', 'I am a Methodist' or 'I am a Pentecostal'. Those attitudes dissolve in the river of God's Spirit.

In revival times God acts quickly; His work accelerates. The Early Church operating in the power of the Holy Spirit saw 8,000 converted within a few weeks (Acts 4:4; 5:14). When Paul left Thessalonica after just a few weeks of ministry, he left behind him a virile church whose quality can be gauged from 1 Thessalonians 1:3. No wonder he asked them to pray that 'the message of the Lord may spread rapidly and be honoured, just as it was with you' (2 Thess. 3:1). The truth of the gospel makes rapid strides in times of revival. People are born again and grow quickly at such times.

Holiness, another characteristic of revival, will add a sharper edge to Christian living bringing a clearer line of demarcation between the Church and the world. Love flowing between believers will show itself in ways that defy human analysis and cause unbelievers to say, 'How much they love one another.'

'How much they love one another.'

Yet another characteristic of a Church in revival is a responsiveness to God's Word. A powerful sense of God's presence imparts new authority to the truth of His Word. Whereas before, the Word of God made only a superficial impact, now it searches the hearts of the hearers to the depth of their being. At Pentecost, and for several decades afterwards, the Word of God touched the hearts of people in a dynamic way. The apostle Paul thanked God that when the Thessalonians heard the Word of God they accepted it not as from men but as the very Word of God (1 Thess. 2:13).

Duncan Campbell describes the condition of the Church during the revival that took place in the Hebrides in this way:

I would first like to state what I mean by revival as witnessed in the Hebrides. I do not mean a time of religious entertainment, with crowds gathering to enjoy an evening of bright gospel singing; I do not mean sensational or spectacular advertising. I do not mean high-pressure methods to get men and women to an enquiry room – in revival every service is an enquiry room; the road and hillside become sacred spots to many when the winds of God blow. Revival is a going of God among His people, and an awareness of God laying hold of the community ... the fear of God lays hold upon the community, moving men and women, who until then had no concern for spiritual things ...[1]

Listen also to his description of a scene that took place during the first days of the movement of the Spirit in the Hebrides.

A crowded church, the service is over: the congregation, reluctant to disperse, stand outside the church in a silence that is tense. Suddenly a cry is heard within: a young man, burdened for the souls of his fellow-men, is pouring out his soul in intercession. He prays until he falls into a trance and lies prostrate on the floor of the church ... the congregation, moved by a power they could not resist, came back into the church, and a wave of conviction of sin swept over the gathering, moving strong men to cry to God for mercy. This service continued until the small hours of the morning, but so great was the distress and so deep the hunger which gripped men and women, that they refuse to go home, and already were assembling in another part of the parish. A feature of this early morning visitation was the number who made their way to the church, moved by a power they had not experienced before: others were deeply convicted of their sin and crying for mercy, in their own homes, before ever coming near the church.[2]

But revival will not only affect the Church, it will affect the nation too.

Revival in the Church has always had an ethical and evangelistic overflow into the world, often of great power. In terms of evangelism it is the spiritual fulfilment of what happened in the post-Exilic restoration:

This is what the LORD Almighty says: 'In those days ten men from all languages and nations will take firm hold of one Jew by the hem of his robe and say, "Let us go with you, because we have heard that God is with you."' Zech. 8:23

Our nation needs God, that is for sure. We are slipping into apostasy, sin is rampant and rife, young people have no clear ethical guidelines, postmodernism rules in our colleges and universities, moral absolutes no longer prevail, there is an undermining of so many things. How can we reach them if there is no revival? How can things change?

We can't look to the nation to correct itself morally on its own. The answer to our morality does not lie entirely in the Houses of Parliament but in the house of God.

How would revival influence our nation? One of the best answers to that question I know, was given by Dr W.E. Sangster. One Monday morning in the mid-1950s, the nation woke up to read in a number of national papers the substance of a sermon preached by him the previous day. Some newspapers printed the main points of his sermon on their front pages. His theme was: 'Revival: The Need and the Way'.[3]

Sangster raised the question: What would a revival of religion do for Britain? He gave the following ten answers:

1. It would pay old debts.

He pointed out that in the days of the Welsh revival those who dismissed it as a wave of emotional fanaticism changed their minds when they heard that wherever the revival went

'A lifting of common morality.'

℘

people were paying old and neglected debts. 'A lifting of common morality,' he said, 'is an early and inevitable consequence of born-again religion.'

2. It would reduce sexual immorality.

Quoting from *English Life and Leisure*, Sangster said there were 10,000 prostitutes in London alone and 250,000 men were estimated to make use of them every week. (Nowadays, those figures have doubled.) This foul traffic, he claimed, was an offence to God and while figures and complaints could do nothing, a revival of religion would. Men and women touched by the Holy Spirit would learn that in God there is power to obey the commandments of God.

3. It would disinfect the theatre and the press.

The Christian faith has never had a quarrel with drama as such, claimed Sangster, but it is deeply concerned when the stage is misused for the deliberate inflaming of lust. Our newspapers include some of the best in the world and some of the worst. Those in the latter class are so sex-sodden that they come close to pornography. In Sangster's day television was in its infancy. What would he say about some of today's programmes which are peppered with four-letter words and portray scenes that are an offence to decency and civility? A revival of religion would cause men and women to turn from such things.

4. It would cut the divorce rate.

In the 1950s divorces ran at a much lower rate than they do today. The texture of society gets flabby, said Sangster, when divorce gets common. Young people who enter marriage with their eye on the backdoor and say to themselves, 'Well, if it doesn't work out I can always get a divorce', make for it when things get difficult more quickly than they think they will. Those who pray together are more likely to stay together.

5. It would reduce juvenile crime.

It was in the 1950s that the 'adolescent thug' began to appear. And the cause? Without doubt the breakdown in family life. It is rare indeed that a thug comes out of a Christian home. It can happen, and sometimes does, but not often. No one is safe in goodness unless he or she wants to be good, said Sangster. And what makes people want to be good? Faith in Christ.

6. It would lessen the prison population.

Here in the UK the prison population in the 1930s stood around 15,000. In the 1950s it was 20,000. Now, in the first decade of the twenty-first century it is getting close to 75,000. Is there not some connection between the fact that as churches have been emptying our prisons have been filling? Sangster claimed that in his day the moral capital built up by generations of God-fearing people was nearing exhaustion. Were he alive today he would see that it has become bankrupt. Only a revival of the Christian faith can turn the tide.

7. It would improve the quality and increase the output of work.

The Christian faith makes a difference to work. How? Because a man or woman who is committed to Jesus Christ works not just for wages but for God. Men and women need wages of course, for no one can live without money, but the highest motivation to work and to do a task well is to do it for God.

8. It would restore to the nation a sense of high destiny.

During the 'Empire' days the British people believed they had a special and high destiny in the world, but some aspects of the idea were somewhat foolish. Thankfully much of that imperial pride has gone. What is our destiny in today's world? We still have an important role in world affairs but how much more powerful that role would be were it to be energised by the stands of biblical faith.

9. It would make us invincible in the war of ideas.

In Sangster's day the war of ideas was between communism and capitalism. Both creeds had their passionate proponents, some even willing to die for their cause. Sangster pointed out that the real war in the war of ideas is whether or not there is a God, whether a man is what he eats and whether the last explanation of the universe is material or spiritual. The Christian faith has a secret that no other ideology knows – how to die to self. The finest schemes fail on the selfishness of mankind. The possession and practice of that secret would make us invincible in the war of ideas.

10. It would give happiness and peace to the people.

Throughout time men and women have sought to find peace in their hearts. But peace can be found only in a relationship with the Prince of Peace – the Lord Jesus Christ Himself. In the world of the 1950s almost the only hope of happiness was to win something big on the pools. Today it is the lottery. The Christian faith offers a peace that does not depend on circumstances. Wars may rage around us but peace can stay with us – if the peace we have is from God.[4]

Britain, said Sangster, speaking in the 1950s, has many needs, but her greatest is revival. Today, close on five decades later, the needs of the nation are much greater and our greatest need is still revival.

We have watched our country slipping back for a generation. And without doubt complacency and lukewarmness gnaws at the door of the Church. It is a lot to believe that humility, believing prayer, radical repentance and cutting out everything God does not want in our lives can change things, *but not to believe it would make God a liar*.

God longs for revival more than we do.

℘

God longs for revival more than we do. 'Return to me and I will return to you,' He said in Malachi 3:7.

So let's not settle for the spiritual status quo, a mediocre, weak and anaemic brand of Christianity, when God wants to make available to us the same kind of power that energised the Early Church. Dr Martyn Lloyd-Jones said on one occasion that the Christian Church is like a sleeping giant. If that is so then it is time for it to awake.

There have been two great spiritual awakenings which have affected Britain in the last 500 years. One was the Reformation in the middle of the sixteenth century, triggered by that great reformer, Martin Luther. The second was the Evangelical Awakening in the eighteenth century under such men as John Wesley, George Whitfield and others. Now in the twenty-first century we are ready for a third awakening, one which will turn the tide and make the Church once again the power God intends it to be.

To absorb ideas about revival costs nothing, but to enter into revival costs everything – our time, changes in our behaviour – and we shall be very guilty if having come to understand revival and be convinced of its need we then do nothing about it. Let us report for duty in the battle for our nation's soul.

Let the prayer of Isaiah become our prayer.

Oh, that you would rend the heavens and come down, that the mountains would tremble before you! ... come down to

make your name known to your enemies and cause the
nations to quake before you!   Isa. 64:1–2

Whatever the needs of the Church and the
nation, our greatest need is revival.

Hear the merciful promise of our Heavenly
Father once again:

'If my people, who are called by my name, will humble
themselves and pray and seek my face and turn from their
wicked ways, then will I hear from heaven and will forgive
their sin and will heal their land.'

Would you join me in this personal prayer?

Heavenly Father, I come to You in Jesus' Name ...
Search my heart at this moment ...
and expose any wicked ways that may be in me.
I want to be
the person You want me to be.
I repent of the wrongs in my life,
show them to me whatever they are;
lukewarmness, indifference to the lost,
lack of prayer, lack of passionate prayer,
neglect of the Bible, compromise, resentment
      toward others, pride.
O God, forgive me for my pride.

I renounce it and turn from it now in
    Your presence.
I bundle all these things together
and bring them to the foot of the cross.
I receive your forgiveness,
help me to start afresh this day.
Change me by Your grace,
forgive me and restore me,
set my heart on fire for You,
that I will be unafraid to witness to my friends
    and family.
May I never be ashamed of You.
Send revival to the land ...
and start the work in me.
In Jesus' Name I pray.
Amen.

Notes

Chapter 1
1. James I. Packer, *God in the Midst* (Milton Keynes: Word Publishing, 1987).
2. Ibid.
3. Duncan Campbell, *God's Answer: Revival Sermons* (Edinburgh: The Faith Mission, 1960).
4. Ibid.

Chapter 2
1. Dr W.E. Sangster, *The Craft of Sermon Construction* (London: Epworth Press, 1949).
2. Dr W.E. Sangster, *Revival: The Need and the Way*, Pamphlet (London: Epworth Press, 1957).

Chapter 3
1. C.S. Lewis, *Mere Christianity* (London: Macmillan Publishing Co., 1943).
2. Charles Swindoll, *Strengthening Your Grip* (Milton Keynes: Word Publishing, 1982).

Chapter 4
1. Dr W.E. Sangster, *The Pure in Heart* (London: Epworth Press, 1954).
2. I am unable to trace this quote.

Chapter 6
1. Duncan Campbell, *God's Answer: Revival Sermons* (Edinburgh: The Faith Mission, April 1960).
2. Ibid.
3. Dr W.E. Sangster, *Revival: The Need and the Way*, Pamphlet (London: Epworth Press, 1957).
4. Ibid.

National Distributors

UK: (and countries not listed below)
CWR, Waverley Abbey House, Waverley Lane, Farnham, Surrey GU9 8EP.
Tel: (01252) 784710 Outside UK (44) 1252 784710
AUSTRALIA: CMC Australasia, PO Box 519, Belmont, Victoria 3216.
Tel: (03) 5241 3288
CANADA: Cook Communications Ministries, PO Box 98, 55 Woodslee Avenue, Paris, Ontario
Tel: 1800 263 2664
GHANA: Challenge Enterprises of Ghana, PO Box 5723, Accra.
Tel: (021) 222437/223249 Fax: (021) 226227
HONG KONG: Cross Communications Ltd, 1/F, 562A Nathan Road, Kowloon.
Tel: 2780 1188 Fax: 2770 6229
INDIA: Crystal Communications, 10-3-18/4/1, East Marredpally, Secunderabad – 500 026.
Tel/Fax: (040) 7732801
KENYA: Keswick Books and Gifts Ltd, PO Box 10242, Nairobi.
Tel: (02) 331692/226047 Fax: (02) 728557
MALAYSIA: Salvation Book Centre (M) Sdn Bhd, 23 Jalan SS 2/64, 47300 Petaling Jaya, Selangor.
Tel: (03) 78766411/78766797 Fax: (03) 78757066/78756360
NEW ZEALAND: CMC Australasia, PO Box 36015, Lower Hutt.
Tel: 0800 449 408 Fax: 0800 449 049
NIGERIA: FBFM, Helen Baugh House, 96 St Finbarr's College Road, Akoka, Lagos.
Tel: (01) 7747429/4700218/825775/827264

PHILIPPINES: OMF Literature Inc, 776 Boni Avenue,
Mandaluyong City.
Tel: (02) 531 2183 Fax: (02) 531 1960
REPUBLIC OF IRELAND: Scripture Union, 40 Talbot Street,
Dublin 1.
Tel: (01) 8363764
SINGAPORE: Armour Publishing Pte Ltd, Block 203A
Henderson Road, 11–06 Henderson Industrial Park,
Singapore 159546.
Tel: 6 276 9976 Fax: 6 276 7564
SOUTH AFRICA: Struik Christian Books,
80 MacKenzie Street, PO Box 1144, Cape Town 8000.
Tel: (021) 462 4360 Fax: (021) 461 3612
SRI LANKA: Christombu Books, 27 Hospital Street,
Colombo 1.
Tel: (01) 433142/328909
TANZANIA: CLC Christian Book Centre, PO Box 1384,
Mkwepu Street, Dar es Salaam.
Tel/Fax (022) 2119439
USA: Cook Communications Ministries, PO Box 98,
55 Woodslee Avenue, Paris, Ontario, Canada
Tel: 1800 263 2664
ZIMBABWE: Word of Life Books, Shop 4, Memorial
Building, 35 S Machel Avenue, Harare.
Tel: (04) 781305 Fax: (04) 774739

For email addresses, visit the CWR website: www.cwr.org.uk

CWR is a registered charity – number 294387

**Jonah –
God of The
Second Chance**

Selwyn Hughes

Price: £4.99

ISBN: 1-85345-258-0

This study of Jonah is an inspiration to anyone who has ever made a mistake, had a regret or failed God. So this is a book for everyone!

Learn to experience the mercy, grace and forgiveness of God and find freedom in His restoring love. A fascinating look at a favourite Bible story.

The 7 Laws of Spiritual Success

Selwyn Hughes

Price: £7.99

ISBN: 1-85345-237-8

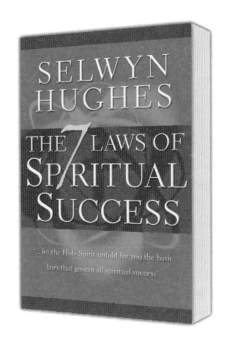

This book has been described by the author as his legacy to future generations. This is a book for men and women of all ages and every stage in their Christian walk. Selwyn Hughes brings a lifetime of experience and ministry to this work, which became an instant bestseller. Explore seven essential elements for a successful Christian life; worship, thankfulness, forgiveness, perseverance, servanthood, repentance and continual growth.

Christ Empowered Living

Selwyn Hughes

Price: £5.99

ISBN: 1-85345-201-7

Transform your life with essential principles of Christian living and develop to your full spiritual potential. These biblical insights will revolutionise your approach to the way you live and help renew your mind.

Trusted
All Over the World

Daily Devotionals

Books and Videos

Day and Residential Courses

Counselling Training

Biblical Study Courses

Regional Seminars

Ministry to Women

CWR have been providing training and resources for Christians since the 1960s. From our headquarters at Waverley Abbey House we have been serving God's people with a vision to help apply God's Word to everyday life and relationships. The daily devotional *Every Day with Jesus* is read by over three-quarters of a million people in more than 150 countries, and our unique courses in biblical studies and pastoral care are respected all over the world.

For a free brochure about our seminars and courses or a catalogue of CWR resources please contact us at the following address:

CWR,
Waverley Abbey House,
Waverley Lane,
Farnham,
Surrey GU9 8EP

Telephone: 01252 784700
Email: mail@cwr.org.uk
Website: www.cwr.org.uk

CWR CRUSADE FOR WORLD REVIVAL *Applying God's Word to everyday life and relationships*